The Madman, The Marathoner
(The Life of Marathoner Don McNelly)
By Juanita B. Tischendorf

This is the Second Edition. Originally published by Tate Publishing, LLC. In January 2017 Tate ceased operation

New Cover design using the drawing done by Yardley Jones, the cartoonist who, in 1998, sketched Don McNelly and has given his permission to use this sketch for the book cover.

Published in the United States of America

ISBN: 978-1-928613-36-7

1. BIOGRAPHY & AUTOBIOGRAPHY / Sports
2. BIOGRAPHY & AUTOBIOGRAPHY / Adventurers & Explorers

DEDICATION

This book is dedicated to those who were not afraid to try new things. The marathon was a classic drama of equal doses comedy and tragedy, euphoria and agony, and like every part of life, it takes willpower along with dedication to face the unknown.

ACKNOWLEDGMENTS

All the material in this book not derived from my own observation are either taken from official records or are the result of interviews with the persons directly concerned, more often than not numerous interviews conducted over a considerable period of time. Because these collaborations were identified within the text, it would be redundant to name them here; nevertheless, I want to express a formal gratitude to everyone who gave of their time to share information, for without their patient cooperation, my task would have been impossible.

I would like personally to thank Joanne Holler of the Seneca Park Zoo, who arranged for me to speak with Rachel Baker August, Sharon Peterson, and Amy Carnahan, all of whom willingly shared their experiences with Don McNelly.

I would like to include a special thanks to two individuals who did not know me or Don but who were willing to provide needed information for the book. Thank you to Shawn Wedge, the Administrative Assistant of Sulphur Grove UMC in Huber Heights, Ohio, for filling me in on the location formerly known as Sulphur Grove, and to Bob Lichty of motorcarportfolio.com, for verifying the make, year, and model of Don and Phyllis's first automobile.

In addition, when I was unable to get all the details I wanted to present on the Columbus Marathon, Cherie Koch came forward with information. Thank you.

Thanks to Jim Ralston, the race director for the Niagara Fallsview International Marathon, and Meredith Maxwell, for their support in arranging credentials for me to do the marathon with Don and attend the special media functions. The opportunity to participate at Don McNelly's side was priceless in the gathering of material and an insider's view of the marathon world.

To Rich Benyo, editor of *Marathon and Beyond Magazine*, who offered to express his opinion on the final manuscript, thank you.

A special thanks to Yardley Jones, the cartoonist who, in 1998, sketched Don McNelly and has given his permission to use this sketch for the book cover. Yardley Jones was a Canadian political cartoonist whose work was seen in the Edmonton News and other papers throughout Canada, as well as in the National Cartoon Museum in Boca Raton, Florida. He and Don McNelly ran together several times in Nanisivik, Northwest Territories. He surprised Don with the sketch done from a photo and memory and used for the cover of this book.

Last but not least, a big thank you to Maggie Richey for her suggestions to help fine tune the contents of the manuscript.

Nita Tischendorf

TABLE OF CONTENTS

DEDICATION...3

ACKNOWLEDGMENTS 5

TABLE OF CONTENTS 7

FOREWORD 12

INTRODUCTION..16

NIAGARA FALLSVIEW CASINO RESORT INTERNATIONAL

MARATHON..18

    THE RAINBOW AWARD 27

BROOKVILLE, OHIO 40

    THE 4-H CLUB AND CAMP HOOK 45

    GENERAL MOTORS INSTITUTE 48

LOVE AND MARRIAGE 52

NAVY LIFE 60

LIVING THE AMERICAN DREAM 71

EDUCATION IS THE KEY 78

THE EYE OPENER 80

THE 1969 BOSTON MARATHON 90

THE MADNESS BEGINS..103

    THE GREATER ROCHESTER ROCHESTER TRACK CLUB.....107

    JFK 50 MILER ULTRA-MARATHON 116

    1975 SKYLON MARATHON 122

    IT WAS MORE THAN JUST THE JOY OF RUNNING.............125

    SUMMARY OF 1970 128

1980S AND THE FIRST 100 130

    THE OLYMPIC TRIALS 131

    THE NEW YORK CITY MARATHON 140

    RACING UP THE EMPIRE STATE BUILDING 148

    GRTC HALL OF FAME 1982..159

    CROSS COUNTRY RUN 160

    EMPIRE STATE GAMES 170

EMPIRE STATE SENIOR GAMES 173

THE MIDNIGHT SUN DOUBLE MARATHON 174

RACE UP MOUNT FUJI...178

SAD NEWS & GOOD NEWS 186

NUMBER 200..187

1988 HOLDS ITS OWN...191

DEALING WITH CANCER 193

SY MAH 195

50 & D.C. MARATHON GROUP 200

SUMMARY OF 1980...202

1990S & NUMBER 500 204

FRANKFURT, GERMANY..205

EVERYONE NEEDS A HOBBY 207

NUMBER 300..208

PANAMA CITY INTERNATIONAL ULTRA MARATHON...........................209

BANGKOK, THAILAND MARATHON 212

NOTHING WENT RIGHT IN BANGKOK 214

PARIS MARATHON 216

ROTTERDAM MARATHON 218

RUNNING IN LONDON..218

BIG SUR 219

NORTH AMERICAN RULES 221

LISBON PORTUGAL MARATHON 224

SHOWING RESPECT GAINS REWARDS...227

VENICE MARATHON 230

TIM HORTON'S VALLEY HARVEST MARATHON 231

1995 THE LAST MARATHON 233

LAST CHANCE, FIRST CHANCE MARATHON 238

THE MOST UNFORGETTABLE MARATHON EXPERIENCE.....................239

FIRST GLOBAL AUTUMN MARATHON 243

NUMBER 500..244

NUUK MARATHON...245

PAFOS MARATHON (CYPRUS MARATHON)..246

CHANGES AT HOME 247

SUMMARY OF 1990...249

2000 AND BEYOND 251

FREESCALE AUSTIN MARATHON 252

THE OKLAHOMA MARATHON 253

600TH LIFETIME MARATHON...254

WINEGLASS MARATHON 257

RUNNING IN JAPAN IN 2003...257

100 MILE ROADRUNNING CHAMPIONSHIP 261

REKYJAVIK MARATHON 262

LIFE CHANGES...264

NANCY ANN FILBRUN MCNELLY 265

2006 AUSTIN MARATHON 268

SURFSIDE MARATHON 269

2007: ANOTHER BATTLE TO DEFEAT..270

THE COLUMBUS MARATHON 271

THE PORTLAND MARATHON 275

GIVING SOMETHING BACK 277

THE NIAGARA-FALLSVIEW MARATHON 278

SUMMARY OF DON'S MARATHON CAREER 284

A Family Affair.. **285**

The One That Got Away **286**

DON IS A PUBLIC FIGURE...289

THE NEED TO KNOW ABOUT RUNNING **293**

2017 - SAYING GOODBYE **300**

LIST OF MARATHONS **301**

FOREWORD

It was indeed an honor to include the following forewords written by these outstanding individuals. Their personal experiences in the life of Donald P. McNelly sum up how extraordinary this man has become.

Having the privilege of conducting a comprehensive medical evaluation as well as a measurement of fitness on Don McNelly February 21, 2008, was an unexpected pleasure. Even though he had been coming to our clinic since April 29, 1975, he was being seen by one of our other physicians.

In evaluating his history and conducting a very extensive examination, I was first of all surprised to learn of his unbelievable marathon accomplishments. This would be phenomenal for a man of any age, but particularly one who was 87.

I was even more amazed to document his record marathon performance, but shocked to see that he had multiple medical problems, including heart disease (including a very high coronary artery calcification score), chronic lymphatic leukemia, and borderline anemia. He even had a reduction in the blood platelets (which account for blood clotting) and a history of prostate cancer. Also, there was a question of glaucoma, a history of paroxysmal atrial fibrillation, and high blood pressure, all being controlled with medications. In medical terms, he would be described as a "walking miracle"!

His cholesterol and other blood lipids were surprisingly normal, most likely due to his medications. Yet he still has room for improvement.

I am both honored and pleased to provide a foreword for The Madman The Marathon since I am so proud to convey his story. He is truly one of the most amazing men with whom I have had the privilege to work.

Kenneth H. Cooper, MD, MPH

Chairman & Chief Executive Officer

The Cooper Aerobics Center / Cooper Clinic

My only hope is that my lifestyle and over forty-four years of running/jogging will enable me to enjoy life to the fullest when I am Don McNelly's age. If so, I might be able to run or fast-walk marathons again!

In my thirty-two years of practice at the Cooper Clinic, I have taken care of thousands of patients from around the world. Among those thousands, several hundred have become very good friends, returning to the clinic year after year, as we discuss not only exercise, nutrition, blood pressure, and other medical topics, but wonderful vacation spots, children, grandchildren, and values, as well as personal triumphs and failures. Among those several hundred, a few stand out above the rest. Don McNelly is in this group.

His accomplishments in the exercise arena were legendary and are chronicled in this book. The discipline of completing so many marathons, of which many have been after the age of eighty, puts him among the elite of the elite. His explanation of how he has accomplished this unbelievable thing—"left foot, right foot"—humbly avoids the truth: this was a man with a driving passion for achievement, excellence, and accomplishment.

My admiration for Don, however, does not center on his exercise performance.

He stands out among those I have been privileged to come to know because of his character. He is one of the most genuine, warm, caring human beings I have encountered. As we talk each year, he as much concerned about me, my welfare, and activities as I, the physician, am concerned about him and his doings. Our discussions quickly migrate to discussions of common friends, their trials and achievements, his favorite humanitarian and charitable causes, his spiritual aspirations, family, and the deeper issues of character.

Don loves life and is a wonderful commentator on the human side of what is happening in the world. Being around him always lifts me up and brings additional light into my view of the world. His optimism is part of the light he brings into his relationships. Major medical problems such as chronic lymphocytic leukemia, atrial fibrillation, and coronary atherosclerosis were taken as minor inconveniences along the road. Certainly, he takes care of his health and his medical problems studiously, but he does not dwell on them or let them cloud his ambition, his plans for his next marathon, or his optimistic view of what was coming around the next corner. To watch how he has dealt with what would be major medical setbacks to others—reasons to head for the rocking chair and a cautious view from the sidelines—has been a textbook in perseverance and resilience. No wonder being around him is so pleasant.

This remarkable man has made the life of this physician, and his other friends, much richer and fuller, and has given all who know him a desire to stretch ourselves a little further, keep going a little longer, and dig inside ourselves a little deeper, in the important pursuits of life.

Larry W. Gibbons, M.D.

Moscow, Russia, April 29, 2007

We first met him on Saturday, 10 October 1997, at Sakura Hotel in Tokyo. We ate a fried pork and rice (*katsu-ju*) lunch with beer at a small, traditional restaurant. Don was a member of Full Hyaku Club (Japan), and this was his first visit as a member of the club, although he had been to Japan before. We had exchanged some e-mail to get to know each other. My basic attitude toward him was respect as a man and a runner.

The next day, we ran the First Global Autumn Marathon Kokyo (Imperial Palace) with some other runners, including the president of Full Hyaku. We reached the finish line at the same time: 6 hours, 23 minutes, and 36 seconds. Don said he ran at 50 percent of his maximum heart rate. We knew how old runners ran safely. The race was operated by the Global Marathon Club—which organizes a huge number of marathons and running races around Kokyo and other places in Tokyo—together with Full Hyaku Club.

Hiroyasu Enomoto (Yasu)

The Full Hyaku in Japan

INTRODUCTION

The way in which people make sense of their lives is valuable historical evidence that can fade over the years, so when I began interviewing Don, I was amazed at how accurate his memory remained. The story I am about to tell you has many levels of interest, and I hope that I can do it justice, because this story is about life and how to live it.

When I decided to write a book about Don McNelly, a man who has achieved success as a husband, father, and as a marathoner, I realized that this would require more than your average research. I could write about husbands, having one of my own, and I could write about fathers, but I had no experience in marathons.

I used to jog when I was younger, but I knew that would not be enough to write this book. I walk as part of keeping in shape, but only up to an hour each day, which is a far cry from the hours to walk 26.2 miles. Lucky for me, I am willing to try most things at least once and usually without giving much thought to the outcome, since I do it for myself.

I have known Don for some time now, having first met him when he took a computer class that I taught at the high school. Later we conversed as I worked on his computer system, and after each conversation I realized how much this man loved his life. Don knew the secret of balancing life with zest and determination, and I wanted to know how it was done. So, being an adventurous person, it was easy for him to convince me to write his life story. That motivated me to go the distance.

When I decided that the only way to experience what goes into a marathon was to be in one, I had a good motivator. Don, who in November of 2006 would turn eighty-six years old, was now walking the marathons, so that gave me confidence that I just might be able to succeed at this feat, but more importantly, I had to succeed in order to see what Don saw and feel what Don felt when he entered a marathon. Some may see this as crazy, but as I said, I do many things just for myself and not to influence anyone else.

By the time of publication, Don will have traveled around 19,500 miles in marathons and an additional 5,850 miles in ultra marathons for a grand total of 25,350 miles. His formula for changing his running shoes will amount to a little over 50 pairs as he journeyed on his way. As for his favorite footwear, they would be called "anything on sale." There is a reason for this, since he wears a size 15 wide running shoe, and stores usually stock up to size 14 making the choice very slim.

When Don entered his first marathon, his youngest child was twenty years old and he and his wife, Phyllis, were empty nesters. I hope you will learn from Don McNelly how it is possible to be a success in more than one part of life. I hope he inspires you to take a "leap of faith" in yourself and go the distance. Don did it at home, at work, in the service, and in marathons. You can do it too. For me, it was easy to try and go the distance, as I had Don encouraging me all the way

NIAGARA FALLSVIEW CASINO RESORT
INTERNATIONAL MARATHON

This was one of Don's favorite marathons because of the course and the people who put on the marathon. I had read, I had trained, and I was ready to get started, but also ready to meet Jim Ralston, the race director, and Meredith Maxwell, his assistant, who had graciously supplied the marathon credentials and were allowing me to walk with Don.

I knew very little about marathons but recognized the importance of certain details, one being the words, "a Boston marathon qualifier." This term I referenced to be similar to the old computer term, "IBM compatible," and I wasn't far from wrong.

Exclusive of the Olympics and various championship races, the Boston Marathon is the only marathon in the USA that upholds qualifying times and requirements. While the specific requirements change from year to year, the requirements generally state that a runner must have completed a qualifying marathon within the year and a half before the upcoming Boston Marathon.

Training to run any marathon takes commitment in terms of both dedication and time. Training to run the Boston Marathon, however, is something not all runners are capable of doing. In earlier years, when marathon running was not as popular, almost anyone could run the Boston Marathon. Whether through official registry or running without an official race number as a "bandit," runners were generally allowed to run the race. Over the past few decades, marathon running has grown in popularity, with new races popping up each year. With the number of marathon runners eager to run in the Boston Marathon, it has become stricter about allowing only official registrants to enter, by limiting registrants with difficult qualification standards. To qualify to run the Boston Marathon, a male age eighteen to thirty-four must run a different marathon in a time of three hours and ten minutes or less, and women of the same age group must run another marathon in three hours and forty minutes or less. Considering the quick pace needed to attain these times, training for the Boston Marathon is normally only possible for experienced runners who have already completed several marathons. The Niagara Fallsview Casino Resort International Marathon is a Boston Marathon qualifier. The history of the Niagara Fallsview Marathon as shared by Don, Jim, and Meredith is interesting because of its unique course layout.

The marathon began in 1974 when a group of local runners wanted to hold the first cross-border marathon. When it began, a percussionist was credited with its creation, and so it was appropriately called The Buffalo Philharmonic Marathon. Later it would be renamed and called the Skylon Marathon (after the Sylon Tower in Niagara Falls, Canada). Beginning during the first wave of the North American running boom, this marathon quickly became a favorite, and it gained notoriety when in 1980 and 1984, it was used for the US men's Olympic marathon trial.

By 1976 the "cross border" marathon attracted more than three thousand runners, surpassing that year's marathoners in New York and Boston, and the name was again changed, this time to the Buffalo-Niagara Falls International Marathon. Its popularity again grew when headlines were made in 1985 when Mark Coleman, a social worker from Newburgh, New York, won the Buffalo-Niagara Falls International Marathon, finishing in 2:30:30. Only that wasn't the reason for the headlines. The marathon that year was indeed newsworthy, as over fifty finishers were led over the wrong course. Don was there that day, but because he was not with the front-runners, he was not affected and managed to stay on the correct course.

What actually happened that day began at the six- and seven-mile marks of the race when a police escort led the runners down the wrong street, adding an additional 1.8 miles to the course before race officials were able to redirect the remainder of the field. To compensate for this error, the finish time for the front-runners was adjusted accordingly.

The marathon ceased to exist after 1986, only to be revived in 1998 as the Buffalo-Niagara Falls Ontario Marathon, with Casino Niagara as the title sponsor and the starting line changed to downtown Buffalo, then later move to the Albright Knox Art Gallery.

Don had completed every edition of the old Skylon race, as the Niagara Fallsview Casino Marathon was called, and most of the ones since its resurrection in 1998.

Marathons would give out perks to certain runners, which might include free entry into the marathon, their hotel accommodations covered for two nights, no charge to enter the pasta party, and a special invite to the Friday night VIP reception. Then on race day there was usually complimentary transportation to the starting line.

In most circumstances when there were special considerations given to a handful, other participants would scream, "It's Fixed." Not the case for marathons. It was more a rite of passage for those whose marathon accomplishments shine.

Don and his long-time friend Norm Frank fell into the category of the elite, since they would be stepping into history yet again when they crossed the finish line that Sunday. Norm, at age seventy-five, would be marking 928 completions of certified marathons, which no one else in North America had ever done. Don, at eighty-five, would complete his 714th marathon, making him third on the all-time North American list. Don also laid claim to having completed more marathons than anyone else after reaching the age of eighty, which is 142 marathons.

Records are important to marathoners, and some make their own that might be odd or quite an accomplishment. Don was known for the amount of marathons and ultras since reaching seventy. A marathoner named Tom "HiGuy" Matti holds the record for running 123-plus miles in sandals; Leslie Miller for being the youngest female to complete 100 miles; Bill Whipp who claims 156 marathons/ultras on total knee replacement; Mike Wojcio for carrying two American flags for close to ninety-five miles, and Norm Frank for running more marathons than anyone else in the United States. There are many more, and every one of the records are personal goals that each runner set for him or herself.

Marathons come and go, and some are replaced, and just as frequently, the marathon routes might be changed.

On Sunday, October 22, 2006, the route for the Niagara Fallsview Marathon began on Lincoln Parkway in Buffalo. Originally called North Park and now known as Delaware Park, this green area was designed by Frederick Law Olmstead, who also designed New York City's Central Park and Brooklyn's Prospect Park. The park includes Lincoln Parkway, the Buffalo Zoo, and several sports fields and picnic areas.

Interestingly, Delaware Park was the site of the 1901 Pan American Exposition, which was designed to improve relations between North and South America. While visiting the exposition, then-President William McKinley was shot and died in the John G. Milburn home, located a few blocks from the exposition. That same day, Theodore Roosevelt took the oath of office to become President of the United States of America at the Wilcox Mansion on Delaware Avenue. The site where President McKinley was shot was located just two blocks from the starting line of the marathon.

As runners wait for the start on Lincoln Parkway, they stand between two very interesting and historic structures. To the left is the Delaware Park Casino and Rose Garden, which attracts thousands of people on summer weekends, and on the right is the world-famous Albright-Knox Art Gallery, which houses one of the finest collections of modern art in the world.

The first two miles of the race are run on the mansion- and tree-lined Lincoln, Chapin, and Bidwell Parkways. As runners turn onto Bidwell, on the right they see a modern-looking, low brick home designed by the famous architect Frank Lloyd Wright. From there, the route goes to Richmond Avenue, a stretch that in Victorian times was famous for its magnificent homes and horse-drawn sled races in winter. At the south end of Richmond lies Symphony Circle, home of the First Presbyterian Church. Directly west of the church is Kleinhans Music Hall, which is the work of Finnish architects Eliel and Eero Saarinen. Once past the customs barrier, the course goes under the bridge and heads south along the lake. This is the point where Don and I would meet up with the rest of the marathoners, having completed the same distance as these runners had, but doing it only in Canada.

Having done this marathon many times before, Don knew the best places to stay to cut down on expenses but still have a clean room. It was not an inexpensive hobby or form of exercise, since the average cost to enter a marathon was between $75 and $100. Then there was the additional cost of attending the pasta party ($15-$25), and meals and transportation to take into consideration, turning this financially into a family vacation for two.

Though the Niagara Fallsview Casino Resort was the "in" place to stay, Don suggested the Fallsview Motor Lodge, where my husband and I were in Room 9 on the first floor. Don and Phyllis were in Room 12 on the second floor.

Today, Don is a commanding figure, standing over six feet tall, with a fringe of white hair around the perimeters of his well-shaped head. He sports a white beard that reaches up to merge with his side hairline. His top lip is hidden behind a full white mustache, and his eyes sparkle through large framed glasses that rest easily on the bridge of his nose. There are character lines creasing his forehead, and the creases at the sides of his mouth deepen when he smiles, something hard to glimpse in the many pictures of him. At that moment, his expression could only be described as that of someone who had a secret to share, and that turned out to be not far from true.

As had been previously discussed with Jim Ralston, Don, Norm, and myself would be doing the whole marathon on the Canadian side since we would be starting out earlier than the rest of the runners. Don entered our motel room and explained that the starting point for us was not well marked since we would be covering the distance entirely on the Canadian side, using the certified course that was laid out when security concerns closed the Peace Bridge to the race in the weeks following the events of September 11. This route would take us through residential areas before connecting to the regular course on the Niagara River Parkway. It was a concession that Jim Ralston, the race director, was happy to make and worked best with our plans to start the race much earlier than the published time of 10:00 a.m. We planned to set out at 6:30 or 7:00 a.m., which would allow us to cross the finish line within the allotted time span set for the marathon.

At Don's suggestion, we climbed into the car and drove the route to eliminate any surprises later when we set out in the dark. Along the way, Don pointed out the side roads where my husband could wait with the car in case I was unable to finish the marathon. He told my husband that we would be doing approximately nineteen- to twenty-minute miles, so that he could figure when to expect us at each location. This would put us at nine hours and twenty minutes to make it to the finish line. Satisfied that we knew the route, we made our way back to the motel.

The Niagara Fallsview Casino Resort International Marathon had also made a change to the regular course, with the new finish line set at Table Rock House, near the brink of the Canadian Horseshoe Falls, the same finish line for the marathon in 1974. This change marked an 800-meter (2,624.67 feet) move north skating pass the major work going on at the old Toronto Powerhouse, where the race had been finishing since its resurrection in 1998.

On Friday we got into the swing of the marathon weekend as we took in the Health and Fitness Expo in the Grand Hall at the Niagara Fallsview Casino Resort. We arrived early, which did not stop Don, who walked to the entrance, grabbed hold of the door handles at the double-door entryway, and swung them open. He stood at the threshold for a moment and then gingerly stepped into the room and matter-of-factly announced that he was looking for Meredith Maxwell. In seconds, Meredith appeared, and her expression was one of excitement at seeing Don McNelly. This was the first time she had met the notorious man.

"Jim talks so much about you, so I was anxious to finally have the honor of meeting you," she said. Before long, Jim Ralston came to join Meredith, and Don and I listened as they talked easily amongst themselves. Don introduced me, and I was supplied with the credentials needed to fully cover the marathon along with Don.

The Queen Victoria Place is a historic building located on Niagara Parkway, directly across from the falls and named after Queen Victoria, the head of the Canadian monarchy. This would be the location of the VIP dinner that we were to attend. As we sat in this place honoring their queen, the room was filled with only marathon staff, media, or marathon celebrities. We heard a steady hum of conversation as runners met up with others they knew, and Don was often caught up in conversations, giving me a chance to watch him in action. Cocktail parties may have taken a little break during the 1960s and 1970s, but since then they had regained their popularity in full-strength, especially at social gatherings where the guests may not know everyone. With wine, beer, mixed drinks, and finger food, a cocktail party allows everyone to move about and get acquainted or catch up with what has been happening in their life.

This party was no different. Along with the drinks, they served shrimp tooth-picked to a tower of pineapple and trays of all kinds of cheeses, fruits, and vegetables. We were offered chicken and beef on sticks and other tidbits too numerous to mention. I spent a lot of time surveying the people around me and sensed the comradeship instead of competitiveness. These runners were friendly and respectful of each other as they moved about the room striking up conversations and laughing easily together.

A look of recognition lit up Don's face; and when I turned to follow his gaze, I saw a man I had seen in many pictures with Don. The man approaching us was Norm Frank. Norm stood six-foot two-inches and weighed around 175 pounds, his physique resembling a marathon runner in body type, but not in age, as he was seventy-six years old. His hair was mostly brown, with a touch of gray, and he wore brown-framed glasses and sported a well-manicured beard that was almost all gray. In a matter of minutes, I could sense the respect these two had for each other and why they had remained friends for over thirty-eight years.

People continued to stop to chat with these two marathon icons. Joe Hvilivizky, who wrote the pre-marathon piece for *The Review* on both Don and Norm, stopped for a bit. Then Art McCarffery of the Great Lakes Sports Publication Company joined us and asked Don and Norm if he could interview them, to which they both replied, *"Certainly."* I watched as they were whisked away to a quiet corner of the room.

When Jim Ralston picked up the microphone, the hum in the room was silenced as he welcomed the runners and introduced promoters and staff members, and then the highlight of the evening began.

The Rainbow Award

The Rainbow Award was given to the individual who had contributed the most to marathons. In 2002, the award went to Bill Rodgers, a spokesman for *Running Times* magazine, and, of course, Bill Rodgers Running Center. In 2003, the award went to Tania Jones, a world-class marathon runner and motivational speaker, as well as a valued friend of the Running Room. In 2004, Kathrine Switzer received the award. Kathrine will always be known as the woman who challenged the all-male tradition of the Boston Marathon and became the first woman to officially enter and run the event. Then in 2005, John Stanton received the award. John Stanton was the founder of Running Room & Walking Room. In 1984, Stanton opened a store and meeting place for runners, and more than two decades later, his company had grown into one of North America's most recognized names in running. John Stanton had run more than sixty marathons in his lifetime.

Then came the moment that everyone was waiting for, as Jim Ralston began the presentation for the 2006 Rainbow Award.

"This year The Rainbow Award is being given for the first time to two individuals. The recipients of the award are Don McNelly and Norm Frank."

Don and Norm were both speechless with surprise, as they looked at each other and smiled. At the microphone Jim Ralston began with a presentation of their credentials.

###

Don McNelly is eighty-five years old and has run 713 marathons. Norm Frank, at seventy-five, has run in 913 marathons. Just to put this into perspective, one must realize that the normal marathoner runs in two marathons per year. To match Don, a marathoner would have to run fifty-nine years doing one marathon per month. To match Norm, a marathoner must run seventy-seven years doing one marathon per month.

At the conclusion of his introduction, Jim Ralston asked Don and Norm to join him at the podium, and the thunderous applause began. The award was a crystal sculpture representing Niagara Falls flowing onto a black onyx base; quite majestic in appearance, but at that moment it was more impressive to watch the faces of the runners and other people in the room. They clearly had trouble wrapping their minds around such an accomplishment. showing their respect and agreement at the announcement.

Figure 1: Don McNelly & Norm Frank Receiving the 2006 Rainbow Award (Jim Ralston in Center)

For some reason I think of a quote I once heard: "They may forget what you said, but they will never forget how you made them feel." At that moment, I knew this to be true.

There was the pasta party, a tradition at marathons, held at the Brock Plaza Hotel.

I needed to ask a question of someone who had entered this race to win the prize money, so I mingled, listening until I heard the words, "Yes, I think I can win!" I stopped and listened, then asked, "How do you do it? How do you run so far and so long?"

There was a thoughtful pause as the runner collected his thoughts. "Let me put it this way. The body of a runner, including his mind, performs on automatic pilot. It's at mile eighteen, twenty, or twenty-four that most runners hit the proverbial wall, forcing the mind to kick into full gear, as the body wants nothing more than to stop the pain. It's either get the mind in override or quit. You see, its all about mind conrol if you want to be first across the finish line."

I stood next to woman in line at the buffet and told her that I planned to do my first marathon and could not quite wrap my mind around what it would be like.

She said simply, "If you've never done a marathon, you couldn't possibly understand the mindset of a marathoner. If you've done one marathon, though, you will likely do another because you discover yourself. You test your limits and you find out what you're made of."

On the other side of me I eavesdropped on a conversation.

I set small goals for myself so that I can concentrate on getting to a place on the course that I can see in the distance. I concentrate so hard that it blurs the pain in my legs. I keep doing this until I cross the finish line.

Don had told me, "Not many things in life push us to the brink. Not many things test our nerve like a marathon, and that's one of the main reasons why I do them. You can make it a good experience or a bad one just by your mindset. It was a matter of showing your body who's boss."

I returned to my seat at the table, sitting next to Don, and knew that my mentor had the information I needed to cross the finish line, so I asked him for any last-minute advice.

Remember from your first step that you're in it for the long-haul, so we start out slow and steady. You aren't going to win the race, but if you go too fast you won't live to race another day. Even though we're going to walk, you should still compete to be your best. Most of us never win a marathon or our age group, but we can set a PR (personal record) or make progress from our last effort. You'll find that whether it's a physical or mental challenge, trying to do our best drives and motivates us.

Though Don was not shaped like these marathoners now that he was older, there was still strength in his body that was younger than his years, and I had seen that, to his peers, Don McNelly was definitely one of them.

At 6:16 a.m. on Sunday, October 22, we drove down the highway to the Brock Hotel to pick up Norm Frank, who was starting the marathon with us. Two friends who can banter back and forth can be so much fun to listen to. They began a conversation about how dedicated some marathoners can be. Don told of a Japanese marathoner who was around fifty years old and owned his own business in Japan but was never there since he was always traveling. Don estimated this runner was back and forth to America at least five to six times a year and knew that at one time he had been to Europe at least four times in one year. "He must be crazy," Norm said, laughing.

Norm next shared a story of the car accident he'd had recently. After letting us know he had not been hurt, he told us that when the car was hit, the air bag was released, filling the car with white powder and making it hard to breathe. If the accident hadn't injured him, the airbag was definitely trying to do him in.

It was the same type of exchange that people have on an ordinary day, though this was not just an ordinary day. I would have thought they would talk about what they would need to do to finish the marathon. Instead they talked of everything but what we were about to do.

Outside it was raining in earnest, setting the three of us to rummaging through the bags we had received at the expo and pulling out the yellow ponchos. Norm reacted to the weather, saying, "You can't catch a good day with this marathon. Usually there are great autumn days with nice sun and the leaves changing as you're running along the Niagara River. But not on race day!" Don agreed as he checked what looked like a wristwatch, but wasn't.

"What's that," I asked. Don replied, "It monitors my heart."

Heart rate monitors gained popularity in the mid-nineties when people found them useful while training and doing workouts. Over the years, they became standard on many exercise machines. There were several types of monitors to choose from. The most common were the heart rate monitor watches and the strapless heart rate monitors. The watches are lightweight and can be used by anyone who wishes to lose weight or increase cardio training levels. In Don's case, he wore it to monitor his heart rate, so he had a chest strap, which was a sensitive piece of equipment that actually registered the heartbeats and transmitted the rate to the receiver in the apparatus on his wrist.

Soon it was time to debark from what had become the only dry space in this universe, and as my husband pulled the car over to the side of the road, for a moment I wanted to stay inside.

We started out in the dark in our yellow rain ponchos, which made a swishing sound with each step we took. All I could do was shake my head in frustration and trudge on. I was prepared for the cold weather, but that didn't mean I liked it. On the contrary, I had specifically tried to avoid it. But here I was, my first time out, walking in a marathon through cold rain drops, even colder wind to come, forcing me to keep walking to stay warm.

It rained frequently, everything from light mists to torrential downpours. High winds transformed tolerable conditions into miserable ones as we tried to adjust to the weather. I had to keep reminding myself that it was worth it, as I would be able to study Don in his natural environment and learn more about marathons than I could in any other manner. Only I was having doubts.

There were water stations that were entertaining with music, supportive shouts, and costumes. There were runners that passed by, giving us words of encouragement as they went by. Before Don said, "Look, here come the other runners!" I was already staring at them in disbelief.

The weather was 40 Degrees F. (4.5 C), a light rain falling and the prediction of increase winds on the Niagara Parkway just ahead of our location. These runners passed us in sleeveless shirts and very short, shorts, looking oblivious to the weather. Others behind them had short sleeve shirts under their yellow rain ponchos. Later runners on the course had leotards under their shorts, but nowhere near the amount of clothes that we wore.

The first wave of runners passed by us easily, which was not surprising. Don, Norm and I wore long pants or leotards to keep our legs warm. We also had on lightweight winter outdoor attire from hats, gloves and coats and of course our rain ponchos. It seemed so appropriate on that day with What did surprise me was

To take our minds off the rain, Don told a funny story about the first time he ran in a French-Canadian marathon.

I had quite a few marathons under my belt and felt confident I knew everything there was to know about marathoning. Everything was as expected until I reached the first water stop. I could hear them as I approached, yelling "Eau," and as I took the water offered, I figured I hadn't heard them correctly and kept on running. I was feeling good as I came to the next water stop, my mind elsewhere as I reached for the water and barely heard them yell "Eau." By the time I reached the next water stop, I was feeling ignorant as they continued to yell "Eau." It was either I wasn't hearing them correctly or something was wrong with either them or me. I heard the same thing over and over again and finally gave up trying to understand something that had no meaning whatsoever. It was later as I crossed the finish line that I finally figured it out. They weren't crazy and I wasn't hearing wrong. They were yelling "Eau", which is the French word for water.

No more did I doubt there would always be surprises, even doing something over and over again.

We walked in silence for a while before Don told me another story.

Whenever Don thought of the Portland Marathon, he thought of the music at the water stops, and that thought would lead him to tell a story of Noriega.

Former Panamanian leader General Manuel Noriega had failed in an attempt to secure an early release from prison in the United States. At a parole hearing in Miami, where Noriega was serving a thirty-year drug trafficking sentence, officials heard arguments for and against his conditional release. But the petition was turned down apparently after concerns were raised about the security risk his release could pose to the former US President George Bush. It was Mr. Bush who in 1989 ordered US forces to invade Panama, which led to Noriega's arrest. He was brought to Florida for trial in January 1990, and subsequently convicted on drug-trafficking charges. He was initially sentenced to forty years in prison, but this was later reduced by a US judge to thirty years. According to US parole guidelines, the general would now remain in prison until 2007, when he might be released if his behavior in prison was considered acceptable.

Noriega was Panama's chief of police from 1971 to 1984, when he took command of the army, and in effect, the country. He was still wanted in Panama on charges of executing army officers in 1989, and the Panamanian authorities in 1999 requested his extradition from the US. What sparked this memory was that Noriega surrendered at a Dairy Queen, and they got him to get out by playing rock and roll music turned up loud. Music played a big part in the Portland Marathon.

I realized how unique Don was to be doing what he was doing at his age. As I walked beside him, I felt a need to thank him for being a friend and allowing me to share this opportunity with him. I was reminded of a quotation by Sir Isaac Newton as I walked in the rain and heard the swishing sound of the cellophane rain gear. "If I have seen farther than others, it is because I have stood on the shoulders of giants."

We passed by many water stations, which where more than just that. From Harley riders, to clowns, to a Mustang Club, to crazed high schoolers, the volunteers were great fun and so upbeat, helping to take our minds off the rain and our aching bodies, and Don told me about his brothers who sometimes ran with him.

The McNelly brothers got together at marathons about three times a year. They compete in the marathon and ultra marathon in and around Ohio. One time that Don recalled was when the brothers met at the fifty-mile ultra marathon in Hagerstown, Maryland, and then got together in Toledo, Ohio, in June at the Glass City Marathon. They had been doing this since their youngest brother (fifty-two-year-old Dick) started running in 1975.

[Note to layout: Subheading] *Runners World* Twenty-Four Hour Relay

One time, Don said he entered the *Runners World* Twenty-Four Hour Relay, designed for anyone who liked unusual and challenging events. The twenty-four hour track lapper has had forty-two teams from fifteen states and Canada, but had yet to have a five-brother team compete. The course was open for six hours, set for a thirteen-and-a-half-minute per mile pace, with four miles done on a crushed limestone Towpath Trail, of which the first two miles were on flat land, followed by a three-mile densely wooded San Run Park, before lots of rolling hills. The last two miles of the course were a long descent to the finish line. Don looked forward to running this relay race with his brothers.

The course had four exchange zones for the relay, which was run along with the marathon. These exchange points had vans to transport runners back to the start or finish line. So the runner had the option of stopping at certain points along the way.

It was a marathon that had the team members run one mile and hand off the baton on the fly, and because you only had to run one mile and had time to rest, you would run wide open. So, Don and his brothers were out to set a world record, because a team over fifty had never done it before.

This would not be the only time that Don had family companionship. At times when Don ran in the fifty-mile ultra marathon in Dayton or Kettering, Ohio, or Hagerstown, Maryland, his brothers, Dick, who was born in 1928, and Byron, born in 1929, would join him. That would make these ultra marathons special and a lot more fun, and Don would say, "A family on the run, I suppose you could say."

Once at the *Runner's World* Twenty-Four Hour Ultra Marathon, the brothers—Don from Rochester, New York; Byron from Kettering, Ohio; Dick from Elyria, Ohio; Larry from Victor; and Robert, who lived in New Lebonon, Ohio—made up a five-member relay team, the first ever with all brothers. Running in Kettering, Ohio, they were half way through when Larry was picked up by his nephew Steve, who was taking him somewhere, and they ended up smashing the car. They were lucky; no one was hurt, but it meant they would not get the "family" record. Not ones to give up, they went back the next year and did it together again getting the record.

The rain just kept coming, and then it was accompanied by a tailwind, making it hard to remember why I was out here doing this. Between water stations, crowd support was non-existent, and by mile fifteen I was beginning to feel the strain.

Don was not running out of stories to share as we kept going. He asked if I remembered the movie *Uncle Buck*, which came out in 1989, and I wasn't sure, so Don filled me in.

Don explained that the parents of the woman who played the mother in *Uncle Buck*, lived down the street from him on Pinegrove. Don's wife, Phyllis, was close to Elaine Bromka's mother, and they used to go out to movies and shopping.

By mile twenty, Don and I walked mostly in quiet, with only words of encouragement that we were getting close to the finish. Then, ahead, we could see the spray from the falls, and we knew we were almost there. We had been walking for over nine hours when we finally crossed the finish line.

Before reaching the finish line, I had noticed a few walkers behind us. One couple seemed to be helping each other along the final leg of the journey. I would have liked to watch them cross, but I was busy accepting the thermal blanket that someone threw around my shoulders. Then I managed a few more steps to collect a bag of snacks and the medal before joining up with my husband, who drove us back to the motel.

The first thing I noticed once I was seated in the car was that my legs ached. My body was stiff from my head to my feet. This was unexpected, as usually my body tended to recover quickly once I stopped walking. I had a feeling this wasn't going to happen anytime soon.

Once inside our room, I quickly stripped off the wet clothing that was plastered to my body. I couldn't get into the shower fast enough, as I hoped the warm water would help loosen my stiffening joints. I remember thinking to myself this must be how the tin man felt in *The Wizard of Oz* as he waited to be oiled, only my fix did not solve the problem. I could barely lift my leg over the edge of the tub, dry myself off, and put on dry clothing. If Don felt this way, I couldn't imagine him wanting to do another. Then I remembered the difference wasn't in age; it was in fitness. Don was probably past the point of dealing with my symptoms.

I did one more thing before allowing my husband to help me in the car. I assured myself that the camera and the recorder had done their job. They had. All that was left to do was say goodbye, and then, as I barely managed to step over the edge of the sidewalk, I watched as Don climbed down the flight of stairs that led to his room. How did he do it, I wondered as I folded my body and managed to fall into the passenger seat next to my husband. Don came over to the car and we said our goodbyes. He leaned in and added, "Don't worry, you'll feel like your old self again". I thought I heard a slight chuckle in his voice, but I could have been wrong.

The experience was one I knew I would never forget, and it helped tremendously in seeing Don on another level. He wasn't a total mad man, but there was something crazy in all the marathoning he did. I had wondered if I could make it through just one, and he had done many. I smiled, remembering something he had said: "If God brings you to it, he will bring you through it."

BROOKVILLE, OHIO

Any marathon in Ohio was a homecoming for Don, who was born in Brookville.

Brookville was an expanse of fertile farmland that dots the horizon, a haphazard hamlet situated sixteen miles from Dayton, Ohio, and an area where the historical tornado activity was slightly above Ohio state average. Here, the ordinary life consisted of farming, hunting, attending school, and meetings of the 4-H Club. It was in this farming community that this story begins.

Don's parents had taken up residence in the Brookville area, since it was where they had spent most of their life. His dad, Russell, had gone through the sixth grade before dropping out of school. Now with a family to support, he rented a one-hundred-acre farm. His mother, Harriet, having attended a "normal school" that had been established to train elementary school teachers, and in some cases provided a year or two of training beyond secondary school, had the credentials and accepted a position as an elementary school teacher to help support the family.

It was from this background that Don was nurtured. With an intellectual mother and a hardworking industrialist father; he could observe firsthand the differences an education could make.

If strength is in a name, Don's parents chose a whopper, naming him Donald Pershing McNelly. His first name is from the Gaelic name Domhnall, which means "ruler of the world," and two kings of Scotland have borne this name. His middle name is claimed from John Joseph Pershing. General Pershing was born in Missouri and would become known as John "Black Jack" Pershing for the role he would play as Commander in Chief of the American Expeditionary Force in the First World War. But a lesser known fact is that Pershing entered the military service as a means of achieving an end. Coming from a humble home of nine children, John Pershing would grow up helping to work the family farm, and later he would become an outstanding figure in American History by accident when he responded to an announcement of an examination for admittance to West Point, which was what changed his life.

Donald Pershing McNelly was born on November 11, 1920, on the family farm in Brookville, Ohio. The year was memorable as the decade known as the Jazz Age or the Roaring Twenties, which began with the election of President Warren G. Harding and culminated in the catastrophic stock market crash of 1929. America had just seen the end of World War I, and having survived that and the worldwide influenza epidemic that followed, they were ripe for good times.

Mark Twain once said, "Keep away from people who try to belittle your ambitions. Small people always do that, but the really great make you feel that you, too, can become great." That was as true as trying to live up to the name you were given. Donald Pershing McNelly would begin his life not that unlike John Pershing's upbringing in Southwestern Ohio. Don was raised in a small rural area called Brookville.

On the McNelly farm was the farmhouse, with a barn nearby for horses, hogs, milk cows, and hay, along with sheds to store grain and farming implements. Close to the house was an orchard of apple trees, a few rows of berry bushes, and a chicken house. Beyond that were the fields for rotating the planting of corn, clover grass for grazing, hay, and wheat. The farmhouse had four bedrooms, which could get mighty cold during the winter, since the house was heated by a wood stove on the main floor which called for constant attention to keep the fire going.

When Don was born, there was never a question of what he would do as soon as he was able. He would help out on the farm. Two and a half years after his birth, Don had a sister whom his parents named Ramona. Three years after Ramona, came his brother Bob, followed by Dick, Byron, and Doralene.

But farm life wasn't all work and no play. From as far back as he could remember, music played an important part in the McNelly household. When Don was quite young, his father purchased an old Nickelodeon piano for his mother, who played beautifully.

Don loved that old piano and remembered that on the day of its delivery, he watched as four men were needed to carry it into the living room, as the piano weighed around five hundred pounds. That was a payday to Don. As he followed the men into the house, he could hear something loosely moving about inside the piano. Curiosity kept him close until finally the piano dropped nickels on the floor and he turned to get the okay from his dad before gathering up the money.

By the mid 1920s, American business seemed to have entered a golden age that would go on for some time. New industries were booming—automobiles, radios, motion pictures, household appliances and the like—and the public was buying more than ever before. Yet, in reality, business was not as rosy as it seemed. While the new industries were flourishing, some more basic ones, such as farming, suffered a steady decline in prices that gradually undermined the country's entire economic structure.

Farmers like Russell McNelly faced an economic slow-down. People had no money to buy the crops and animals that farmers produced, and many farmers lost their homesteads. In foresight Don's father took a job at the Frigidaire Division of General Motors in Dayton as a blue-collar group leader in charge of a line that machined compressor bodies. He was not aware of what this change would eventually mean for his son.

Russell showed his children the ropes in farming. The older children were assigned responsibilities such as feeding the farm animals or working in the fields. One of Don's jobs was keeping the wood box full, which he did faithfully along with his other responsibilities. One day on Don's eighth birthday, his mother said to him, "Donald, there was no wood in the wood box."

Don replied innocently, "But it's my birthday!" Don was confident that this was an excellent reason, so he was unprepared for her response.

"Well, Donald, then you are old enough to work on your birthday."

There were generally six to eight good milk cows on the farm that not only supplied the family with fresh milk and butter but furnished some cream or butter to sell. Of all the jobs, milking the cows was a least favorite chore. As an incentive on the McNelly farm, the rule was that when they were old enough to milk their first cow on their own, they got a dime from their mother. A dime back then was an impressive amount of money, which short-sighted the children, who later learned that once they earned that dime, they were destined to milk from that point on.

Life went on following the same pattern most days, but every now and then there was a treat. For Don the best treat of all was when he was around seven years old, he was allowed to spend a lot of his time at his aunt's new home site at the edge of town where she was building her house. Don liked to help the contractors and often pretended that he was supervising the project. That along with 4-H Club became the highlight of his life.

Figure 2: The McNelly's Line Up By Age

There was one outing that remained constant, and that was going to church every Sunday. Church played a major role in the McNelly upbringing, and that required the purchase of an automobile, since it was too far to walk. Because of the size of the family, Don's father purchased a 1909 seven-passenger Plymouth. This was a big deal, as not until the late 1920s was there reported to be one automobile for every five Americans, and the McNelly's car, therefore, represented a step up in the social structure.

Every Sunday the family got up early, dressing quickly for the ride together to church. Yet, even though they liked riding in the car, like most children, the McNelly brood was no different in dreaming up excuses to stay home. Rarely did they succeed in remaining behind, and when they did, his parents had rules. They had to be "can't get out of the bed" sick and could not, under any circumstances, preview the funny papers until everyone returned home from church.

Figure 3: Four Generations of McNellys

Around this time, another family tradition developed: taking family pictures. There was a routine established that required each family member line up by age for the picture. If anyone was missing and unable to be part of the family picture, they would leave a space where that person would normally stand in the lineup.

Don worked, played, and sheltered his siblings during those early years, and the farm work helped to strengthen his body. Considering what was left to do for idle hands and minds, working on the farm, going to church, and attending school were worthy outlets.

By 1938, Harriet and Russell would have their last child, Larry.

The 4-H Club and Camp Hook

Not surprising, farm life led to joining the 4-H Club, and Don became an active member, not only to hone his farming skills, but to make contact with other children his age. Early 4-H programs emphasized skills for the farm and home, and only later did they adopt a broader opportunity for training.

There were projects for 4-H members, and for Don there was also Camp Hook, which he would attend faithfully for several years. There he was around other children who understood what it was like to roll out of bed at five o'clock a.m. and have more to think about than a bowl of cereal for breakfast, since there were hungry cattle to feed in addition to their rumbling bellies. It didn't matter that 4-H was a working club. Don, like other 4-H youths, enjoyed raising animals, crops, and creating old-fashioned arts and crafts that seem quaint in this age of iPods and touch phones. Being a member provided an outlet for creativity as well as a means of learning responsibilities and strong work ethics.

One year, Don decided to try something new and chose to raise a prize steer. This was a long-term project for Don, not one for completion in a year. His project was for a market steer, which meant he had to select and feed it for market weight and be the one responsible for caring for it. The work was time-consuming, but his efforts paid off when at age fifteen, Don's steer was named reserve champion[i] out of at least sixty entries. His steer wore the purple ribbon for second place.

Figure 4: Don with his prize 4-H Steer

Such an outcome gave bragging rights at Camp Hook that year, but more so it made him stand out from the crowd. Like most 4-H camps, this one was co-ed, housing the boys on one side and the girls on the other side of the camp property. Like most other camps for children, there were camp leaders and adult supervision. The campers were not always separated, since they ate their meals, swam, and played sports together. Knowing that for most of these members, paying a fee was a hardship, the camp accepted not only cash. In lieu of a money exchange, a camper could supply fresh vegetables, such as a bushel of tomatoes, beans, or corn, which would be served as part of a meal.

The older campers looked forward to attending the nightly campfires. Something about a roaring fire and the darkness surrounding the perimeters enhances the need for companionship with the opposite sex. The campers knew this and, therefore, had their blinders off, searching for the one they hoped to sit next to on that log in front of the fire. Don had his eye on one girl with whom he hoped to be paired, but he was shy and had only taken notice of Phyllis and did not make his move before the moment passed.

He eventually became a Camp Hook leader and had a group of younger people under his command. In this role, he was involved in providing leadership for 4-H and other youth programs and organizations. He gained information and experience for planning, conducting, and evaluating camp responsibilities, activities, and programs. Although he didn't know it then, 4-H was about to shape his destiny.

General Motors Institute

As a result of those famous words of Roosevelt, "I pledge you, I pledge myself to a New Deal for the American people," 1937 proved to be a landmark year for the labor movement. The country was recovering from the Depression. The sensation of prosperity was real enough during this period in Don's life and had an intoxicating effect as he had harbored a desire since the fifth grade to be an engineer. Don had looked beyond farming for several reasons, but mainly because he felt that by becoming an engineer, he could help solve problems that were important to society and be active in creating advanced technologies. He also knew that engineers had significantly higher starting salaries than college graduates with bachelor's degrees in many other fields. Engineering seemed a more secure career choice over farming, even though society would always need both occupations. Being strong in both mathematics and mechanics made this an excellent career fit.

In 1937, Don was ready to continue his education beyond high school, and an opportunity revealed itself for a way to attend engineering school. Russell McNelly was working at General Motors, a company that was presented with a vision from a man named Kettering, who believed in combining learning with practical needs. This theory took root and led to the birth of the General Motors Institute (GMI) in 1926. Kettering once said, "I think that the greatest education in the world was the education which helps one to be able to do the right thing at the time it has to be done."

Don's father had been a blue-collar worker at the plant when it became one of the emerging champions of the workingman in the mid-1930s. General Motors, along with U.S. Steel, made an early move to sign union contracts to unite the voice of organized labor. What became more important to the family was that Russell was able to open the door for his son to continue his education.

Don attended the General Motors Technical Institute for eight weeks at a time in Flint, Michigan, and then worked for eight weeks at a time at Frigidaire, which General Motors Corporation purchased in 1919. In 1921, General Motors moved the company to Dayton, Ohio, as a subsidiary of its Dayton Electric Light Company (Delco), a convenient solution for Don, who could spend his eight weeks living at home working at Frigidaire and on the farm.

His engineering training was extremely technical, with math and science taking up most of the curriculum. Therefore, some general subjects, such as English, were not emphasized.

Although this was a busy time for Don at home and at school, as a social person, he slipped in one more commitment, and that was joining a fraternity. He managed all his responsibilities without letting his grades slip, a necessity during this period when there were more people looking for jobs than there were jobs available. It was part of their training to be told that if they did not shape up, seventeen other individuals could take their place. With this threat hanging over his head, he did only what he could do successfully, but luckily this included many of his past commitments, such as 4-H Club and Camp Hook.

In 1937, a fire broke out at the McNellys' Brookville home, which was located in a remote area near the edge of town. It happened one day as his father, Russell, and Don were mowing the lawn and happened to look up and see smoke coming out of the upstairs of the house. Russell sprang into action, and taking the garden hose, he turned on the spigot and began running with the hose. Don ran with his father, focusing on the smoke above them and not aware of the hose wrapping around one of the clothesline poles. Before reaching the house, the hose had wrapped itself tightly, forcing his father to pull harder until he found himself being jerked backwards, knocking his father on his rear end and loosening his lips. It was comical to watch, but the situation called for quick action. His father down, Don was in shock, but not so much that he hadn't heard the words that burst out of his father's mouth.

In seconds, the two of them were again racing toward the house, knowing as they looked up that the fire was out of control. Flames now licked across the roof, engulfing it in waves of black smoke that could now be seen beyond their property and soon caught the eye of a neighbor down the road, who put in a call to the fire department.

Luckily no one was hurt. When the firemen arrived with their equipment, they soon had the situation under control, but not before the flames had burned through the upstairs of the house, filling it with smoke and leaving major damage in its wake. Later when it was all over, Don remembered those forbidden words his father had blurted out, realizing that was the first and would be the only time that he heard his father swear.

LOVE AND MARRIAGE

The 1930s were a period in history that saw rapid change to the simple way of living.

The hard work of farming was not looked upon as a chore, but more a necessity and a way of life. This had been the way for so long that the simple changes brought excitement, one of which was indoor plumbing, which the residents of the town had enjoyed for some time, but the families on farms were just experiencing the joy of not having to make that cold, long walk during the winter to the outhouse.

The reason for the delay had been the wait for the electrical lines to reach the rural homes, and once that had taken place, indoor plumbing was not far behind. Don's parents remembered that day and spoke of the change to electricity as though it were a miracle, especially the wonderful instant when the lights came on, allowing Don to turn on the "juice" for the first time. But there was so much more on the horizon.

Electricity led to a radio in the home. For entertainment, there were movies with sound, and even though the sound didn't always work, it was still worth going. Movies became another important form of entertainment for everyone of all ages. In Don's home, there was work to be done and attention to school, but now and then there was a chance to go into town and see a movie. They provided an escape from the hardships of the Great Depression, if only for moment.

The Great Depression changed the lives of people who lived in town and those who lived in the rural farm areas. Harriet would tell her son, "No one had any money. We were all in the same boat. Neighbors helped each other through hard times, sickness, and accidents. Farm families got together with neighbors at school programs, church dinners, and dances. Children and adults found ways to have fun for free—playing board games, listening to the radio, and going to outdoor movies in town. The sad part, though, was that many people put off getting married because they had no money to start a home and family.

By the time Don was ready to date, life was far easier, and there was much more to do than sit around and talk.

"Behind every successful man," the saying goes, "there's a good woman." I once saw a magnet that said, "Behind Every Successful Man was an exhausted woman." Yet as clichéd as this saying was, Don's life took on new meaning once he met Phyllis.

They were teenagers when they really met. Don was between his freshman and sophomore years in college when he first approached Phyllis Jean Filbrun, a high school senior. They sat beside each other at 4-H camp and talked.

Don and Phyllis were no longer strangers. This was not the first time they had seen each other, but it was the first time that they showed more than a passing interest. Campers knew everyone at the camp, as the same ones came year after year, and beyond a nod of recognition when their paths met, what they were thinking was never spoken until that day.

Don would tell me his version of that day and what happened afterward.

###

It was August of 1939. That year when I attended the 4-H camp I was a camp leader, and that made me feel important. That evening I put on my fraternity T-shirt and wore it to the campfire. I saw Phyllis seated at the campfire, and I sat down beside her, and being a college kid now, I tried to be laid back and sophisticated. From that first moment, I knew she was special, and I told her about myself and my family. She responded by telling me about herself and her family. Just that allowed us to see how much we had in common. It was a good basis to hope she would say yes when I asked her out.

I was so happy when she said yes that she would go out with me, and even to this day I can remember the date. We had our first official date on September 3, 1939, the date when Britain and France declared war on Germany.

Figure 5: Don & Phyllis on a date (October, 1941)

###

Phyllis would agree with some of what he said when she shared her version of meeting Don McNelly.

###

I noticed him before, when attending 4-H camps, but we didn't meet until one evening at a campfire program when Don chose to sit beside me and start a conversation. Now, six decades later, I'm still not sure why. I was a certifiably shy high school senior, and he was an outgoing college sophomore and a camp leader. Mostly he talked and I listened. I agreed to a date the next Saturday if he could get the family car. Having never dated before, it would be a new experience for me. He lived on the far side of the county, and our farmhouse had no phone, so I waited, never really expecting to see him again. But he did come! We drove to Dayton in the huge car, saw a movie (Nelson Eddie and Janet McDonald in *Blossom Time*), and stopped for fudge cake a la mode en route home. It was a pleasant first date, and the rest was history.

###

Tension filled the air Sunday morning, September 3, 1939. At 11:15 a.m. the Prime Minister of England interrupted the regular radio broadcasts to announce that Britain and Germany were at war. Don had gone over to the Filbrun farm, which was twenty-five miles from his parents' home but still in the same county. He borrowed his parents' hulking green automobile with its three rows of seats, knowing that it wasn't the most romantic means of transportation, but it was all he had at his disposal.

If the war encouraged anything, it was the need to act quickly on one's choices. With the real possibility of being drafted any day, or feeling the urge to enlist to defend our country, it would be stupid to not act swiftly when you knew who you wanted in your future. Phyllis expressed how it felt to be engaged.

Figure 6: The Engagement Was Announced

###

After college, we were engaged and each living at our family homes. We both worked at a General Motors plant in Dayton, I as a secretary and Don a tool designer. With World War II raging then, it had been converted from making refrigerators to machine guns. Almost everyone was working six days a week, but we managed to get a Friday and Saturday off for our wedding. On the day of the wedding, at my family home where it was to be held, Mother cooked and baked, Dad repaired the sagging yard gate, big sister cleaned, and little brother struggled to make a chain of tin cans. It was for tying on the rear bumper of the groom's car. A rural custom back then, it was to sound off the alarm should the couple try to slip away early for their honeymoon. I shortened my new dress. Ever practical, I had selected a heather blue crepe, which I could and did wear often thereafter. I also gathered flowers from the long row in the garden and otherwise fussed about. Don, it turned out, had to go to work that morning of our wedding. His family, all eight of them plus grandmother, arrived shortly before. So did the friends we had chosen to act as our witnesses. They were a couple of schoolmates with whom we had double-dated at various times. Last came the minister from the church near our farm. All seated themselves in the living room while the minister, Don, and I stood at the doorway. The ceremony was short and no-nonsense like my dress, but rather elegant in its simplicity. Afterward we chatted, opened gifts, and feasted at a long table on the screened-in porch. The feast included roast beef, chicken, and many noodle, vegetable, and dessert dishes, which was just like my mother. She was a fine cook and always went that extra distance to please her family. Even her prize-winning angel food cake with spun sugar icing seemed better than usual. Shortly after that, Don and I met quietly outside at a far corner of the house and sneaked to our car. But our brothers were waiting for us and dashed after the car, yelling, pounding on buckets, and otherwise slowing us down on our way out the long lane to our new home and life.

###

War caused a shortage of funds for wedding expenditures; so many marriages were celebrated at simple, tasteful gatherings held at the bride's home with all the family there. It was a wedding like thousands of others performed across Europe, the United States, and Canada in the years during and after the War. Time, money, facilities, and place dictated how people arranged and celebrated the most significant experiences of their lives. Strangers in hotels took the place of family, and tradition was a luxury that had to be put in the back of a closet, to be pulled out sometime in the future when the heart of the world beat more regularly once again. So in many ways, Don and Phyllis were lucky to have family with them on their wedding day, April 25, 1942.

After the wedding, life went pretty much back to normal. Don was still in school, finishing up his senior year in college; so after their marriage, Phyllis stayed at her parents' home until he graduated. She had been attending Ohio Wesleyan University but quit when they got married. She still did not have much idle time, but during the time she did have after working all day, Phyllis, an organized individual, set all family pictures in albums with notes so that there was no mystery to what was happening in the picture. Don loved her organization and so much more about her. He would say she was indeed a beautiful woman, inside and out, and the joy of his life.

With his schooling completed, Don and Phyllis settled down in Dayton, Ohio, during their early married years, with both holding down jobs at Frigidaire. Two years later, their first son, whom they named Thomas McNelly (Tom), was born on April 2, 1944, in Dayton. The McNelly's would move a few times during those early years.

Don and Phyllis were living the American Dream of success, happiness, and financial comfort. They were in love, had good jobs, a home, and a child.

NAVY LIFE

In September 1939, the war in Europe began when Germany invaded Poland with a massive and quick attack. Poland was defeated; Germany took the western portion, while the Soviet Union took the eastern part. France and Britain responded by declaring war on Germany, and later, in the summer of 1940, Germany launched an air attack on Britain. In a massive air war, the Luftwaffe, the German air force, began to mount assaults on British RAF (Royal Air Force) stations. The French had hoped to hold off the Germans by use of a strip of defense along the French-German border, which proved futile, as the Germans simply proceeded around it and into France. France had fallen.

Japan decided to cut off vital Chinese supply lines from Southeast Asia. The U.S. responded by cutting Japan's supply of American goods. Japan wanted to return to its expansion plans, so it turned on the one force that could thwart them: the United States Navy.

The war in the Pacific began on December 7, 1941, when warplanes from Japan launched a surprise attack on the U.S. Navy base at Pearl Harbor, Hawaii. They sank four battleships and destroyed nearly twenty aircraft. The next day, the U.S., Canada, and Great Britain declared war on Japan.

In 1942, the United States and Japan engaged in a series of naval battles, climaxing in the Battle of Midway, in which Japan suffered a defeat. Three events helped turn the tide on the Japanese. One of them was the Doolittle raid in which sixteen B-52 bombers surprised Tokyo. It was of little military value but psychologically of great value. The second event was the Battle of the Coral Sea, which halted the Japanese attack on Port Moresby. The third was the Battle of Midway, in which Japan sent a large fleet to capture one of the Hawaiian Islands, but the Americans intercepted the plan and prepared for a surprise attack. In 1943, Germany was forced into a full-scale retreat.

On the homefront, the lives of millions of Americans were changed, heightened, and sped up by war. Shortly after the birth of his first son, Don made the decision to serve his country while Phyllis did defense work in Dayton and cared for their son on the Filbrun farm in Wayne Township.

Figure 7: Don Is A Navy Man

It was June of 1944, and Don was overseas by early September. His brother Bob also joined the navy. During wartime, the term of duty was served until the War ended, which meant they were in for the long haul. Don's first position in the navy was ensign, since he had a background in engineering. Within six weeks of enrollment, Don was shipped overseas.

Figure 8: Don OnBoard The USS Kyne

Don McNelly served in the navy as a lieutenant during World War II as chief engineer on the USS Kyne, a Destroyer Escort, DE744. It was one of our many ocean-going ships in service during the war, smaller than a Destroyer. It was used primarily for screening convoys of supply ships to provide anti-submarine protection but designed for limited conventional fighting if necessary.

During the first typhoon, Cobra, in December of 1944, Don's ship was anchored in the semi-protected area of Ulithi, an atoll in the Caroline Islands of the western Pacific Ocean. The semi-enclosed area outlined by Ulithi was eighteen miles long and nine miles wide, forming a lagoon that was the fourth largest in the world and was located near Japan and was the main anchorage for the third and fifth fleets during the later part of the war. In this area in Ulithi, the ships were protected to a degree

Don's ship, the Kyne, was at sea near Okinawa during the second typhoon, where they experienced the full force of that severe weather. Six sailors were killed by what the navy dubbed Typhoon Viper; thirty ships were damaged and seventy-six aircraft destroyed.

Don served under Halsey and also under Vice Admiral Slew McCain, who reported directly to Halsey.

Operating together with support units, the Kyne departed the atoll Ulithi in February to provide a screen for refueling operations during the Iwo Jima invasion. When that island was secure, giving the United States an air strip vitally needed as base for future B-29 raids on Japan, Kyne returned to Ulithi in March. Sailing again as a screen to oilers, she made her way to Okinawa—the last step on the road to Japan. She continued screen and patrol operations for the support unit throughout most of the Okinawa campaign.

The Kyne cleared San Pedro Bay in the Philippine Islands in June to screen escort carriers as they provided air support for the invasion near Balikpapan, Borneo. Following the Borneo landings, she returned to the logistic support group during July, as planes of the fleet rained fire on the Japanese home islands. Upon cessation of hostilities in August, and after forty-three days at sea, the USS Kyne arrived in Tokyo Bay as part of the occupation force. It departed Yokosuka in October and arrived in Philadelphia via Pearl Harbor and Long Beach.

During his commission on board the Kyne, Phyllis was able to keep abreast through newspaper articles:

Ensign McNelly on First Destroyer to Enter Tokyo. During the recent occupation of Japan by the US, Ensign Donald McNelly on military leave from Tool Design Department Plan One was aboard the first US destroyer to enter Tokyo Bay.

Brookville Star Newspaper and Frigidaire Bulletin, September 1945

Ensign McNelly has been overseas for 13 months and was a veteran of the Philippines, Iwo Jima and Okinawa campaigns. He is the son of Russell McNelly, Dept. 12 Plant One, and the brother of Ramona McNelly, Dept 217 Plant 2. His wife Phyllis and son, Tommy, reside at Sulphur Grove.

Brookville Star Newspaper and Frigidaire Bulletin, September 1945

Valley Man in Jap Waters - Aboard the first U.S. Destroyer to enter Tokyo Bay Aug 28, 1945 was Ensign McNelly of RR 9. His ship entered the area at the head of the convoy that brought the first occupational troops to Japan. Ensign McNelly, son of Mr. and Mrs. Russell McNelly of Brookville, attended Brookville High School and General Motors Institute before entering the service and going overseas 13 months ago.

Dayton Daily News, September 1945

Since women's participation in the war effort was essential for an Allied victory, gender roles were dramatically altered, at least temporarily.

Phyllis chose to work, and she stayed with her parents until the end of the war and Don's return to civilian life.

Phyllis worked in the office of General Motors, preparing the paperwork needed by the company managers. Her days away from the plant were filled with caring for her family. To get around, Phyllis had the car that she and Don had purchased and that Don had used to drive back and forth to school. Although it wasn't new, it was to Don and Phyllis, since it was the first car they had ever owned. Their 1934 black Chevrolet coupe was eight years old with only one row of seats and a rumble seat. They loved it.

Figure 9: Don & Phyllis's first car - 1934 Chevy with rumble seat

As time grew near for Don's return to the States, Phyllis received word that he would be stationed in Florida. The next move was to find an apartment before sending for his family to join him. Being a stranger to the area, this took some time since he wanted a safe and nice neighborhood. When he finally secured a place, Don sent for his family and without hesitation, Phyllis began planning for the move.

Since she had been living with her parents, Phyllis and Don hadn't accumulated much that she would have to take with her beyond personal items and small treasures, and all of it packed easily into the car. The first thing she needed to do was give notice at work, which she did immediately and used the next few weeks to get all her affairs in order and finish packing their belongings. Finally she was ready for the long journey ahead, but the last preparation would be the hardest since Phyllis had never been far from her family and friends. It was hard to move on, as tears and instructions to keep safe were repeated until finally Phyllis was on her way with baby Tom in tow.

The weather was warm that day as Phyllis drove down the family driveway and turned onto the dirt road, so happy to be on her way to reunite with Don, but sad at the same time. It did not matter that this was the first time she would be driving such a distance alone or that it would be the first time that she had traveled beyond the Ohio State limits. She started with confidence, beginning on Route I-70 and then taking 1-75 to Dayton. On she drove through Lexington and Richmond, Kentucky, stopping only for gas, since her mother had prepared food for them to take on their journey. Then it was on to Nashville and Chattanooga, Tennessee, before entering Georgia, and finally she was making her way into Florida. The total trip took her over 785 miles of long hours behind the wheel.

Phyllis occupied her time seeing to the needs of her son and enjoying this newfound freedom. She knew that many wives had remained home while their husbands were stationed overseas, and like herself, they would be reuniting at the military posts, some as far from home as herself. But she felt lucky, since other wives of enlisted men had nowhere else to go but to follow their husbands. Phyllis had her family. Being able to stay with relatives was the best alternative, since the servicemen received little for family maintenance: minimal travel allowances and inadequate or no housing.

The closer she came, the more excited she felt, until soon she was in St. Augustine, Florida, where Don had rented space in the Homestead Guest House, a century-old Victorian building. This was to be her new home, and Phyllis was determined to make their new living arrangement comfortable, and she did.

With unpacking behind her, reuniting with her husband made it all worthwhile and there was something more. She had never been this far from home before or lived in a suburban setting, which she found quite different from farm life, since there was much to do and see, all of it within close range. St. Augustine had the distinction of being the oldest continuously occupied settlement of European origin in the United States. By the mid-twentieth century, Americans took to the highways in search of a vacation land, and St. Augustine became a destination for automobile-borne visitors.

The area was attractive, and its beauty did not go unnoticed as Phyllis found time to take in the sites with baby Tom in his carriage. Right from the start, Tom was a healthy, bright, and active child, and for Phyllis, who now wanted to spend as much time as she could taking in the sites, Tom was a blessing. At Ponce de Leon's Fountain of Youth Park, Phyllis and Tom viewed the excavation of the actual stone cross that Ponce de Leon and his men laid out in the sand upon reaching Florida shores. Nearby, Nombre de Dios marked the first Spanish Catholic Mass and Mission on American soil. They went for walks almost daily to the Our Lady of La Leche Shrine, which was the Ancient Mission of Nombre De Dios where Father Lopez de Mendoza Grajales offered the first mass. This was where she lived now, in this breathtaking setting, and here she would remain for the next four months.

Don's ship had returned to the United States after the war with a very commendable accumulation of six battle stars. Each day, Don drove the fifty miles from Green Cove Springs, Florida, and back to be with his family in St. Augustine until his discharge papers were in his hands. Now it was only a matter of time before they could return home.

On Tuesday, April 2, 1946, shortly after the decommission ceremony, Don was ready to move with his family back to Ohio. The town, family and friends, were there to welcome the McNellys back home, and once settled in Don would take up where he left off as a tool designer for the Frigidaire division of GM. An article appeared in the Brookville paper, running with the title, "Chief Engineer on Destroyer Returning to Job in Dayton."

Recently released to inactive duty in the Navy at the Jacksonville, Fla. Naval Personnel Separation Center, Lt (jg)

Donald Pershing McNelly of Dayton will now resume work as a tool designer for the Frigidaire Division of GM. In the Navy, Lt (jg) McNelly served as Chief Engineer aboard the Destroyer Escort Kyne during the invasion of Iwo Jima and Okinawa strikes against Luzon and Leyte and the bombardment of the Japanese coast. Just returned from the occupation of Japan, Lt (jg) McNelly received his release from active duty Tuesday, April 2. He is the son of Mr. and Mrs. Russell R. McNelly of RR 6 Brookville and is married to the former Phyllis Filbrun of Dayton. They have one son, Thomas.
Dayton Daily News and Frigidaire Bulletin in 1946

During the Eisenhower era, America experienced a time of prosperity, and the McNelly's were home to enjoy it. Comedian Mel Brooks said it best: "When I was a little kid fifty years ago, in 1946, I had just got out of the Army after two years fighting in the war. The American Dream was a house and a car. Today, the American Dream is winning American Idol. It's changed slightly. In another fifty years from now, when the economy collapses and everything is in threads and torn, the American Dream then, in 20-whatever, will be a house and a car."

On the date of his release from the service, Don's son, Tom, turned two years old. The day they celebrated his birthday was a happy one, and there was a special birthday cake, thanks to Phyllis. Phyllis had been washing the dishes while listening to her favorite radio station when an announcer came on, informing the audience that the radio station was holding a contest. Phyllis stopped what she was doing to listen and heard the announcer say that if your child was celebrating a birthday on April 1, you could win a birthday cake for the celebration. "Just mail in your child's birth date, your name, and address to participate in this promotional event."

At first Phyllis sighed as the birthday was announced. It was a day earlier than Tom's birthday. She continued doing the dishes, but she couldn't keep her mind off that cake. How special would it be to have a beautiful birthday cake for Tom's second birthday, a day they would be sharing with his father? She found herself toying with the idea of the promotional and finally decided to send in her entry, as it was just one day earlier than Tom's actual birthday. Why not?

The wait was stressful. The idea that she entered the contest sort of illegally had her regretting taking such a bold step. Then she thought, if it were not to be, it would not be. If she did indeed win, then God wanted this for her family. And she did indeed win the cake. So on Tom's two-year-old birthday, with both Phyllis and Don present, there was a beautiful cake with two candles for him to blow out.

The birthday, and the fact that Don was home to share the day with them, was not the only reason for Don and Phyllis's happiness. They had learned that they were expecting again. Phyllis was due in November, so the McNelly's were soon to have another important celebration. On November 3, 1946, Daniel McNelly (Dan) was born in Dayton, Ohio.

Phyllis and Don easily continued where they had left off before he went into the service. They accepted each other unconditionally in a marriage that was filled with love and happiness. They wanted a family, and that wish had come true for them. In short, their marriage was a source of joy and fulfillment.

It was a year of firsts. The first celebration of Thanksgiving as a family since Don's return from service went smoothly in some ways, but it took twice as long to get the dinner on the table. And then came Christmas, days in between filled to the brim as Phyllis even amazed herself at how well she managed to handle it all and make it happen in the knick of time.

Don was drawn away from home by his job, leaving Phyllis to manage the homefront. He knew it wasn't easy for her, even though anyone could tell she loved taking care of her family. He was so proud of how well she handled everything, from changing diapers to putting the finishing touches on each meal, and doing it with a smile. She was to Don an incredible woman even then before the madness began.

LIVING THE AMERICAN DREAM

Between 1946 and 1960, every pointer for national wealth and prosperity had risen. The stock market was more than twenty times higher than during the depression year of 1932. The gross national product was almost 250 percent higher than at the end of World War II, and the median family income had almost doubled. What this meant for a majority of Americans was a material life of incredible abundance. By 1960, America was the richest nation the world had ever seen.

For the McNellys, life too was getting better and better. After the birth of their second son, Don had not only completed his schooling, but had served his country as well.

He was an engineer, and as such he liked developing economical solutions to technical problems. It was his joy to work through the dynamics and come up with a finished product. Don had his sights on a supervisory position, allowing him to employ all the elements of his talent. He had heard the jokes about engineers but still wanted to join their ranks. Things like, "For an optimist, the glass is half full, for a pessimist, it's half empty, and for an engineer, it's twice bigger than necessary," and his personal favorite, "A scientist can discover a new star, but he cannot make one. He would have to ask an engineer to do that."

Don found his training as an engineer was about to pay off, that plus his dedication to the job would open doors for him. When those doors did open, it came with another change and that was to move his family once again.

Ohio had been home to Don and Phyllis since birth. Here they had grown up on the farms of their parents and enjoyed a life that was about to change dramatically, but in a good way. There had been a short time during the service when they called Florida home, but they had always planned on returning to Ohio. Only now this was a promotion that required them to move out-of-state and settle in Hartford City, Indiana, where Don would begin work as an engineer with the Fort Wayne Corrugated Company. The year was 1948.

Hartford City, Indiana, in Blackford County, was seventeen miles north of Muncie, Indiana, and sixty-three miles north-east of Indianapolis, and the area's claim to fame was its large natural gas reserve. Following the same pattern as before, while Phyllis finished up in Ohio, Don was busy finding a new home in Indiana. Again it was a matter of seeking a home in a strange place and to make it the best choice for his family. By the time set for the move, Don had found and purchased a house on a half-acre lot that was located on the borderline between Hartford City and the country. There was one possible problem with the location, and it was that the children in this rural area attended a one-room schoolhouse located within walking distance of their home. This caused him concern, since he knew something about one-room schoolhouses.

So Don did some checking and was able to get Tom into a bigger school, where the educational environment was more to their liking.

From the moment they moved in, the McNellys felt right at home. Having been raised on farms, Phyllis and Don went about planting crops for the joy of seeing them grow and to feed their family. As past 4-H members, they had competitive natures, so not all the crops were consumed; some were entered into the growers' competitions. They won a blue ribbon for their tomatoes and later won another one for their kola rabbi crop. Since they were the only ones to enter this category, they just might have had an edge.

What was but a new experience, soon became very much a part of their life as they piled up fond memories in Indiana that made it more than a stopping off place, for here Phyllis gave birth to their daughter, Nancy Ann Filbrun McNelly, on October 31, 1949. This would be the last addition to their family.

Three children with three different personalities kept Phyllis on her toes night and day. Don did his part too, but sometimes there was a home project or two requiring his attention, and though most times he was able to fix whatever was broken, it didn't always work out that way. Such a project happened to surface for Don in 1951 when he noticed that some trees in the backyard were interfering with the powerlines. Deciding he needed to clear away some of the trees, he went about cutting them down, but what was left was tree stumps in the backyard that needed to be removed. That would require some help.

Don had met a friend at the paper company in Jacksonville by the name of Ked Martin who told him he had been a demolition expert in the army, so Don gave him a call to see if he could help him out. Ked said, "Sure." A few days later, the two drove the 138 miles from the plant to Don's house in Hartford City. There Ked looked over the job and off they went on the five-mile-drive to Montpelier, where they purchased the dynamite and blasting caps needed to do the job, which was perfectly legal back then. After signing for the dynamite and the blasting caps they had purchased, they drove back to Don's house, set the dynamite charges, ignited them, and went for protection. The dynamite went off, blowing out windows and scaring the life out of Don, who thought the house was going to go up in flames.

After that fiasco, some pesky stumps were still left. Don was not about to call on his buddy again, but instead decided to do it himself. One stump in particular was right next to the house, so he dug around the base of the trunk, cut the dynamite into little pieces, and put them in. When he ignited them, they blew the dirt away from the stump so that he could chop off the roots and remove the remains. That chore done, he tackled another stump that was under the telephone wires in the back of the lot. He followed the same steps as before, only when the stump blew up, it flew into the power lines above, and fragments of wood were all over the place, with some tangled in the wires themselves. He felt sure the police would cart him off to jail when they saw the mess he had made of the wires, so he stood below them and kept throwing things up at the wood pieces, and eventually he was able to untangle the branches and chunks of wood so that they fell harmlessly to the ground. He now had thoroughly learned his lesson and vowed never to attempt that feat again.

For Don, being in charge of quality control at the Ft. Wayne Corrugated Box Company became a demanding job, and even more so when in 1948 he found that he was constantly on the road traveling between plants in different states. This continued through the years as 1949 became 1950 and then it was on to 1951 and 1952. His love of the job didn't change. It was what he was missing in his personal life that worried him. He was only catching glimpses of the children growing up and had so little time to spend with his wife. It was not the life he intended to continue.

He was thirty-two years of age when the opportunity presented itself to accept yet another promotion within the company. In 1952, Don was promoted to production manager in charge of manufacturing boxes for the company. In his new position, he would manage box factories in Rochester, New York; and later in 1955 he was given charge of Pittsburgh, Pennsylvania; Springfield, Massachusetts; Hackensack, New Jersey; Baltimore, Maryland; and Wilmington, Delaware. The position called for him to manage a testing laboratory with five young women as testers, and along with traveling to the out-of-state plant locations each month, his plate would be full and he still had to find time in his schedule to prepare written reports for management.

With each promotion came more responsibility, but Don and Phyllis adjusted and kept the family on an even keel, with Phyllis taking on more and more of the responsibility of raising the children. While on the road, Don kept in contact, and while home, he spent his time catching up with the family's activities. Each promotion was a result of his work ethic and personality, allowing him to provide his family with a better living. This was something that both Don and Phyllis respected, even if it meant making sacrifices since it would all pay off in the long run.

It was a hectic schedule, but Don loved a challenge. With the job and the travel, he needed to consider another move that would lessen the distance of travel, and after discussing this with Phyllis, the plans began. This time moving would be more involved since they had to consider the needs of their three children and the fact that they had accumulated more than just personal belongings. There was also the house to be sold before the family of five could make the move.

What Don had discussed with Phyllis was that to be centrally located, the family would have to move to New York, and they made what would be their final move in 1954 to Rochester, New York. There they rented a house for a year in the suburb of Greece while they familiarized themselves with the area. Each week they went looking at homes, and the suburb of Irondequoit caught their eye. They fell in love with a house that was only a year old and was the last house on a dead-end street called Pinegrove Avenue. The location was great for raising children, and the quality of the school system was well in line with what they had hoped for their children.

From the moment they had settled in, Don's job had him on the road again. Don was constantly traveling between the factories and spending many nights away from home. The children were now ten, eight, and five, and it took all of his wife's time to stay on top of their homework and their outside activities. And then something wonderful happened when in 1955 Don was promoted again, this time to General Manager for Production and Sales for the total packaging company operation. His overnight traveling lessened, allowing him to spend more time with the family. Most days he had sales trips to Buffalo and Syracuse, which he could complete in a day and be home for supper.

Then in 1959, the company was sold to St. Joe Paper Company. This change had little effect on Don, since he remained General Manager, doing exactly what he had been doing before.

St. Joe Paper Company in Rochester, New York, was a company born in the Great Depression that prospered and expanded into a billion-dollar conglomerate under the iron hand of Ed Ball, who was DuPont's brother-in-law. It was a company with a future that met Don's career objectives.

Don was now an involved father, and he loved it. He wanted his children to be well behaved, appreciative of the past and the present, and generally have a wealth of knowledge, so Don and Phyllis wasted no time setting the stage.

When entering the McNelly home you could hear music, classical music floating through the air as the phonograph played the vinyl recordings in a strong analog sound, the needle moving along the spiral grooves. Almost every day the music played, and the children grew to like it, even missed it when the phonograph was silenced.

Magazine subscriptions were purchased and placed around the house to catch the attention of the children. There were issues of *Scientific America*, a popular science magazine that had articles about new and innovative research for the amateur and lay audience and *National Geographic,* which provided free maps, photos, videos, and daily news stories, as well as news articles.

Making these articles available to the children and taking the time to talk to them about the music they heard or the articles they shared became valuable family time. But Phyllis did not stop there. The library became Phyllis's second home as she made trip after trip to sign out books to read to the children at first, then later books that they could read on their own.

Don knew he was fortunate having a mother who, as a teacher, had done an outstanding job instilling his appreciation for education. Now he saw this same personality in Phyllis as she provided a rich educational environment for their children.

EDUCATION IS THE KEY

The year was 1961, and just as Don's family had grown, so had the company he worked for continued to expand, opening several new plants. Don was still a General Manager and still traveled extensively to the plants currently under his supervision. He was friendly, forthright, and capable, which may be the reasons he was chosen to handle the opening of new plants, adding onto his already-full schedule.

He was there when they opened Memphis, Tennessee. Then, due to an internal management problem, Don was asked to take charge of the Pittsburgh Plant when their manager was fired. As the years progressed, Don found himself filling in several times while the company searched for new management at other plants, and his willingness to accept the responsibility advanced him once again. Before the end of the year 1961, Don was promoted to Regional Manager in charge of six plants, which put him on the road again, traveling every week for two or three days and staying at home on Mondays and Fridays. He was becoming an expert at balancing his career with his family life. Although it was hard, he was always conscience of his responsibilities as a husband and father, making sure that his family was not negatively affected by his career.

Don was doing everything right, and it was proven when in 1966 his progression up the corporate ladder continued with a promotion to vice president and a member of the Board of Directors of St. Joe Paper. He had chosen the right career and landed the right position in a company that recognized and showed its appreciation for his ability.

At the age of forty-six, Don had achieved more than most people would expect. He was at the top of his career, his children were following in their parents footsteps as they sought the best education possible. He was happy in his marriage, his home life, and on the job. There was no reason for him to anticipate anything going wrong.

THE EYE OPENER

Don's generation had earned their leisure after facing the results of the Great Depression and the challenges of World War II. In the 1960s, prior to the White House Conference on Food, Nutrition, and Health, the importance of nutrition had yet to be fully appreciated. Instead this was the decade of change, with the introduction of different foods and cooking habits in the consumer's kitchen. Consumption of meat and sugar reached record levels, probably in reaction to the years of rationing. Sliced white bread gained popularity, and cereal makers branched out from the familiar corn flakes and whole wheat breakfast cereals to produce sugar-coated cereals. For those in the corporate world, beef-eating was almost portrayed as a patriotic endeavor, the power lunch of the executive, and there seemed to be no reason not to indulge.

A heart-attack is a frightening event, especially back in the 60s, and more likely to happen due to unhealthy eating habits. Yet it was easy to assume it wouldn't happen to you even if statistics said it could. Unlike today, facts and statistics were not well known, nor were the symptoms common. People believed that a heart attack was sudden and intense, like a movie heart attack, in which a person clutches his or her chest and falls over. The truth is that many heart attacks start slowly, as a mild pain or discomfort, which is why people don't know right away they are having one. These symptoms can come and go for quite a while until it is too late to turn it around.

For some, the warning comes from another direction, and they react to that wake-up call. The narrow escape of a mishap, the close avoidance of a loss, helps us realize how fragile life is, and how close we are to death at any moment. For Don, a friend's death started him thinking about a change in his personal lifestyle.

It came out of the blue and frightened him so deeply that it would change his life dramatically. Ken Evans had gone to General Motors Institute with Don and lived in the same fraternity house. Don graduated in 1942, and Ken, just a year or two behind him, left General Motors Institute and went to work at Rochester Products (now Delphi), a block north of St. Joe Paper Company on Mt. Read Blvd. They were now both engineers with good paying jobs and had kept in touch.

The Evanses had a cabin in the Adirondacks, and they often talked about vacationing together, as their wives were also friends. The vacation in the Adirondacks was a way to relax, play, and hike through trails leading to majestic high peaks, isolated waterfalls, or forest glades. Even the drive there was breathtakingly beautiful from all angles. There they could see the St. Lawrence River and the Tug Hill Plateau in the west, and Lake Champlain and Lake George in the east. After spending time there, it was much easier to return to their demanding jobs and lifestyles. It was just such a vacation that Ken and Don had planned with their wives when the call came from Ken's boss at Rochester Products. This couldn't be happening. He must have not heard him correctly. Only when the words were repeated, it was perfectly clear that he had heard right. Ken had died. He had a heart attack!

After he hung up, Phyllis could see that something was wrong, but she gave Don a minute to recover. Then, he turned to her and said, "That was Ken's boss, and he said that Ken, that Ken was dead." "What, Phyllis, asked?" "Ken had a heart attack and died. I can't believe it." At first, Don was shocked by the news, and then he felt guilty, wondering what he could have done or said to prevent this from happening. Because they were friends, living basically the same lifestyle, Don began to wonder if he should be worried about his mortality. For the first time, he realized just how fragile life could be. If this could happen to Ken, it could happen to him, so Don decided to turn his life around. There had to be something he could do to improve his life expectancy.

He did not waste another minute. He had an appointment for a physical with family physician, Dr. Leo Stornelli. This was the best preventive medicine of the time.

When that day arrived, Don went to his appointment praying for a clean bill of health, and in a way his prayer was answered. Dr. Stornelli told him he needed to exercise, cut down on his fat intake, and try to lose weight. This was not the first time Don had heard these instructions from his doctor, but the difference was that now he was listening and intent on knowing what exactly was required to eliminate the possibility of him having a heart attack or facing any other physical problems. Yet he had to admit, he wondered if all those changes were necessary. Did the good doctor want him to tackle it all at once? His doctor told him that there was only one way to go about lessening the possibility of having a heart attack, and that was by reducing the risk. If he wanted a guarantee, he needed to start taking control of his life, lower his blood pressure, reduce his blood cholesterol, and, above all, become physically active each day. Dr. Stornelli was running three miles a day himself.

And so his fitness regime began when Dr. Stornelli gave Don a book entitled *Aerobics*, by Kenneth H. Cooper, M.D., M.P.H. Today, aerobics has become a way of life, but keep in mind that Don was introduced to this book in the '60s. Cooper published *Aerobics*, his first bestseller, in 1968, but not only did he introduce a book, he introduced a new word and a new concept to America. It caught on like lightning as millions of people started exercising. They were motivated by his preventive-medicine research and public appearances, and this motivation fueled a worldwide fitness revolution. After reading this book, Don saw the light and knew what he must do.

An engineer at heart, Don loved statistics, and this book had one that Don still recites: if you get yourself in shape, your resting heart rate will go down ten beats a minute. In his book, Dr. Cooper went on to point out that the average adult heart beats about 60 to 100 times a minute at rest. The resting heart rate usually increases with age, and is generally lower in physically fit people who exercise routinely or take medications that slow the heart; then the rate may drop below fifty-five.

All Don knew was that the cardiogram clocked his heartbeats at seventy-two. Never settling for less or in this case more, Don wanted his heart beat lowered. He reasoned that if God had assigned him a certain number of healthy heartbeats and he was already borrowing more, he had best climb on Dr. Cooper's bandwagon.

"Where to start?" was the question in Don's mind as he wondered which course would lead him down the path of success to change his life.

This was ground zero, as he hadn't any fitness routine set up, and the more he checked around, the more confused he became. He could join a gym and work out with other sweaty men in a confined area. He could purchase equipment, and he read up on the value of doing lunges to work the major muscle groups in his legs: quadriceps, buttocks, and hamstrings. There were cardio exercises to strengthen his heart, sit-ups to firm up the midriff, free weights for upper body strength, running and walking, aerobics, and on and on. It was too much to research, so he took the easy way out. He would do what his doctor did: run.

Don couldn't help thinking about what Dr. Stornelli had told him. "An aging body gradually slows down." Don was nearing the end of his forties, so the time had come to get in motion.

He had his game plan in place. He would be a runner, but early on he found exercising was arduous, and finding time to exercise was challenging. After all, he had a job and a family to support. Yes, it was easy to find reasons to hold him back from starting, but he just had to remind himself to think about what his family would do if he were to die.

He ran slowly at first, until he began to build up his endurance; speed would come later. He was determined to be content with gradual improvement so that he could sustain his new lifestyle. Besides, he wasn't in training for a race of any sort; he was in training to save his life. He ran when he could, but not with any routine, and then he was again given a sign. Just a week after hearing about Ken's death, another close friend died of a heart attack.

What was this? One shock was enough to get the message through he needed to exercise and he was doing it. But now, he figured God didn't think he was doing enough. Why else would the shock come in pairs. Whatever the reason, Don was not going to wait and see anymore.

He was going to get physically fit no matter how long or how hard he had to work at it. He for one, wanted to be around to see his grandchildren.

When Don began to run in earnest, he was thirty pounds overweight.

Don drove to West Irondequoit High School's quarter-mile track and stood looking around the oval path, holding his towel and stop watch. He was feeling good standing there in the warmness of the day and wearing what he thought was the best pair of shorts and top for the job ahead of him. He had invested in a new pair of running shoes that felt good on his feet. Not sure exactly what to do, he mimicked other runners he had seen pressing one heel and then the other heel to the ground to stretch their Achilles tendons. He followed this manuever with that of raising his arms over his head and lacing his fingers together as he leaned to the left and then to the right. That done, he stood a moment, trying to think of what else he should do, but nothing came to mind, so instead he stepped onto the track and began to run. Anyone seeing him could tell he was an amatuer. He started out running quickly, not slowing down as he completed one lap, but he could not run any farther. This was unexpected. Here he stood breathing heavily, trying to slow his breathing down but unable to. As he leaned over and placed his hands on his thighs to keep him from tipping over, it didn't help much, so he stood up and tried to take a step. His legs felt like lead weights in those expensive running shoes, refusing to make a step forward. At that moment all he wanted to do was climb into his car and head home; only he didn't think he could make it to the parking lot. Instead he concentrated on breathing properly, and slowly he found himself in control once again, so he decided to take a step, and then another, until he knew he would not give up. He didn't, and he was smarter as he took it slowly, walking and running around the track three more times until he had one strenuous mile under his belt.

He should have been proud of his accomplishment, but he wasn't. He had not thought that a one-mile run would be asking too much of him, and thought that a quarter mile would be a breeze. Winded and tired, he climbed into his car and headed home. He was in worse shape than he had imagined, putting on such an embarrassing performance. Not used to losing, Don vowed it would not happen again.

But, of course, it did. The following evening when Don returned to the track he found that he could not complete a mile without periods of walking in between, but he knew there was always more than one way to look at a situation. As he thought it through, he realized he had made improvement. Even though he had done some walking, he had run a bit farther before having to give in to walking again. With a new attitude, round and round the track Don went until the mile was completed. This time when he climbed into his car to drive home, he was happier with himself.

From that day forth, Don could be seen every evening jogging around that high school track, always going farther and farther before giving in to walking. He eventually managed one lap at a slow run; he got so excited that he wore himself out but refused to quit as he walked the last three laps around the track. He continued pushing himself. Closing in on his forty-eighth birthday, in November of 1968, Don ran five miles without having to slow down to a walk. The moment was monumental, as he reached up over his head and ran as though he were crossing a finish line. In a sense he was, because at that moment he felt in control. He was a man who had never been serious about working out and had never taken part in athletics until he started running, because, until now, he never had time for sports. That was a major accomplishment that he was not about to let pass idly. He would celebrate by sharing the news with his family and anyone else who would listen.

Don slowly increased his endurance until he became hooked. He no longer had to force himself to run; instead he found himself looking forward to the moment when he was free to pursue his new sport. On that Thanksgiving Day weekend in 1968, Don did his first five-mile run off the track without stopping. That day his children and extended family were home for the holiday, looking forward to the Thanksgiving feast. Don decided he had time enough to run around the block before the festivities would begin. Phyllis, Tom, Dan, and Nancy were used to this madman who needed to run, so while he took off, they went about preparing the meal. Only he went farther, as he ran down Pinegrove Road until he reached St. Paul Blvd. There he turned left and kept straight onto Cooper Road. He ran along Cooper road until reaching Titus Avenue and there turned left. On he went, feeling as though he could go forever and found himself turning right onto South Kings Hwy and knew it was time to turn back. It was quite cold outside, but Don had dressed appropriately with leggings under his shorts, a light weight but warm coat, a knit hat pulled down over his ears, and gloves. Now as he retraced his route back along the path he had taken, he knew he had done his first five-mile route, and it would remain his standard route for some time afterward.

Don would remember that first five-mile route run fondly; expecially the part where he happened to look down and noticed that his sneaker had come untied, but he didn't stop; he continued to run with the lace dancing back and forth until he was at his own front door. Then he walked in and said to his family, "Guess what I just did?" No one replied; they just looked at him as if he were insane as he announced his latest accomplishment. In his family's defense, it was a family holiday, and Don thought it might have played out differently if it were not Thanksgiving Day. From that day forward, when he put on his running shoes and headed for the door, they would say, "There goes Dad again."

Don had set no minimum speed, weight limits, required distance, or number of goals. He had no specific form, mandatory gadgets, or experience level that would make others assume he was a runner. Don believed that if you have ever run, and if you run, you can consider yourself a runner. You can even skip a day, week, or months of running and still be a runner. You can run fast or slow and some days even walk. You can run in races or avoid them entirely, and yet you are a runner. For Don there was only one guideline worth following, and that was that he ran his run. And if he chose too, he would run his race.

It surprised even him when he realized that he wanted to run in a race now that he was a runner, after all his purpose was only to get physically fit and avoid an early trip to the grave. But now he seemed to have a different agenda in mind, one that he never realized had made an appearance. So he started looking for races to enter to add another level to his running, but he quickly found they were hard to come by, especially when he wanted to run long distances. Some were three miles, others were five, and they always had a special race for the men over age forty, which was Don's category. He remembers entering a race called the Rose

Festival, which had a predominantly flat course and a moderate incline at mile two, something Don ran almost every day. This gave him encouragement as he signed up for the race.

On that cold, rainy day, six men were running in the over-forty category. As they stood together at the start line, the other men complained about their aches and pains. One said he had a bad knee; another said his back hurt. Don was quiet, thoughtfully listening to all the excuses, and slowly the idea dawned on him that he had a chance. He just might win. They fired the gun, and they all took off, leaving Don in their dust, moving farther and farther ahead until he no longer could see them. He was stunned right up until he crossed the finish line and overheard the runners talking. They had not been spoofing him; they did not want to look bad in front of the other runners, so they had made excuses in case they did not do well.

That was a lesson he never forgot, so when he was again in a race with the same five men, he paid no attention to the complaints; instead he focused on his personal aim. They had five trophies to hand out. Don already knew these five men were faster than he was, so if he wanted one of those trophies, he needed to concentrate on beating at least one of them. With that in mind, he planned on running as fast as he could, but something happened that day. One of the runners named Rodney Carter, God rest his soul, got lost and went off course, so Don won fifth place to receive his first trophy. That, for Don, was his lucky day, and somehow that day marked the beginning of marathons.

THE 1969 BOSTON MARATHON

Running had been the furthest thing from his mind, and Don never fantasized that someday he would be running in a marathon. He had a barrel of excuses for why it seemed impossible. When he was younger, he was too busy bailing hay, chasing cattle, doing homework, and learning as much as he could. Then his career demanded time for him to become secure and able to support a family. When his children came into the picture, he treasured moments spent with each of them, so that took up even more time. He had long ago convinced himself he had no time for exercising until he was forced to recognize what he was doing to his body. Even then a marathon was too foreign to imagine, but as it turned out, in April of 1969, Don would enter the Boston Marathon.

Mention to anyone the word "Marathon" and immediately they think of the Boston Marathon because it is the oldest of the marathons. At the first annual Boston Athletic Association on April 19, 1897, this United States marathon was born to commemorate the famous 1775 ride of Paul Revere. The topography of the 24.7-mile course—Metcalfe's Mill in Ashland, Massachusetts, to Boston's Irvington St. Oval—was similar to the Athens course, although 250 meters shorter. Fifteen runners started that eventful race, but only eight finished the 39,751 meters.

A problem arose later when it was noted that this marathon did not match the distance set in London at the 1908 Olympic Games. Not everyone was in agreement to make a change, but a standard needed to be set. After sixteen years of debate, the 42.2K (26.2 miles) distance was established as the official marathon length at the 1924 Olympics in Paris. Following this decree, the Boston Athletic Association officials adjusted their course distance in 1924 to what they thought equaled the official

26.2-mile distance. They were wrong. The Boston Athletic Association discovered a few years later that the Boston course was 161 meters short; again they went about making a change, and this time the distance was correct. As a result, records for a full 42.2K marathon cannot officially be taken from Boston marathons until after 1927, but even though the distance wasn't correct, this is still the oldest marathon in North America.

For marathoners who set a record prior to 1927, this decision had to be devastating, especially since they had done nothing wrong. Imagine what was required to run in a full marathon without walking or stopping for about three hours, only to have that achievement go unrecognized. However, having a standard proved to be important, especially with more and more marathons being born.

From a small percentage of participants, the Boston Marathon grew, and with more competition, some marathoners were finishing in slightly over two hours, but the truth be told, only a small percentage of marathoners break the three-hour mark, which soon became the goal for the faster marathoners.

Year after year the popularity of the marathon was recognized by the number of entries continuing to grow, until it was necessary to find some method of control or elimination. What was done was setting requirement to qualify for the marathon.

To qualify for the Boston Marathon, athletes must meet the designated time standard that corresponds to their age group by September of the previous year subject to review and verification. In addition, runners in this marathon must be eighteen years or older on race day. The B.A.A. first introduced qualifying times to the Boston Marathon in the early 1970s, along with setting a maximum field size of twenty thousand entrants.

Once he started running and his motivation to take control of his body became powerful, the miles became easier to put behind him. He found he no longer had to push himself to run; he enjoyed doing it. One April day, Don was in Boston for a visit with his son Tom at MIT. He stood with his son in front of the fraternity building when the marathoners came running by.

Tom had often brought pictures he had taken of the runners home to show his father and his sister, Nancy, who attended Boston University, frequently talked about the Boston Marathon. This, of course, could be considered normal since almost everyone living in Boston finds the marathon fascinating, whether they have entered it, known someone who has, or caught a glimpse of it.

This marathon became *the* marathon to enter, and even non-runners wanted to experience the race either as walkers or spectators. To Don, the Boston Marathon was like the World Series of running, but at the time, his only interest was in the spectacle of the race itself, since he did not consider himself World Series caliber, and it surely was not on his list of goals or even a dream.

So what was the difference between a goal and a dream? Some say that goals are dreams with deadlines. Winston Churchill said, *"Success is not final; failure is not fatal: it is the courage to continue that counts."* One reaches success or conquers a goal by just trying.

When exactly the Boston Marathon became more than a spectacle to talk about with his children, Don cannot say. Don just found himself thinking more and more about it, and since his nature was to try to be the best at whatever he did, the idea of entering was not easy to shake. This was an extremely high goal; he knew he would be shooting for the moon, but he had a safety blanket: if he missed, there were still the stars. He was more than thinking about running in the Boston Marathon, but not because he wanted to be the first man over the finish line. It could happen, but the probability was slim. He did not put himself up there with John J. McDermott of New York, who in 1897, emerged from a fifteen-member starting field and captured the first B.A.A. Marathon in 2:55:10; or the legendary John A. Kelley, who won the race in 1935 and 1945; and the many more who had claimed the fame of being the first one across the finish line.

Once he admitted his goal to himself, he tailored his training for that race; running, stretching, and running more until he could run a good distance. He was able to find out about the course, knew what to expect weather-wise, and somewhere had heard that he should run the first half slow even though it would be very flat. Don added plenty of downhill runs and uphill runs to his training. He was careful not to push himself too hard so that he wouldn't risk an injury. And more importantly, he knew that his training was to strengthen his quads and control his mind for the difficult Boston course, as well as the distance.

When he shared his plans with the family, no one laughed, and no one tried to discourage him. In training for his first Boston Marathon, Don set out with Phyllis, who opted to ride her bike. They traveled down his normal running route with Phyllis leading the way down Pinegrove to the Irondequoit Town Hall and back. On one such occasion, trying to keep pace with Phyllis's pedalling, Don's foot hit the back wheel of the bike and sent Phyllis tumbling over the handle bars, landing on the ground in front of her bike. Don was quickly at her side, asking, "Are you all right?" Phyllis said her wrist hurt, and Don could tell with one look it was already swelling. Here they were away from home without a car, at a time before cell phones, and with a bike to boot. Phyllis felt she could make it, as they weren't far from home, so they walked back to the house and Don went in to get his car keys. Soon they were on their way to the emergency room. The outcome was that her wrist was broken, and soon she was sporting a cast.

For nine months he worked hard at preparing his body and mind for the competition. He was not determined to win, but he was determined to finish. When the April 1969 marathon was announced, Don was ready to run the whole twenty-six miles and 385 yards. He was ready to try his first marathon.

Figure 10: Don Running In His First Boston Marathon in 1969

Don had lost weight, felt good, was more alert, and quickly becoming the talk of the office and his neighborhood. He was now forty-eight years old and planning to run a marathon, but not just any marathon—the Boston Marathon. Until that day he was positive he was ready, but it soon became apparent that he was not mentally prepared as he went out that day, nervous and tense.

The Sunday just before the race, he had run and walked twenty miles, doing a five-mile loop four times, and was proud to have survived. Although he was doing well, he was not certain he could complete the marathon in four hours, which was the specified amount of time allowed. Later he learned he had made a wise move, since that year marked the last year that one could enter the marathon without qualifying first. By 1970, a four-hour qualifier was necessary to compete in the marathon, but this April of 1969 that rule was not in place.

In the years following, that Boston Marathon qualifier would be set even lower and on the official entry form for the Boston Marathon it stated:

"A runner must submit the certification…that he has trained sufficiently to finish the course in less than four hours…"

Only Don did not know this yet.

Runners from all over the world compete in the Boston Marathon each year, braving the hilly New England terrain and unpredictable weather to take part in the race that begins at noon in Hopkinton, Massachusetts. The Marathon was considered one of the more difficult marathon courses because of the infamous Newton, Massachusetts, hills along Commonwealth Avenue that culminate in Heartbreak Hill near

Boston College. The course was modeled after the original one in Greece, which was generally flat for the first half, with a series of hills between miles fifteen and twenty and a steep descent to the finish. It is demanding even for a well-trained marathon runner, which many describe as fourteen miles of fun, eight miles of sweat, and four miles and 385 yards of hell.

Along the entire stretch of the race, thousands of fans and well-wishers line the sides of the course to cheer the runners on, encourage them, and provide water and snacks. The fans were even more encouraging for the amateur runners taking part in the marathon for the first time.

Don had to keep reminding himself that he would do his very best and would run as though he could win a prize or be first across the finish line, because that was the mindset he needed. After a year of running, his physique had changed. There was less flab and more muscle on his six foot one frame, and his abdomen was flatter, but Don still saw himself as having an unnatural athletic body. So you might ask, what was a forty-eight-year-old, less-than-a-year runner thinking?

On the day of the marathon in 1969, Don got in the middle of the crowd, which was less than a thousand participants. At noon, the gun was shot to start the race, but Don did not even see the starting line for another several minutes, and when he did, he had to battle for footing as they headed downhill toward Ashland, two miles from the starting point.

First mistake realized. He went out with the crowd but soon knew he was too big, too heavy, and admittedly slightly older. Don was sucked into the beat of the runners that were moving way too fast for him. However, he could only see two choices: slow down and get trampled or keep up. He opted to keep up. Wrong from the start, he was about to face the second mistake in his first marathon. After the first two miles, they were going uphill.

The biomechanics of running uphill were very different from running on a flat surface. When going from flat ground to uphill terrain, the physical demands on the muscles change. Even if runners are in shape, when they do something new, they tend to be sore from it later. When running uphill, the ground rises in front and forces runners to raise their legs higher and then lower their feet back on the ground. This motion works the hip flexors and stretches the gluteus (buttock) muscles. The starting uphill phase of the stride also requires more force since runners are trying to move their bodies forward while also going uphill. Now they have to use the gluteus muscles, the hamstrings, and the calves to achieve their goal.

The stride length will shorten, causing leg muscles, especially hamstrings, to work in a much shorter range than they are used to, which leads to fatigue more easily. A shorter stride also results in taking more steps than normal to cover the same distance, which, in turn, requires muscles to work harder over the same distance. The steeper the incline, the more obvious these changes become. Before runners know it, they are experiencing lower back pain.

Not surprisingly, Don was about to pay for his error in judgment. With one mile left to go before reaching Farmington, which marked six miles, Don was walking and feeling he could not go any farther.

However, he was smart to prearrange for his family to wait at the ten-mile marker in Natick. There they would cheer him on and give him water. Don was confident that he could do the first ten miles and that his problems would come past that marker. He also knew that he would require hydration at that point and might need some support to keep going.

Just shy of six miles, he was not so sure he could make it. He needed mental stability to keep himself going, and the thought of his family waiting for him in Natick was enough. He had to get to Natick, and then he would quit.

Determined, Don headed toward Framingham, too tired to appreciate the scenery or even the relief on this two-mile stretch of flatness, only knowing that Framingham marked six miles, leaving four more miles to get to Natick. Exhausted but anxious, Don found himself running downhill and then felt the ground under his feet return to flatland again. He was very close to his destination, but something had happened. Ten miles was coming up; Don was not feeling good, but he wasn't feeling bad either. He did not know what this meant exactly, but at that point, he knew he was doing okay. A little over two hours had passed, and he had covered ten miles.

A voice in his head whispered that he still had 16.2 miles to go, but he tried not to listen, as a bit of confidence started building. And then Don was at Natick, accepting water from his family and surprising himself as he told them, "I'm hanging it up, but I think I'll go another three so I can say I did half the marathon. Meet me at the thirteen-mile mark."

No one knows Don better than his family. They could see he was pushing it, but he also had that gleam that said to them he did not want to admit defeat, at least not yet. They watched as he continued through Natick. Don was unable to appreciate the scenic Lake Cochituate as he passed by. When he finally reached Wellesley, the halfway point of the marathon, the screams of encouragement in front of Wellesley College filled his head while he searched the crowd for familiar faces. He saw his family and an arm outstretched with a cup of water, but before he reached them, someone else had taken the cup. Somehow it didn't matter, not because plenty of water was being offered, but from a feeling within that became clear when he heard himself say to his family in passing, "I think I'll try a bit more." Without a pause in his step, he was on his way again.

He was going more slowly than his previous pace, but the time no longer mattered. The hills were coming, and he still wanted to do a few miles at a faster pace without risking burning out too quickly. He stopped all thoughts of running, keeping his mind occupied with pleasant memories, which seemed to work as he kept a steady pace, with the down-hills forcing him to run a bit faster. To cool off he doused himself with water he grabbed from an offering hand connected to someone, but he only noticed as far as the arm length.

Mile sixteen was almost all downhill; Don pressed hard, but his hamstrings were beginning to tighten, so he slowed himself down and tried to relax. The pain in his legs was manageable, as was the pain on the balls of both feet, which had now become a constant companion, and he wished he hadn't just chosen a pair of running shoes by what was on sale. Only ten or so miles were left, and Don knew he could finish. Pain was the least of his worries as he crossed into Newton and the hills started in earnest. He was struggling up the first of the four major hills. Hill number two was better, but Heartbreak Hill loomed large; even though he couldn't see it, he knew it was there. Then there was a slight downhill length before Heartbreak Hill that seemed like a gift as he pressed on.

He was committed, but not quite aware of how deeply, as he had the family playing hopscotch with him, giving him water and meeting him at the next designated point. What a supportive family they were, as they left the decision of how far he would go up to him.

The crowds of spectators cheered the runners on and did their best to encourage each one of them not to quit. Don needed those cheers, as most of the runners did, especially as they approached Heartbreak Hill. After running twenty miles to be faced with Heartbreak Hill, ascending 0.4 miles is enough to break the experienced runner. It is the last of the four "Newton hills" that begin at the sixteen-mile marker and rise eighty-eight vertical feet from an elevation of 148 feet at the bottom to 236 feet at the top, which is not so very much to face if it weren't positioned at a point on a marathon course where muscle glycogen stores are likely to be depleted. Don was physically at that point, often referred to as "hitting the wall". His lungs worked overtime performing their role of assisting with breathing in fresh oxygen for the bloodstream and breathing out unwanted carbon dioxide. With each choking breath it felt as though he would be suffocated, but he was determined. Breathing wasn't the only problem he faced as his leg muscles twitched involuntarily, and his mind roared for relief. He reached the top only to face the 236-foot drop that would punish his body in a way he could not imagine if he didn't maintain stability of his body during the descent. He had to avoid heel striking or he would have to contend with painful knees and quads. He made it downhill and pushed on, hardly recognizing when he passed Boston College. He was in control of his mind and body now as he headed into Boston. He was running into Cleveland Circle, located in Boston's Brighton neighborhood, in very close proximity to Brookline, which he passed through heading toward Coolidge Corner, perhaps the most well known neighborhood of Brookline, MA, located at the intersection of Beacon Street and Harvard Street.

Pushing on, Don found himself at Kenmore Square the 25.3 mile mark, where three main throughways - Commonwealth Avenue, Beacon Street, and Brookline Avenue - all converge into a lively congestion of shops, restaurants, bars, hotels, clubs, and educational institutions, but all of that was lost on Don as he forged on. Boston University, was only a block away as he reached Boylston Street, that began at the intersection of Park Dr. and Brookline Ave. and would take him to the Boston Public Library, and there ahead he could see the blue and yellow painted line on the street that said "Finish."

Exhausted beyond words, he gladly clicked the button on his stopwatch as he crossed the line. The race was over, and he had stuck it out. He had started out in a sea of runners, but as he reached the finish line, nobody was there to see his finish in 5:01:00. Still, it was a victory that changed his life. So what if a fellow from Japan named Yoshiaki Unetani made it across the finish line in 2:13:49. Or that one of the three unofficially running women finished in 3:22:46. All that mattered was that he had finished the marathon, even if his run had not been officially recorded, since marathon officials stopped timing at the 3:30 mark.

Barely able to stand and sweating profusely, the forty-eight-year-old Don McNelly realized he had completed his first marathon only nine months after he first began running. He also realized that he had been over his head—or should I say out of his head—by attempting the Boston Marathon so soon. He later described it as god awful, pure agony, and pain with indescribable exhaustion, but to his credit he had finished. He vowed at that point that for the next race he would be physically ready. And that was the first time he heard himself admit that there would be another!

What was it about a marathon that one can describe his feeling of utter exhaustion and only have one thought in mind: "I'll do better the next time!" Add to that the cost to enter the races, the travel costs, room and board, and the clothes, and the wonder increases. Pain, expense, and time all go into running marathons, whether to win or just to be in them. Whatever it was, the feeling was powerful.

Later Don heard that the field topped the one thousand mark for the first time that year with 1,152 marathon participants.

THE MADNESS BEGINS

After his first marathon experience, Don joined the Rochester Track Club[ii]. At the time, the Rochester Track Club was a distance-oriented team, with summer track meets becoming the core of the club's activities. To keep himself in shape, Don began running five miles per day, five or so days a week, whenever he could. His job kept him on the road a lot, but that did not usually stop him from running. He had discovered favorite motels in the cities where he went most often, choosing them because of nearby trails; he laid out running paths that fit his needs. There was a city park in Springfield, Massachusetts, a high school track in Wilmington, Delaware, the beach in Norfolk, Virginia, and a pine forest surrounding the company mill in Port St, Joe, Florida. He also sniffed out places to run when he visited Baltimore, Maryland, and Hackensack, New Jersey.

When home, Don was in his best element, having laid out five or six routes that he routinely ran. His favorite was along New York State's acclaimed Erie Canal's picturesque towpath. Here shoppers mingled with sightseers and exercise buffs surrounded by a spectacular view, which was what marathon routes were like. Yes, the marathon organizations not only concentrate on the exact marathon length; they also try to establish a route that has beautiful scenery. Just like the marathon has more than one purpose, so did Don for his choice of this training path. Situated in Pittsford, New York, this bustling Erie Canal village is one of the earliest and best-preserved collections of nineteenth-century structures in the Rochester region and also happened to be home to Don's son, Dan. On those days when Don chose to run or walk along the canal passageway in Pittsford, Dan was at his side. It was a comfortable time, as they ran in sync with each other, so familiar they need not speak, yet they did. This was part of their life now, and neither would ever break the tradition.

Each time he ran, Don was preparing for another marathon; even though he never said it outloud, it was always there on his mind. His body knew he was hooked before Don allowed the message to pierce his brain. Don wasn't able to define running beyond just doing it. He was running for sport, for his health, and because he just enjoyed running. It didn't make him special, as everyone knows how to run and anyone can do it. The first time he admitted that anyone can do it, something happened to him. He wanted to step out from everybody, because he had never been comfortable just doing what everybody else did. He had to try and improve on the technique or in some way make it his own.

Boston Marathon on April 20, 1970

Don was again running in the Boston Marathon on April 20, 1970. It was a rain-soaked day with a temperature of forty-four degrees, and Ron Hill would slaughter Japan's Yoshiaki Unetani, who had become the hero at the Boston Marathon in1969. It was Unetani's build that matched the physique of so many runners that made Don question just exactly what did he think he was doing. Like Unetani, a five foot nine male weighting 137 pounds was the norm, and he was way out of that league. At the 1969 Boston Marathon, Unetani's time set a new course record of 2:10:30 at the Boston Marathon in 1970. Something else had changed, and that was for 1970, the Boston Marathon instituted mandatory qualifying times. Don was about to learn that that did not deter runners, but made it a critical goal for dedicated marathoners. Qualifying to run the Patriots' Day race requires discipline, patience, and plenty of miles.The field of marathoners was 1,011 starters, quite large considering the entry qualifying time of

4:00:00 hours, but some were running just to be part of the experience, since they had not qualified. Don was one of those non-qualified runners.

An official race number was necessary to enter the corral area, which was where the group of qualified runners were stationed. The Bandits, which was what the unqualified runners were called, were supposed to line up at the end of the corrals, and security ensures that unregistered runners remain behind the registered runners. The field of runners was so large that those who line up at the end of the corrals would not even get to the starting line until thirty minutes or more had passed.

Don was there, a year older but in the best shape of his life. The race was still grueling, but the outcome impressed him. Putting his mind in control of his body, Don was not only able to complete the marathon in a respectable time but found his pace stayed at a jog through most of the course. Tired, happy, and proud summed up his feelings as his running shoes crossed the finish line in 4:50:00.

It was after this marathon that Don felt a change in himself. He wasn't actually sure when it started, but it must have been happening all along. It wasn't an unpleasant change, but quite pleasing really. It was the moment of discovery that running had become fun. He actually enjoyed running and felt a necessity to do it often, and do it in a competitive way. He still didn't see himself as a winning competitor, but the thrill of competing had claimed his soul.

There were many benefits. He noticed that it offered so much more than a flatter stomach, more muscle tone, and a longer and more energetic life. Don had reached the time when his body and soul both tuned in to this stimulating activity. He was no longer just running; he was learning all he could to ensure that he could continue running.

He felt the jarring of his body, how tired he could become, and knew from his readings that there would be changes in his body's structure, functions, and even in his body's chemistry. He had to be one with his body and listen to it since any one of these effects could interrupt or even curtail this sport. By now, the thought of not running was unbearable, so he listened and gave his body the time it needed to adjust. He read and heard the horror stories that could make people think before attempting a marathon. Not blackened and broken toenails, shin splints, sore muscles, or Achilles tendonitis could stem his desire to run the 26.2 miles.

Each year Don entered the Boston Marathon and kept improving. He was there in 1971 at the 75th edition of the Boston Marathon, when in one of the closest finishes ever, Mejía dueled almost the entire way with Pat McMahon, a native of Ireland and local Massachusetts resident. Mejía clocked in at 2:18:45, just five seconds ahead of McMahon. Don was over the finish line in 4:41:00.

Figure 11: Don Enters the Boston again in 1970 and 1971

The Greater Rochester Rochester Track Club

With a mission "To promote and encourage running and fitness in Rochester and the surrounding communities by providing support, information, and events for people of all ages, abilities and levels of fitness," the Rochester Track Club (RTC) was formed July 1, 1958, by Peter Todd. During its first year, the RTC team won a trophy and had seventeen members on the roster, but it remained a basic unknown until the running craze of 1976. In 1976, the RTC merged with both the Rochester Road Runners and Brockport's College City Striders Club to become the Greater Rochester Track Club, and with the help of Bill Quinlisk, the new club was a success.

Exercising was an epedemic during the 1970s, as a fitness craze swept the United States. The era of recreational jogging exploded with widespread excitement in 1973 and 1974, as vast multitudes took to the streets and parks and began logging miles in earnest. In a matter of months, running was transformed from an activity that attracted only serious racers and physical fitness enthusiasts into major leisure-time activity. This led to the running boom that took place between 1976 and 1985 when road running took off as a sport. Along with the running boom came the amazing increase in numbers, size, and quality of local races.

Though marathons had been around for some time, for those few dozen who were enthusiasts it meant battling with traffic as they ran along backroads. For instance, the New York City Marathon held in 1970 had the runners doing laps around Central Park with only fifty-five finishers. It wasn't until 1972 when Frank Shorter won the Olympic Marathon that America took notice of the marathon.

With interest perked, it was suggested that the New York City Marathon invite teams from the the five boroughs of New York City to compete, and that, along with it happening during the American Bicentennial celebration in 1976, helped start the boom.

Athletes like Frank Shorter and Bill Rodgers were invited to participate in the marathon, and it launched the start of the marathon boom.

There were not many marathons to choose from in the early 1970s, but Don was able to find a few for a change of scenery and for more than one opportunity a year to run, since marathons schedule only one yearly competition. On October 10, 1971, he entered the Akron-Canton Marathon in Ohio, which began at the Morley Health Center on Broadway in downtown Akron, passing the University of Akron toward the Mustill Store at Lock 15 of the Ohio Erie Canal. The runners next pass through the Ohio & Erie Towpath Canal Trail and Sand Run Park. Finally the runners are on their way to the finish line as they pass through the grounds of Stan Hywet Hall & Gardens, until finally arriving at the finish line in Canal Park, and crossing the finish line in 3:59:00. His confidence grew, along with his strength, in a repeated entry in the Ohio River RRC, which is Ohio's oldest marathon. The Ohio River Road Runners Club, founded in 1966, represents a group of individuals dedicated to promoting running through its support of marathons in and around Dayton, Ohio, and the Miami Valley. Don would finish in 3:51:00. He was getting faster and stronger.

On April 17, 1972, Don was back at the Boston Marathon, doing much better as he crossed the finish line in 4:18:00. That year women were officially allowed to run, and Nina Kuscsik emerged from an eight-member starting field to win the race in 3:10:26. But marathons were not all that were going on during this period in Don's life.

In 1970, blood glucose meters and insulin pumps were developed, and laser therapy was used to slow down or prevent blindness in some people with diabetes. Since President Nixon declared what he called "war on diseases" in 1972, diabetes had risen over 400 percent[iii]. We were not winning the battle. Diabetes results from having too much glucose, a type of sugar, in the blood. High blood glucose can cause heart and blood vessel disease, which can lead to heart attacks and strokes. Damage to the eyes can lead to loss of sight or blindness. Nerve damage and poor blood flow can cause foot problems, sometimes leading to amputation. The only prevention or delay for diabetes complications was to keep blood glucose, blood pressure, and cholesterol under control. Don's mother passed away from complications of diabetes in 1972 at the age of seventy-six.

No matter where people are in life—young or old, single or with a family of their own—the death of a parent is very emotional. The loss of his mother was a loss of a life-long friend, counselor, and advisor. After the initial shock faded, he began to think of all the upcoming experiences that his parent would not be there to share. Just as it had after the death of his friend, his mother's death brought up issues of his own mortality. He needed time to grieve and say goodbye, and eventually to believe he was doing all that he could to keep his body healthy. And, even though we can see it happening, he eventually was at peace with her passing.

Until this point in his marathon career, Don had done three Boston Marathons, two Ohio River RRC Marathons, and one Akron-Canton Marathon. He was back out running again at the Boston Marathon in April of 1972, finishing in 4:18:00. He enjoyed it, but the truth be told, he wanted new marathons and new courses. He liked the Boston, but he wanted to experience what else was out there. He wanted to run on different surfaces that carried him down different routes in different cities where he hadn't been before. Even though all marathons would take him over twenty-six miles, he knew each would be a new experience for him. Not having access to the computer or the Internet to gather information, this would not be an easy task, but Don was determined, and so began his search by asking around and making phone calls. Eventually his efforts were rewarded. He entered the Milk Run Marathon in Syracuse, New York, in May 1972 and finished in 4:44:00. Then in June of 1972, Don found himself running with 202 runners in unseasonably cool temperatures. He would finish at the Glass City Marathon in Toledo, Ohio, on a course that was flat, fast, and USATF certified (Boston Qualifier). This year the the race and the temperatures were unseasonably cool. The running field included 202, but 179 would finish.

This was a different time in history, as the race results proved. All the male runners were listed by their first and last names, while every female was identified with a Mrs. or a Miss designation. Only Don wasn't concerned with who won, only that he would finish. He crossed the finish line in a time of 4:19:00. The marathon had a scenic riverbank loop course that took the runners through downtown Toledo and a tour of both sides of the Maumee River, through communities along city and country roads that enter Rossford, Perrysburg, and Maumee. The marathon honored the memory of Sy Mah, one of Toledo's greatest running enthusiasts, who once held the Guinness World Book record for running 524 marathons in his lifetime. Don never dreamed that he would someday meet Sy Mah in the flesh, or that he would surpass Sy's marathon record.

Figure 12: Running with Sy Mah, Norm Frank, & Don McNelly

Finally a marathon was held closer to home. In September of 1972, he entered the first marathon in his hometown of Rochester, New York. Here was an opportunity to not have to travel a distance to enter a marathon, giving him the added advantage of being able to sleep in his own bed. The race began at the old Greyhound Bus Station on Andrews Street. From there runners made a right turn onto Liberty Pole Way, then a left onto Franklin, on Main Street, and continuing down East Avenue. The marathon course was relatively flat with some scenic views such as the

Eastman House and the Rochester Science Museum. Don finished in 4:48:00.

Prior to the next year's Boston, Don ran in the Earth Day Marathon in March 1973, finished in 4:31:00. This marathon was first run in the Bronx in 1958 and was known as the Cherry Tree Marathon. In 1971, it was moved to Central Park and renamed the Earth Day Marathon, and in 1973, the Earth Day Marathon was moved to Westbury on Long Island.[iv]

Different scenery, different locations, and different times added a little variety, but in these early days of his running career they were all practice for the Boston Marathon. Something was different this year, as his oldest son, Tom, was doing post research in Zurich, Switzerland, marking the first time any of his children had been so far from home. Don recalls April 16, 1973, as a very hot day. He never felt strong from the very start, and keeping his interest up to finish the race was hard; even though this was the marathon he looked forward to each year, his head wasn't totally into the moment. Then, as if the world itself was off kilter, the Boston Marathon would begin the week with perfect weather. Temperatures in the forties greeted runners as they arrived in town, but then temperatures went berserk when by noon on Patriots' Day, the temperature in Hopkinton was climbing toward 80, sending runners scrambling for the shade. Only Don was in another zone that day, as he put the miles behind him; and it seemed to work in his favor to be preoccupied since he managed to cross the finish line in 4:56:00, a far cry from the time he had recorded the prior year, but then the temperature had been in the forties.

As 1973 progressed, Don entered the Hike for Hope marathon held in Rochester New York on May 6, and he finished in 4:21:00. Then just a week later on May 12, he ran the Plattsburgh Marathon, where he recorded a time of 3:58:00. After an eight-day rest on May 20, it was on to the Yonkers Marathon in Yonkers, New York, which was the second oldest marathon in the United States. Similar to Boston, it has many hills. The course was a two-loop, climbing expedition along the Hudson but with few views of the river. From the start it was uphill, and by mile five runners were doing a forty-five-degree climb in Hastings. A severe downhill decline ended in front of an old cemetery. The back portion of each loop gave a tour of industrial Yonkers, which was a bit dreary. Don crossed the finish line in 4:14:00. Before the year ended, Don completed three more marathons, which included repeating on June 17, the Glass City Marathon in Toledo, Ohio, where he crossed the finish line in 4:25:00. The race was originally designed to be on Father's Day. Two hundred and thirty runners were at the start line, and 186 made it to the finish on this hot June day. This was the third edition of the race, which was now the eighth largest race in the United States and the second largest of the thirty Midwest marathons. On October 6, Don was at the Octoberfest in Kitchener, Ontario Canada, where he finished in 4:14:00 and finally a return on October 21 to run in the Ohio River RRC Marathon in Xenia, Ohio, finishing in 4:39:00. Don had another lucky day at the Xenia, Ohio. He had talked his brother Byron into entering with him. This marathon would be Byron's first, and Don hoped it would be great. They rented a motel room and got a good night's sleep before heading out the next morning and registering for the marathon. As they looked around, they saw twenty trophies set up on the table. Byron said to Don that he would give his soul for one of those trophies. When they were standing at the starting line, Don realized only seventeen runners had entered the race. He did not say anything, nor did he know if his brother realized that all he had to do was cross the finish line to make his dream come true. They ran, competing with the other runners, and at the end they each received a trophy. Bryon was happy to have earned that trophy, and Don admitted that he finished fourteenth, but he still had a trophy to show for his efforts.

Don was ecstatic with his accomplishments. He ran those miles effortlessly, feeling good about himself and his health; running became something he had to do. He felt indestructible, as each day he put more effort into his running and witnessed the miracle of his body obeying his commands. Although some days he felt sluggish or downright fatigued as the pressures of every day bore down on him, he didn't allow it to stop him in his tracks. Admittedly he was not always able to master his body, and on some days he found his legs feeling so heavy that reluctantly he could not push himself and farther. But that only happened when he was training, and not after entering a marathon. It was at these times he reminded himself that whatever he accomplished would be better than doing nothing at all.

Don knew he was doing more than the standard amount of marathons, so it was important that he understood what his body was telling him or he might have major consequences. So he continued to read up on the sport to pinpoint the causes of any stumbling blocks that appeared. He learned that fatigue resulted from too little blood sugar, too much lactic acid, too little water, too few electrolytes, too little glycogen, too much heat, and too many metabolic wastes. This made him think back to that day in the doctor's office when he was told all the things he needed to do in order to keep himself fit. Now the list was growing longer. He realized his body needed time to recover with his schedule of marathons. Studying books on how to run effectively, he began to concentrate on his running shoes. Although the running shoes he bought were good ones—he believed they were Nike—they were not meant for the distances he was running and were causing blisters. He learned that the running shoes had to be properly padded to cushion the shock when his foot came down on the pavement. They needed to have a stable heel to keep lateral sway to a minimum and reduce wear and tear on his leg muscles. If he wanted to continue running, he had to take good care of his feet. Don was willing to invest in a good pair of running shoes, but he also wanted to get a good buy.

When he first started, he was not doing much stretching, but he read that stretching was crucial to avoid injury. This activity added more time devoted to his exercise period, as Don arrived at the track and stretched his calf muscles and Achilles tendons by standing about three feet from a tree. With his feet flat on the ground, he would lean in until his legs hurt slightly. He would hold this position for ten seconds and then relax before repeating the exercise five or six times. To stretch his hamstrings, he would sit on the ground with both legs straight and bend his head forward toward his knees until he felt the strain. He would hold this position for ten seconds, then repeat the exercise five or six times with each leg. To stretch his lower back and hamstrings, Don would lie on his back, arms down by his sides, and bring his legs up with his knees straight and try to lower them over his head as far as he could. He would hold this position for ten seconds and then repeat five or six times. Finally, to strengthen his stomach muscles, he would do twenty or so sit-ups with his knees bent. As a result of first doing this routine at the track, Don eventually began stretching at home and realized it helped increase the distance he could run.

Don was doing only marathons—no 5Ks or 10Ks would suffice. He knew that his training program covered a good mileage base, which was recommended for a faster recovery after the marathon, and just as important was what he did the first few hours and days preceding if he wanted to run the next without muscle soreness, fatigue, or feelings of depression. He was willing to put in the time, not taking proper training lightly. He was in great shape and even enjoyed the running, exercising, and resting required to make it back out there for the next marathon. Sometimes, though, the next one was sooner than expected.

Most importantly Don was having fun, and those who knew him were aware of that. It came as no surprise to his family and friends when he made the decision to reach for the stars.

Don ran on March 16, 1974, in the Shamrock Sportsfest marathon in Virginia Beach, where he crossed the finish line in 4:14:00. It was only after entering the Shamrock Sportsfest marathon that he learned of the JFK 50 mile marathon being held in Hagerstown, Maryland, on March 31.

JFK 50 Miler Ultra-marathon

Don could see himself accomplishing great goals because he felt like an athlete. He had wasted a lot of time getting started running, and now he didn't want to let time slip away before he reached his next plateau and at that moment the next step was to do an ultra. He only had fifteen days to recover from the Virginia Beach marathon and prepare for the JFK ultra if he indeed intended to enter. He must be mad! At least 90 percent of all runners will never attempt an ultra because they perceive it as something too difficult and unattainable, so why at his age and having just completed a marathon did he even give it a thought?

He knew the answer was because it was his goal to do an ultra, and even though he had fifteen days, he didn't doubt that he would be ready. He knew about pain, fatigue, and broken bodies, but he also knew how it made him feel young and capable. He had what it took and that was the desire, discipline, and dedication to work hard to prepare his body and his mind for the ultra.

Technically, any distance beyond a marathon (26.2 miles) is considered an ultra, but usually the distance for ultras is 50 kilometers (31 miles). Most ultra-runners consider ultras to be a distance of 50 miles or longer, and if there had been a 50 kilometer ultra he knew about, he wouldn't hesitate to try that first, but that was his circumstance now. That said, he knew he would be entering the ultra.

Don knew how to train and knew he would need to include walking as well as running distances in his preparation, because he'd be a fool to assume he'd be running all the way. His wife, Phyllis, along with his sons, shared in his workouts as they had done before, and Don enjoyed the company even though he was sure they thought he had lost his mind. Don began in earnest running and walking for as much as four hours at a time and being sure to add in a hill or two for good measure. If he wanted to cross that finish line he needed to spend more time on his feet or else he could kiss seeing that finish line goodbye. He began early to cut out caffeine, sodas, and alcohol and started drinking sports drinks and lots of water. Though he was living a full life with his job, his family, and his marathons, it all seemed to be in balance, because he projected his ambitions to his coworkers and his family, leading to their support in his preparation.

His plan was to run for at least twenty-five minutes and then walk for five or longer, so he trained in that way, not worrying about the amount of time because his goal was just to finish in a reasonable amount of time. Somewhere he had read that his aim should be to double or triple his marathon time. This meant anywhere between nine and thirteen hours would be respectable for him.

This ultra marathon began in 1963 by individuals answering President John F. Kennedy's call for Americans to rebuild their failing fitness. Kennedy discovered that President Theodore Roosevelt had required military officers to be able to cover fifty miles on foot within twenty hours. Kennedy challenged his officers to reach the same standard, and soon fifty-mile hikes were all the rage. After Kennedy's assassination, people lost interest in the hikes, but one that went from Boonsboro to Hagerstown, Maryland, via the Appalachian Trail and C&O Canal survived. This ultra was renamed for Kennedy and in 1968 became a marathon. Today the JFK fifty-miler is the nation's oldest ultra. The route travels along Washington County (Boonsboro) across the Mason Dixon Line that separates the boundaries of Pennsylvania and Maryland, the Appalachian Trail, Harper's Ferry, and many other notable sites.

What was it like to run fifty miles? Participants might find themselves running at a respectable pace of around five- to six-minute miles, but by thirty-eight miles that pace slips drastically to seven to eight-minute miles. By the forty-four mile aid station, they were dead on their feet and shuffling at nine- to ten-minute miles. For certain, Don had no idea how his body was going to react. Completing the Appalachian Trail without falls and injuries would be enough of an accomplishment.

The day arrived, and Don would soon know his fate. The morning of the race, Phyllis and Don went down for breakfast. Don ate heartily then checked to make sure he had stocked his fanny pack with his protein bars. His pre-check on the course produced enough water stops so that he would not need to add that to his load.

More than ever his shoes and his clothes were important, so on the day of the race, Don wore Nikes that happened to be on sale and gave him adequate stability and traction on the different surfaces. He put on his wool knit cap to keep his head warm and his Gore-Tex waterproof mittens to hold in his body heat. He would need a hat and to carry some sunglasses, and since it was March it would probably be cold, so he put on a lightweight capilene long-sleeved turtleneck shirt, non-binding shorts that he had adequately tested in his long runs over tights. Over the top of all of this he had a Gore-Tex jacket.

It was a cold, rainy spring day with mud everywhere and over 1,700 runners. His son Dan and he were in the back, and the course was a sea of mud by the time the 1,600 runners ahead of them chewed it up. He started out strong, and by the end of fifteen miles, Don still had lots of adrenaline pumping. He had followed everyone's advice and walked up most of the hills, with a little running on some that were not too steep. He ran on the level and downhill parts, including running slowly and carefully down the switchbacks of the cliff-descent portion. The Appalachian Trail was very rocky, so it required short, quick steps to keep running, with an extremely limited reaction time, because the runners in front blocked the view of more than four feet out. The course required almost total concentration on each step during the entire downhill portion of the run. Even a slight distraction or not completely lifting feet off the ground could result in at least a stumble or fall.

Not long after reaching the 26.2 marathon marker, Don started feeling tired and wondered what he had gotten into. He felt his first doubt about the possibility of finishing the distance. He began running and walking at intervals to catch his breath. He told himself that he had to maintain this discipline if he was going to succeed, and he did for the next few hours.

The end of the Chesapeake and Ohio Canal confronted Don with a long, steep hill that climbed away from the Potomac River up to the rolling Maryland countryside; the paved country road passed through farmland and a small town to the finish. On those last eight miles, mile markers counted down the remaining distances. They made it to Snyders landing, 34+ miles in 10:44 and quit. He had made it, and though the training and the ultra was behind him, there was the need to take care of his body if he planned to ever walk again. Don knew there was a two-hour window during which his body would absorb the protein and carbohydrates lost during the ultra and the first thirty minutes of that window were the most critical because his body was capable of absorbing almost 100 percent of the carbohydrates and proteins it needed. After that period of time, the level of absorption decreases as the two-hour window progresses. So he began replenishing his body by consuming protein and carbohydrates and later in the hotel room he prepared to take an ice bath from his hips down to reduce swelling and muscle soreness. That done, he was ready to revel in his accomplishment.

Ironically, five years later as Don prepared to run again in the Boston Marathon, Phyllis was out training with him, only this time she rode her bike behind Don. Either something caught her attention or her mind drifted just long enough so that she ran into her husband, hitting his heel and causing him to fall forward. Don came out luckier than she had since he only scraped his knees and hands as he tried to break his fall.

Don was back out putting in more miles on April 15 at the Boston Marathon, where he clocked in at 4:06:00, and then after a month's rest, on May 19 he was again at the Milk Run in Syracuse, NY, finishing in 4:18:00. On June 2, he crossed the finishline in 4:07:00 at the Yonkers Marathon, and fourteen days later he ran in the Glass City Marathon, finishing in 4:06:00. On September 2, he was back home for the Rochester Marathon, finishing in 4:01:00. Started in September of 1972 and held in Rochester, New York, the Rochester Marathon could be a cool 50 or a high 80-degree marathon, and it was the mystery that added to the fun. It was still cool when Don arrived at the start of the race, shivering in the cool, gray dampness as he looked around at the runners waiting for the race to begin. The temperature was 59 degrees when the horn marked the beginning of the race. The field was small, as the group slowly accelerated from a walk into a jog past the banner. Don felt good. His legs felt strong and pain-free as downtown Rochester moved by slowly; the course had been mostly downhill until reaching Pittsford, where he saw the entrance to Nazareth College of Rochester. Soon after, he was running next to the Erie Canal on a gravel path, giving a new feel to the race and keeping him focused. Cheering groups of well-wishers were few and far between, and the lay of the land was absolutely flat. He passed the twelve-mile marker, enjoying the ease of the course and the added life when the sun came out. After mile fourteen, the drudgery of the canal run with its brown water and flat gravelly footing ended. He was now in the park where people were cheering and holding out water to the runners. Then it was up a little hill out of the park and onto a bridge that led into the village of Fairport before heading toward East Rochester and mile eighteen, where the terrain was constantly rising and falling, until it became a steady incline as he neared mile twenty. It continued uphill for the next five miles, running through the Rochester city limits.

Soon he was turning right off Broad onto Allen, and soon it was over and he had completed another marathon, but this time on familiar ground.

With almost a month off, Don next was at the Ohio River RRC Marathon on October 20, where he finished in 4:23:00, then six days later he crossed the finish line in 4:14:00 at the Buffalo Marathon in Buffalo, NY.

Don was at the Glass City in June of 1974 when a record 252 runners started with 215 crossing the finish line. It was a clear, cool day that year, and Don would cross the line in 4:06:00.

Don was different from most marathoners from the beginning of his running career. The number of marathons that he ran in a given month was more than most ran in a year. His aim was to be a part of the marathon field, and to cross the finish. From that first marthon in 1969, his goal for all his marathons was to do his very best in his age group. Then in 1973 he began what would make him stand out even more in the marathon arena; he did his first marathon outside the United States in Kitchener, Ontario, Canada, and this would become the first of many marathons he would run outside the United States.

1975 Skylon Marathon

In 1975, he found another marathon that had a different challenge. This one was called the Skylon Marathon, today known as the Niagara Fallsview Marathon, the only marathon in the world that starts in one country and finishes in another. The course is considered flat and fast and it is a Boston Qualifier, something that was very important to a lot of runners.

On that windy October morning in Buffalo, New York, Don stood with other runners waiting for the race to begin. The runners crowded onto a bridge next to the Albright-Knox Art Gallery, which would take a little over six miles to shuffle off through Buffalo and arrive at the Peace Bridge that would take them into Niagara Falls, Canada, and up Niagara Parkway to the falls. It was here that the course got worse. The turn to follow the Niagara River to the Falls came later after a short lap Fort Erie way and then there came the strong wind. To keep his mind off the cold and the wind, Don concentrated on the beauty of the Niagara River that ran along the path until finally, already cold he could feel the spray of the Falls on his face. It was a challenge, and Don loved a challenge.

That was in October of 1975, and Don was six years into his marathon career.

More and more was being printed about runners in the news. For instance, in 1975, sixteen students from Rochester Institute of Technology who were on the cross-country team decided to run a relay across the United States; with two RVs, they headed for Los Angeles, California, with plans to run to either Baltimore or Annapolis, Maryland. These were students in their prime, making a statement. Don read about these adventurous students but didn't give the matter any further thought; at least then.

Though by rights, going over 26.2 made his first JFK Ultra Marathon count, Don was not happy with the fact he hadn't done the full designated distance so he returned on November 15, 1975 and did the 50 in 13:13:00.

It was getting easier to sniff out marathons, and there were indeed more to choose from and some run in untraditional ways, and the New York Road Runners Club organized one such marathon. Its first route did laps around Central Park, including some grueling hills in the northern section of the park, but it wasn't until 1976 a road route was set up that led runners through five boroughs, snaking over five bridges to its end point in Central Park.

In 1976, his run in the Boston Marathon was again not one of his best showings. At the start of the marathon, the temperature in Hopkinton had reached a record 96 degrees with the heat shimmering over ground surfaces. Hydrants had been opened around Hopkinton, and many of the runners soaked themselves, trying to stay cool.

The race began with a sea of runners ahead of him. At the Framingham checkpoint around six miles, Don took water at every possible stop and ran through every garden-hose shower encountered. Earlier, race officials had placed a scribbled sign on the front of their bus reading "Hose the Runners," and spectators complied. In Natick Center, where the traditional orange triangular marker in the middle of the road read "16 2/3 Miles To Go," Don was still running but with effort as he entered Wellesley. He was hot, but managed to keep going, and four miles later, near the landmark firehouse on the corner of Commonwealth Ave., the hills began and Don had all he could to keep going. At mile twenty-two his calves began to cramp, but he kept on going until he finally stopped running only because he had reached the finish line. This was a memorable year for the marathon itself, as it was not only America's Bicentennial year but provided Boston's hottest race conditions ever. The race became known as the "run for the horses," with temperatures reaching 100-plus degrees, forcing more than forty percent of the starters to exit prematurely. Don finished in 4:40:00, not his best time, but he did cross the finish line.

It Was More than Just the Joy of Running

There was much to say about marathons, but for Don, the friendships and some interesting experiences stand out most. For instance, there was the time when he was again running in the Boston Marathon in the spring of 1977, and at the eight-mile-mark he saw state police cars up ahead with their lights flashing. His concentration was distracted as he drew closer and saw a station wagon with the back down, and he couldn't help wondering what had happened. Then as he drew closer he could see television cameras.

Don continued, and just as he reached the station wagon, a woman climbed out, moved to the back of the wagon, and started running. Don kept his pace going and soon was running side by side with the woman. He peeked over and thought she looked familiar; but it wouldn't be until he had gone a few more feet that he figured it out. It was Joanne Woodward, and she was making the movie *See How She Runs*. The movie being made would air on CBS in 1978. The movie was about a wife and mother who had devoted her life to her family and suddenly decided to run the Boston Marathon as a self-expression of herself. Joanne Woodward played the role of Betty Quinn, a middle-aged school teacher and divorced mother of two daughters, who lives in Boston.

The man in the station wagon was Paul Newman, and Don could tell that Paul was watching his every move. It was hard to pretend nothing was different from the usual marathon as they ran side by side for a couple of miles. Then, as Don chanced a glance at Joanne, she smiled at him. The moment passed in silence as they each continued on their way. Don couldn't wait for the release of the movie, but he would be disappointed to learn they had cut the scene out.

In October of 1978, Don entered the revised route New York City marathon, completing it in 4:24:00. That was the year that Grete Waitz called the New York City Road Runners Club to get an invitation to run in the marathon. She was turned down at first, but later was contacted to run as a "rabbit." She accepted, and because she had registered so late her bib number was not listed in the official runners list and no one knew who she was. When asked who had won, all anyone said was "Some blond girl." Waitz had set a new women's world record for the distance with a time of 2:32:30, two minutes faster than the old record.

Don was just beginning and already was on his way to being a collector of marathons as he finished his first decade with sixty-seven marathons under his belt, if he included his first Boston Marathon in 1969. During the '70s, he completed eleven Boston Marathons, four Ohio River RRC Marathons, seven Rochester Marathons, seven Glass City marathons, four Syracuse Milk Run marathons, six, JFK Ultra Marathons, four Ohio River RRC Marathons, three Skylon Marathons, four Shamrock Marathons, three Yonkers Marathons, four Syracuse Milk Runs, three New York Marathons and one or two entries into a sprinkling of other marathons, and Don was already becoming a familiar figure at the marathons as he entered some over and over again. More often race administrators would call him by name or take the time to personally welcome him to the marathon. Other runners did not see him as a threat, but a sort of information source on what other marathons were out there or what a certain course was like. If there were local press in the area, Don was someone they took the time to interview. Other runners as well as people staffing the Health and Fitness Expo and the traditional Pasta Party would call him by name, and he felt like he belonged. Not only did he have sixty-seven marathons to his credit, but six of them were ultra marathons. A pattern was beginning to form.

It wasn't about speed, it was about finishing and to the average marathon runner, this was obvious. Don was happy with his fastest time of 3:57:00 at the Boston Marathon in 1975 and the fact that he had managed a 3:58:00 at a marathon held in Plattsburgh New York and another good showing of 3:59:00 at the Akron –Canton Marathon in Ohio. It was enough that he had managed these three below 4:00:00, though none would be considered worthy of bragging rights. He was proud of his 50 mile records that fell between 10:00:00 and 15:00:00, again nothing worthy of bragging rights, but made Don happy. He was hooked on marathons and being able to enter as a runner and not a 'bandit' gave him a sense of pride.

In 1979, Don, at age fifty-nine, was the oldest of the ultra marathoners. What pleased him most about ultra marathons was they were run with his mindset. Rules allow runners to "go as you please." This means they may take walking breaks, pause to drink or eat, and even sleep if the events are especially long, such as multi-day races. Like the marathon, they were run on roads, trails, and tracks. They might be point-to-point, out and back, or even be held on loop courses, like the famous one-mile loop that Sri Chinmoy runners circle sixty-two times in New York. He found there were two types of events - those in which runners set out to cover a fixed distance and those in which runners cover the greatest possible distance within a fixed period of time (such as 24 hours, 48 hours, or six days). Then there was journey running, where the runners set out to cover long distances at their own daily pace.

Summary of 1970

The summary of Don's races from 1970 through 1979 would seem excessive even to the practiced marathoner. He ran two marathons in 1970, three in 1971, four in 1972, eight in 1973, nine in 1974, nine in 1975, four in 1976, eight in 1977, nine in 1978 and 10 in 1979. During the 70s he would also complete 5 ultra marathons and one marathon outside the United States in Canada. Yet a closer look at his pattern will show not only was he doing at least one a month, he was putting in miles at marathons in less than a month. Take his October 10, 1971, Akron-Canton Marathon in Canton, Ohio, that was followed by an October 24, Ohio River RRC Marathon in Xenia, Ohio. The pattern repeated after this fourteen-day span between marathons is almost unbelievable in that Don would run in the Hike for Hope Marathon in Rochester, New York, on May 6, and turn around six days later to run in the Plattsburgh Marathon in Plattsburgh, New York.

From his best run at 3:51:00 in 1971 to his worst timing of 5:01:00 at the Boston in 1969, Don seemed satisfied with his accomplishmetns. His ultra marathons on the other hand were not getting better. He did one in 10:44:00 in 1974, but his worst came the following year in 1975 when he finished in 13:34:00. This pattern would continue year after year as if Don were collecting marathons. This year he would log over 4,300 miles on foot. That, along with working a full-time job and spending time with family and friends, might seem impossible, but it was the reality. He was now ready to see what he could do in the '80s.

1980s and the First 100

So much would happen in Don's life during the next decade as he balanced running with his job and family life. He would enter the Perrier Mardi Gras Marathon held in New Orleans in February 1980. There would be nearly two thousand people lined up on the North Shore of the Lake Pontchartrain Causeway to face the challenge. Little did they know how severe the test would be. The conditions on the Causeway that morning would separate the proverbial men from the boys.

When the race started, conditions were almost pleasant for a non-runner. For runners, the temperature was high—68 degrees. The winds were at their worst, southerly and strong. At the starting line, conversations followed the usual trends of hopes for good times, for personal bests, for finishing well, for beating a long-time rival. The gun sounded, and the reality of the situation became apparent quickly. By mile five, conversations changed from considering personal bests to simply finishing strong. By mile ten, finishing was the goal, and by mile twenty, it was a matter of putting one foot down and then the other foot.

The elements provided the ultimate challenge: man versus nature and, ultimately, man versus himself. The straight, flat course traversing the waters of Lake Pontchartrain became the battlefield. Those not strong enough for the challenge—either physically or mentally—gratefully grabbed rides on the back of pick-up trucks, jammed into vans, or would have willingly become a sardine in a can to escape the storm. The runners who overcame the elements were assured a victory more sweet than a personal best, more savory than vanquishing that long-time rival. They became champions. They bested themselves. They survived the test and proved that finishing was indeed winning. The medallions earned that day were no gift. Don would finish in 4:14:00.

The Olympic Trials

It was 1980, and the Olympic trials were being held in Russia. In 1979, the Soviet Union had invaded Afghanistan, and US President Jimmy Carter's ultimatum was that the USA would boycott the Olympics if the Soviet Union did not withdraw from Afghanistan by February 20, 1980. No Soviet withdrawal was made, and on March 21, 1980, the United States officially announced that it would boycott the Olympics.

Because of this, the 1980 Olympic trials marathon was a sad time for all, since the boycott had already been announced by the US, thus rendering the race a mere formality. No one in this race would be going to Moscow to compete in the Olympic Games.

Yet the US Olympic Marathon Trial was an event that thousands of Americans had been looking forward to; some hoping to go to Moscow, but many more who just wanted to compete in the trial itself. For the elite runners, this would be the culmination of four years of training; and when the hard reality of the government's Olympic boycott began to intrude on the runners' dreams that winter, there was no thought of canceling the trial. Only a few of the top runners elected to stay home, but on the morning of May 24, 1980, 178 of the 222 American men who had met the qualifying standard were in Buffalo, ready to run.

These athletes came to run their best marathon, and the day was filled with personal bests and records. In the trials, winning was being one of the top three finishers, since any of those spots would yield an Olympic berth. It was obvious to Don that when people have a goal, it is astonishing how many will achieve it, and though Don was impressed with the dedication, Don told himself this wasn't for him because he wasn't an Olympian.

Yet the new location put the Olympic trials too close to ignore for a man like Don McNelly. He had to be there, but he also had a need to go and see the Olympic trials in a way that would allow him to have a good view. Remembering his running buddy who owned the *Rochester Business Journal*, Don decided to ask a favor. He called his friend and asked if he would supply him with press credentials; he would be willing to cover the Olympic trials for the Journal, and to Don's amazement, he went for it. Don was excited on that day when he went to the paper to pick up the paperwork. The credentials were on the *Rochester Business Journal* stationary, looking very professional and proper, and whether Don was aware of it at that moment, he was too much of a professional to take any job lightly. Instead of it being about him wanting to get a good seat, it now became an issue of being at the proper location to provide the best coverage he could for the Journal.

With the credentials in hand, Don presented them to the press department for the Olympic trials and was only mildly surprised when they said they had never heard of this magazine, since its circulation was limited to the Rochester area. He stood there, not knowing what to say, or if he should say anything. Finally the suspense ended as he watched them place his name at the bottom of the press list.

With the initial scare behind him, Don's business sense kicked in. Being at the bottom of the list was not what he wanted, so being as tactful as he could, he negotiated to get his position moved up on the list, and then waited again. Finally the press employee stated that the best they could do was put him in the third row of the finish line.

That was something, but not enough, as he had spied the press truck sitting at the curb, and so he negotiated again, boldly asking if it were possible to get on the press truck so he could look back and see the runners. Even before the words came out of his mouth, he knew he was pushing it, but they didn't laugh at him and that was encouraging. He waited, hoping he hadn't ruined his chances. Finally they said that he could be put on the press truck, but only if there was a cancellation. At the moment the truck was full.

This was more than he had expected, and they had been very considerate of the demands of this local paper representative, so he accepted the offer and told them he would wait to see if anyone cancelled.

There was still some time left before the event would start, so Don went to get a cup of coffee and carried it back with him to stand near the press truck. He had only just arrived when he heard his name called. With fingers crossed and trying to not look over anxious, he walked over to the press representative and identified himself. Sure enough, there had been a cancellation and he was given a place on the press truck.

Don had been very particular, not wanting to be taken for an amateur, and obviously he had succeeded with his two Nikon cameras swinging from his neck, each sporting a telephoto lens. As he swung up into the truck, he took the best viewing seat, only to be told he had to move. When he looked up, the man said to him, "That's my seat." Don looked at his credentials and got up. The man was from *Sports Illustrated.*

They fired the gun and the runners took off. Don took pictures like crazy and noticed a strategy of the runners. They were not pushing themselves, but instead would take the lead and then back off and then take the lead back again. That style continued since these runners knew that they just needed to be one of the first three across the finish line in order to make the Olympic team, even if they wouldn't be going to the games. To keep the pace from falling below the desired 2:21:00, there was a pace setter or "rabbit" that the runners followed.

These were the elite, and Don had a bird's eye view of them as he snapped picture after picture, just like the professionals were doing. He was so involved that he hadn't noticed the truck speeding up as they passed the twenty-four-mile mark and then come to an abrupt stop. It was seconds that passed as he looked around him at the other occupants of the press truck, who showed no surprise at this turn of events, as they began to jump out of the truck. Not knowing what else to do, Don followed their lead, finally realizing what was happening. They were now positioning themselves for the best possible location for taking the pictures of the marathoners as they crossed the finish line.

This was far more than he had expected, and it took him a while to get over the awe of the situation. His group stood to the side watching and snapping pictures, and Don was amongst them doing the same, taking pictures of Tony Sandoval, who was first at 2:10:19, Benji Durden, who followed at 2:10:41, Kyle Heffner, at 2:10:55 and then Ron Tabb, crossing at 2:12:39

Later he would learn that the top three finishers ran personal bests and ran what remains the fastest three Olympic Marathon Trials times. Fifty-six men finished in under 2:20:00, another trials record. Of all the pictures Don had taken, the first four across the finish line were his best, which included the rabbit. After that, he continued only trying to capture anyone he knew in the marathon until realizing that the other press members were still madly snapping pictures.

Don didn't want to stand out from the rest, so he decided he would take pictures of anyone he knew from Ohio, even though he didn't know them personally or whether they were in the front heat. So he had pictures of Walt Saeger and Rick Callison, who were among the first thirty across the finish line, and then others who came later. It had been an experience he would never forget, and the *Journal* was happy with his coverage of the trials.

When Don got the pictures developed, he decided to mail them to several of the runners. He met the man who had been the rabbit at a race in Richmond, Virginia, and showed him the twenty pictures he had taken of him, and Don was flattered when he said he wanted all of them.

That encouraged Don, so he sent out five-by-seven inch pictures to other runners, and each one that he sent, he received a wonderful heartfelt thank you. What he remembered from this experience was that one runner wrote back that the pictures he had sent were the highlight of his life, while the man who had been the rabbit for the race wrote back that it was the highlight of his life so far. That last statement stood out in Don's mind for many years, as it said mounds on who would be back in the pack the following year.

In the end, some sixty teams boycotted the Moscow Games. Among US allies, Great Britain, France, Italy, and Sweden did enter, and while some countries did not officially send teams, they took no action against athletes who attended.

There was a change in the procedures, in that if a country won medals, those athletes were greeted on the medal stand by the Olympic hymn and flag rather than their national anthem and flag. [v]

It was a great year for Don as well as other runners, as new marathons continued to pop up everywhere, and along with them came more ultra marathons.

It might be wise here to explain the ultra marathon clearly. Ultra marathon racing was actually a much older sport than the marathon, but it wasn't until 1991 that the IAAF extended official recognition to the 100-kilometer event. Since that time, the 62.1 miles (100-kilometer) event has replaced the marathon as the longest running distance recognized by the world athletics governing body. But an ultra marathon was more than just 62.1 miles. It was any organized footrace extending beyond the standard marathon running distance of twenty-six miles, 385 yards (forty-two kilometers, 195 meters). The typical Ultra race was thirty-one miles (fifty kilometers) and could extend way beyond this, as there was no limit to the distance. There were also different types of ultra marathons. The ultra marathons were run on roads, trails, and tracks. They could be from one point to another point, like the Comrades Marathon in South Africa; or out to a certain point and back to the start, like the Niagara 100K in Canada. Ultras can also be run around loop courses, like the famous one-mile loop that Sri Chinmoy runners circle 1,300 times in New York.

This can be appealing to those who are not trying to be first across the finish, since the standard rules allow runners to "go as they please." This means they may take walking breaks, pause to drink or eat, and even sleep if the events are especially long, such as more than a one-day race. Actually, six days became a major standard racing distance in the last century, when ultra marathoning was known as pedestrianism.

Typically, six-day races started at the stroke of midnight on Sunday night and concluded at the same time the following Saturday night, and now the events have begun to include all other measures of time and distance.

But ultramarathons are not something you do to get or stay healthy. They can really take a toll on your body. You have to be "mad" to do an ultra, knowing there will be blisters to contend with and nothing you can do about them. Then there is the possibiity of nagging pain, stomach aches, hurting tendons, stiffness in the knees, and extremely sore feet. Most will happen, you can count on it, but it really is still possible determining how you handle it. Yet, on the whole, this assumption is well founded, because madness is a term assigned by society to all people who attempt to push themselves, and those who enter ultras do just that. They chance life to discover themselves and prove limits exist only in the confines of the mind.

In July of 1980, Don would enter a new ultra marathon in Hannibal, New York. Hannibal a town in Oswego County, New York, is named for the hero of ancient Carthage, Hannibal. There were only ten runners in the marathon, and Don's time at Hannibal was 9:53:45.

Don's training was up to forty miles a week, keeping him quite fit and not looking to be a man who would turn sixty years old by the end of the year. His workouts kept him limber and alert. His legs were long and muscular, his body thicker than that of the average long distance runner, but lean in comparison to other men his age. Marathon runners on a whole are always rail thin with little muscle mass, and Don didn't fall within that description. His hair was gray and apparent now only around the fringe of his head, which is not the standard age apparent look of a marathoner. But none of that matter because Don had charisma. It was his smile and his outgoing personality that drew people of all ages to him. This was so at the Hannibal marathon, where he was the oldest but also the one whom a troop of Girl Scouts adopted, following his course, counting his laps, giving him water, and cheering him on.

In September of 1980, Don entered the Rochester Marathon in his hometown and finished in 4:27:00. Just as Don was recognized now at marathons, he recognized others such as Norm Frank and Sy Mah; and he would inevitably seek them out. Running was best when shared with fellow runners, and Don liked sharing, especially with runners who were close to his age and out doing more than just one or two a year. These men had another point in common with Don in that they entered to finish and not necessarily to win. Since Norm lived in Rocheter, it was not surprising to see him often. There were others he recognized and would nod, but that would be the limit of familiarity because they were serious runners.

Though the monetary costs of marathon running are not onerously high compared to other activities, there are numerous expenses including shoes, running attire, race entry fees, and often travel, which may be a factor in the need to at least win some "place" money. That may be why many runners are not looking to be friendly with the competition. For example, some runners may be driven by a need to compete against other participants, whereas other runners are driven to improve their own performance, or even health concerns may be of primary importance.

As he joined the runners as they lined up on Andrew Street, recognizing people he often saw out running he nodded. Then it became serious as they poised for the sound of the gun to send them on their way past the historic Erie Canal and two historic canal locks. Though there is much to see, the route will seem long with temperatures a mild 70 degrees on raceday. Starting on State Street at the Eastman Kodak Building, the runners take a left on Main Street. All traffic has been diverted as the runners reach East Avenue and turn right. The field of runners keep going east to the five-mile marker until they reach St. John Fisher College, where they cross over Fairport Road, to Schoen Place. From here they enter the canal path and proceed along the Erie Canal to the ten-mile marker with little conversation between the runners. It is quite warm now and along the way one can see discarded pieces of clothing and more constantly being added to the roadside.

Empty cups compete for space along the route as runners try to keep hydrated, not wanting to suffer the consequences if they don't.

On the path the sound of sneakers against pavement continues, a smacking sound that sometimes is uneven as the pace differs from runner to runner, and each is concentrating on just keeping their pace as they head to the fifteen-mile marker. The stream of runners flow along the route and though some have dropped out before reaching this point, there are still quite a large field keeping the tempo.

On they go, reaching the intersection of Fairport Rd and East Avenue, where the runners veer right and proceed until they reach Park Avenue, always looking forward into the back of runners ahead of them. Now they are close to the end crossing the River to South Plymouth Ave. at the twenty-mile marker. Just a little over six miles to go is what most of the runners are thinking at this moment.

The runners continued along the route with no one talking as they passed familiar faces because they needed to conserve their energy if they wanted to finish the marathon. And finally the end was near for Don as he crossed the finish line at the Eastman Kodak Building on State Street, in 4:27:00. Just beyond that point stood other runners who had completed the marathon and now had time to talk with each other before the ceremonies began.

Don had started the year of 1980 entering on February 10, the Mardi Gras Marathon in New Orleans, LA, and keeping with his track record, he would complete fifteen marathons during that year with two more ultra marathons that he finished in 4:14:00. Don would double up on marathons in June, September, October, and November and travel to nine states to compete in marathons.

The increase of marathons in New York State was very attractive, since now as Don added to his collection, he was able to cut down on travel expenses. But this would not deter him totally from going across the boundary to try new or some of his past favorite marathons.

The New York City Marathon

The Year was 1985, and the New York City Marathon was famous, and most of that was due to the course that had been designed. At the first New York City Marathon, in 1970, the entrants ran four-plus laps in Central Park, and then in 1976, the New York Road Runners (NYRR) moved the marathon to the streets of New York's five boroughs.

The course now covered all five boroughs of the City of New York. The marathon starts in the smallest of the boroughs, Staten Island, with the startline near the approach to the Verrazano Narrows Bridge, taking runners over the bridge; and then descending the bridge, the course winds through Brooklyn for approximately the next twelve miles.

Runners pass through an enormous variety of neighborhoods, and at the 13.1 mile mark they cross the Pulaski Bridge, marking the halfway point of the race and the entrance into Queens. After about two and a half miles in Queens, runners cross the East River on the Queensboro Bridge into Manhattan. This is the point in the race when many runners begin to tire from the climb up the bridge.

Finally, they are in Manhattan after about sixteen miles, the busiest and most crowded of the city's boroughs, and the race proceeds north on First Avenue then crosses briefly into the Bronx, over the Willis

Avenue Bridge, and goes for a mile before returning to Manhattan over the Third Avenue Bridge. It then proceeds south through Harlem, down Fifth Avenue and into Central Park. At the southern end of the park, the race proceeds across Central Park South, where thousands of spectators cheer runners on during the last mile. At Columbus Circle, the race re-enters the park and finishes outside Tavern on the Green. The time limit for this course was eight and a half hours from the 10:10 a.m. start.

Don entered this marathon on June 30, 1985, and took in all the cultural and physical changes along the way. Coming down one of the main streets of Harlem, which parallels the east side of Central Park, Don felt a little unsure, realizing that he was in an area where there were very few whites. He was cruising down the road and to his amazement everybody was nice, cheering him along with women handing out water. To be honest, Don was surprised by their enthusiasm but welcomed it. It was while he was going down the street with his adrenaline kicking in that he heard a voice amongst the crowd's roar say to him, "Go get them, Pops." Don kept running but turned to see if he could locate the person who had called out to him, and when he did he was shocked. There at the front of the crowd was a black man kneeling on a skateboard with black rubber pads on the stumps of his legs that ended just above the knee and leather gloves on each hand that he used to wheel himself forward so that he could be heard. All this was absorbed in one quick moment that touched Don's heart deeply as he thought to himself that this man was cheering him on as a hero, but to Don, this bystander was twice the man he was. As quick as the message reached his brain that he must say something, he found his hand moving up from his side and reaching his forehead, and he saluted before moving beyond the range of sight. The man was close in age to Don, and from that one moment when their eyes met, the memory was burned into Don's brain. Even now, when he relates the story, he can't help tearing up. It touched him very deeply. Don would complete the New York City marathon in 3:54:00, making this marathon his personal best.

Later he would learn that the man on the skateboard had entered the marathon because he heard that the winner would get a car. That was enough of an incentive for him, as he began the race amongst all the other entrants. Of course, the cameras were eating it up. Unsure of the actual fact, Don assumed that the man would go as far as he could and then stop and rest somewhere. He may have even gone home to sleep. Anyway, three days later he was seen coming into Central Park and crossing the finish line. Again, the media was there to capture the picture of this incredible determination, and it was said that the man's first words after crossing the finish line were, "Where's my car?"

Memories were strong and many for Don but the next reality of life would put memories aside if only for a brief time. It's said that being a grandparent is the best job in the world, and Don and Phyllis were about to find out if it was true when Dan and Pamela announced they were pregnant. Baby Nicholas was born August 18, 1985, and that same year Dan and Pamela moved closer to the McNellys, buying a house in Pittsford, New York.

The miles continued to pile up as he completed the Columbus Marathon on October 13, 1985, in 4:08:00, then the JFK Ultra Marathon in Hagerstown, Maryland, in 11:32:00, followed by the Baltimore Marathon, where he would cross the finish line in 4:08:00. By the end of that year, Don had completed fourteen marathons, bringing his total to-date up to eighty-one marathons.

Don was making a name for himself as he continued finishing marathons and ultra marathons, until there were so many it became impossible to mention them all. But there were some achievements that required special attention.

Don was so involved in the sport and was running in marathons all over the country that by now he was known by many and admired by all who had an opportunity to meet him. He saw other marathoners often, and soon he had developed many friendships, such as the one he had with Wally Herman from Canada, whom he counted among his best friends. Wally would become the first marathoner to finish a marathon in all the fifty states and the Canadian provinces by 1983. Even before that feat had been accomplished, Wally and Don were traveling buddies. Over the years, the friendship extended beyond marathons and included their wives, who had also become good friends. The foursome would spend time socially and during the cold winter months in the East would travel together to spend three months in Fort Lauderdale and Pompano Beach, Florida. There they spent time enjoying the sun, playing golf, and running in at least five marathons in Florida.

Just as close a friend to Don was Norm Frank, who also lived in Rochester. Every Tuesday morning for years, Norm and Don met for breakfast and talked about upcoming marathons, their training regimens, and traveling to the events together.

There were friends before marathons, and they were still friends, but not best friends. That was understandable since friendship is a relationship that should be comfortable and relaxed, and in order to meet that objective, friendship requires meeting the needs of both friends. It takes time to build a friendship, and it takes more time to keep friends, especially when lifestyles change, friends move away, or interests are no longer compatible. Change was the worst enemy of friendship, and it became so with Don, but the friendships that he outgrew were replaced by the new friends who shared the same interests. For instance, friends from high school, of which few remain, but who still live in Ohio were seen at times when attending the alumni association gathering. Don at times had contact by email with David Paullin, who was in his graduation class. They remained friends, but interests and geography have made the friendship not as close as it used to be.

Nineteen eighty-one would be the year of Don's thirteenth Boston marathon. It would also represent the first time he would receive official recognition from marathon organizers. That made this one special. For his age group, Don would have had to run a 3:30 marathon, but his personal best ever in a standard marathon was 3:54 reached the previous year at the New York City Marathon. Don was determined to reach this goal of being an official marathon entrant, which meant he would be assigned a number. He wasn't sure he could make it happen, but he was not about to give up without trying. So Don sat down and wrote to Will Cloney, the marathon director, with his entry form and $5 entry fee included. In the letter Don gave Mr. Cloney the facts. He, Don, had run in the Boston Marathon twelve times over the years, and when he completed this upcoming Boston

Marathon, it would be his eighty-seventh completed marathon and he would have logged more than nineteen thousand miles since he'd taken up running. The fact that he had entered the Boston Marathon and had done so many marathons, of which some were qualifiers for the Boston, should show how much he wanted that official standing. He had come close to qualifying once when he missed his age group qualifying time by less than two minutes. That was back when the qualifying time was higher, but still he was close. After that, with runners getting faster year after year, the qualifying time kept getting lower and lower, while he was getting older and older. Don explained that he had no illusions of finishing among the first one thousand runners in Boston, since he would be sixty-one in November of that year and he had not come close to doing that before.

Don sent the packet in the mail and waited, satisfied that he had done all he could to make this goal happen.

Don recalled that Kenneth H. Cooper, M.D., the father of aerobic exercise, had run the Boston Marathon twice when he was at Harvard Medical School in 1962, and he placed ninety-ninth in just under four hours, though the following year he crossed the finish line in 3:24:20. Then in 1969, to limit numbers, the B.A.A. asked runners to certify that they had trained hard enough to finish under four hours, and then the downward spiral began as the qualifying standard was progressively lowered from 3:30 to 3:00 to 2:50. Don knew it wasn't impossible to meet the times, since in 1963 the record was set at 2:18:58. There had been steady increases in spectators and entrants since Will Cloney directed the marathon, so they were not desperate for entrants. With marathons more popular than ever, he knew that it was a long shot at best, but one he had to take.

Don put it behind him until he received a reply back stating that he would be assigned a number and run officially in the Boston Marathon. This was a major leap forward, and Don, who had continued his regular training routine, now had another reason to feel good about himself. He would be running as a qualified runner in the Boston Marathon. All he wanted to do was run his best, which was somewhere between fifty percent and sixty percent from the leader. When all was said and done, Don crossed the finish line in 3:59:00 as a member of the senior division (sixty to sixty-nine). Clive Davies, who was sixty-five in 1981, ran 2:43:56.

The 1970's increased interest in marathons was not limited to the United States, as the need for race categories of age groups and sex divisions, increased since more and more diverse runners were competing. Increased numbers of entries in clubs and organized races forced improvements in race categorization, and the breakdown had become similar to that of the other ones he entered in the States. By now Don had entered most of the marathons more than once and wanted new scenery, so in 1981 he entered the three-year-old Montreal Marathon in Canada and finished in 4:16:00. Kebede Balcha of Ethiopia won that year with a time of 2:11:10, a track record.

At the end of 1981, Don had completed one hundred marathons, including thirteen ultra marathons, and there was no sign of him slowing down.

But it was what he would do next that highlighted the year's accomplishments.

Changes on the Horizon

As the years progressed and marathons grew in popularity, there was more to consider in the arena of long distance running. Not only more, but some were so very different they would not be recognized as a marathon or an ultra marathon.

There had to be rules, and in order to count a marathon, they had to be certified by the USATF (USA Track & Field). This was a part of a limited list at first, but over the years more and more marathons would go through the process of having their route certified by this National Governing Body for track and field, long-distance running and race walking in the United States.

At first this might have seemed to be an intrusion, but the purpose of the USATF course certification program was to produce road race courses of accurately measured distances, thereby guaranteeing a standard for marathoners like Don, who were actively keeping a count.

For any road running performance to be accepted as a record or be nationally ranked, it must be run on a USATF-certified course. No one can truly establish a personal best if the course distance is not accurate and, in addition, if the track does not meet the physical condition requirements. That was why the duration of certification was limited, because courses often degrade over time; all course certifications expire automatically ten years after the year of issue.

By the end of this decade, twenty-five marathons would become certified, and in fact, between 1983 and 1999, there would be 193 marathons certified throughout the world with the first countries added being Netherlands Antilles, Azerbaijan, Bahamas, Bermuda, Brazil, Canada, Grand Cayman, Costa Rica, Ecuador, France, Great Britain, Northern Ireland, Guam, Guatemala, Indonesia, Virgin Islands, Jamaica, Mexico, Panama, Puerto Rico, South Africa, and Trinidad and Tobago.

Then, of course, there had to be a certification organization to coordinate all of these countries' marathons, and there was. The Association of International Marathons and Distance Races (AIMS) was established in May 1982, and today AIMS is an association of more than 250 race organizations located in over eighty countries. Any member organization must have their courses measured by an accredited AIMS/IAAF[vi] measurer.

No one could deny the effort that the following race entailed, or that it was a marathon of sort, only it would not be certified by USATF (USA Track & Field), so could not be counted.

Racing Up the Empire State Building

The Empire State Building Run-Up is a foot race that begins at ground level and goes up to the eighty-sixth-floor observation deck. The event wasn't new as it has been held annually since 1978. Different from the marathon, those who enter the run-up are often referred to as both runners and as climbers. It is a vertical distance of 1,050 feet (320 m) done by ascending 1,576 steps that makes the event unusual. This annual race is the olympics of stair climbing. The athletes and enthusiastic amateurs dash from the marble-clad lobby to the observation deck in a flood of hundreds of runners from around the world. Like marathons, the popularity of the race has increased.

Built during the Depression, the structure was a competition between Walter Chrysler (Chrysler Corporation) and John Jakob Raskob (creator of General Motors) to see who could build the tallest building. The construction began on March 17, 1930, at the rate of four and a half floors per week, following the design of William Lamb, an architect at the firm

Shreve, Lamb & Harmon. By October 3, 1930, there were eighty-eight floors finished, with only fourteen more to go that would form a distinctive tower of glass, steel, and aluminum. It was in this historical artifact that the runners would experieince the joy of taxing their limits.

It was February of 1982, and the event sponsored by the New York Road Runners, who also sponsor the New York City Marathon, would present its fourth run-up event. Runners were routed up the eighty-six flights of stairs to the top of the Empire State Building, where they were greeted by King Kong. Don had heard about the Empire State Building marathon and had filled out an application, hoping to be accepted as an entrant, knowing that space limited the amount of participants to thirty-eight. If chosen, he would be running up the 1,576 steps of the world's third tallest building.

The Empire State Building Run-Up he knew was by invitation only due to space on the stairs being limited. This was one of the main reasons he didn't have much faith he would be chosen; his age he figured to be another. Yet he had to try. For Don, who was now sixty-two years old and still going strong, it would be an ultimate test of his ability. He could recall in detail how he felt when he received a call from the New York Road Runners Club (NYRR). It was the first time he felt that he had a chance to wind, but as his heart bounded he tried to calm himself to face defeat graciously. Besides, the run-up was in ten days. His courage up, he identified himself and listened. He was being invited to be part of that year's Empire State Building Run Up. The voice on the other end of the line asked, would he accept the invitation and without hesitation he said, "Yes!"

He knew that this would not be a walk in the park and would require special training, so Don began thinking about including stair climbing in his regimen, knowing that he would need to consider how he could secure a smooth passage into the stairwell from the starting line in the lobby of New York's tallest building, since all the entrants would be vying to get through that entrance. He planned to train to complete and not to win but knew that a lot depended on luck.

It was too late to do any special training, but he felt confident that he was in good shape, with 21,000 miles in fourteen years and nineteen major road races, marathons, and ultras under his belt. He didn't fool himself into thinking that this was the same as doing the marathon, but he just felt he was ready, and besides, it was an honor to be asked.

He had been going through all sorts of mental calculations for the race, comparing winning times for marathons and 10Ks to his own, and he was sure he would be able to do it in twenty minutes or more, but secretly he hoped to do it in eighteen. That would mean he should aim to do five floors a minute, which could put him at the top in a little better than seventeen minutes. This was striking for his best, so he knew he had to plan carefully, and he did, determining that he should start out moderately, keep track of his time as he reached every fifth floor, and above all, stay focused.

Only thirty-eight invitations, Don thought. He had checked out the field of players, and in the thirty-eight entrants figure, there were nine women, one fifty-nine-year-old man, and several in their forties. Don knew that at sixty-two years old, he was the oldest to have ever entered the Empire State Building Run-Up during the five times it has been held, so whatever he did would be a record for men over sixty for the course.

It was 1982 and in his head, Don began identifying the facts that could keep him from attaining his goal. He, of course, was the oldest; he was also probably the heaviest and probably the tallest at 208 pounds and

6'1". His physique though larger than the thin runner, was still a step above that of the average sixty-two year old.

He had such a short time to prepare for this important race which meant that he needed to get started right way and make very second count. At least that was his plan before something materialized that altered that.

Actually, there had been something that interfered with his training, and that was Nippon Television Network Corporation, headquartered in the Shiodome area of Minato-ku, Tokyo, Japan, owned by the Yomiuri Shimbun.

In 1985, Nippon TV completed a studio in New York City, and it was from that office that they heard about Don McNelly being asked to be part of the Empire State Building Run-Up. Because of the shortness of time, they immediately contacted Don and told him they wanted to do a film on him and the event. When Don agreed, Nippon sent a film crew to Rochester to follow him around. Nippon was preparing a thirty-minute show on the run-up and thought Don was a great angle for the broadcast.

That was how Don happened to have a cold. He had spent four hours outside in the snow while the Nippon crew filmed him for a program that would air in Japan. The TV producer, Tak Inagaki, explained that the theme of the program he was preparing was the *Celebration of Mankind*. He wanted to emphasize what he believed to be a significant trait of the American spirit. When you were born into an older, stable society such as Japanese, French, or German, you knew pretty much what was expected of you, where you fit in, what you do, and what you don't do. Because Americans are such a mishmash, we don't seem to have as many rigid social customs, and that was fascinating to Imagaki, who summed up this

American characteristic in the words, "Why not!" If it was not life threatening, Americans would not hesitate to give it a try.

Now in order to produce the type of segment they wanted, they needed to film Don before, during, and after the run-up. Outside, in the coldness of the wintery Rochester weather, Don ran some and then stood around sweating while they organized the next shot. It was a beautiful day out, with a fresh five-inch coating of fluffy white snow on top of the ten-inches already on the ground, but the cold weather made it hard to enjoy the beauty.

As the cameras ran, Don ran the winding roads of Durand Eastman Park behind his house and the shores of Lake Ontario a short distance further. He couldn't help but be impressed with the Japanese professionalism. They knew what they wanted, yet they were open to any ideas Don had to improve the shots. There were four in the camera crew, and they worked very well together, not missing a step as they aimed and shot over and over again.

They shot Don running for quite some time, then they all returned to Don's house, where they took more shots of him with his wife as they sat side by side amongst a sea of his seventy-eight T-shirts from previous races; but the film crew wasn't done yet.

They positioned Don on roadways and park lanes to get the best pictures they could and later would follow him into work, taking pictures as he went through the corrugated box factory that he supervised. Later, more pictures were taken in his office, followed by shots with his son, who worked at the hospital, and more with half a dozen neighbors out in front of their houses shoveling snow. It seemed important for them to interview Don's family, the people at work, and the neighbors, as they asked them what kind of man he was. If they hadn't known it before, they all knew he was going to tackle the Empire State Building.

On the evening before the big race up, Don stared out the window in his room at the Empire Hotel in New York City. He had flown into LaGuardia that afternoon and set a new personal record for getting from the airport to the hotel and took that as a good sign. That was but one plus for the day.

Outside his window, the sky was blue and the temperature crisp as he took in the beautiful view up Broadway. He turned to the other corner window where he could see the marble building of Lincoln Center, the cultural area of the city. He thought about what he couldn't see, and that was the Statue of Liberty, Ellis Island, and of course the Empire State Building.

Early that morning, he felt a cold coming on and had been chewing vitamin C tablets and taking aspirins in the hope that he could cure himself before the run up. He even considered taking a nap, but he was too excited as he thought about this honor that had been bestowed on him.

It seemed all of Rochester knew of Don McNelly and his invitation to the Empire Run-up and everyone wanted to help. On the morning of the race, the general manager of his company plant in Hackensack, New Jersey picked him up at his hotel and they drove to the Empire State Building. A friend of his, Jim O'Brien, the manager, who also ran some and played racquetball, met them there, since he had offered to be Don's handler. They arrived at the Empire State Building around 9:40 a.m. for the 10:30 a.m. race. Don immediately went to check-in, only to be greeted on his return by his TV crew, who sent him back up the steps to walk down again to the lower lobby to pick up his number and his seventy-ninth t-shirt for the cameras.

It came as no surprise to Don when he was given the highest number, which he assumed would station him last in the lineup. This didn't bother him, since he had been informed earlier that positioning for the race was based upon marathon times and seniority. Don had decided earlier that he would try to give the younger and faster runners an open shot at the stairs. It would be crowded, since the stairwells were narrow with room for only two abreast at one time.

What mattered now was that he needed to get ready. In the basement of the Empire State Building, the runners gathered in a small locker room to get dressed for the run-up. To keep their minds busy, the runners talked among themselves and Don joined in wholeheartedly. He eventually found himself talking with George Spitz, the fifty-nine-year-old man who was entered in the race. George expressed to Don that he was glad to see him there, admitting that he had always finished last and, with Don in the race, there may be hope he now had a chance for the position of next to last. That made Don laugh, and he found himself liking George, who was very helpful in answering questions Don had on how to go about the race. When it was time to make their way to the starting area, they went together.

The lobby of the building was a mad house. There were runners, spectators, and at least half a dozen TV crews with their roving reporters and many cameras flashing in the lobby. Don somehow managed to squeeze through the throng of people and stopped when he spotted Fred Lebow. Fred was born in Transylvania, Romania and had always been an avid road runner. It was Fred who founded the New York City Marathon. Right now, he was talking with Larry Wydro, the race director. Don worked his way over to them and introduced himself, then thanked them for inviting him to participate in the Empire State Building Run-Up.

The time was drawing near, and tension was building while adrenaline rushed through the runners' veins. Don looked around the lobby and noticed they had coffee, ice water, and orange juice available for the runners. He talked to a twenty-two-year-old woman who happened to be standing next to him, and she announced boldly that she would win. He liked that confidence and told her so before she moved along.

Don was wearing wide sole running shoes to give him a lot of surface on the stairs for maximum traction. On the advice of his son, Don decided to wear his glasses to help judge the stairs, something he never did when running.

The waiting for the start was difficult, and finally it was time. The signal was given for the start of the race, and the women were sent off eighty-six seconds earlier than the men, who followed, unceremoniously jostling and shoulder barging one another out of the way in a huge crush and desperate attempt to get to the small-framed door to the staircase first, and Don was thankful he'd be starting near the back. Then it was stair-crazy all the way, once pushed through the door. It was also the portal to begin concentration on settling into a pace and running near his limit. So moving as fast as he could, Don started taking two steps at a time. He pulled himself with the hand railing to take some of the load off his legs. By the time he was settled in, he was on the tenth floor and two minutes had gone by. He was on a minute pace at this point to reach the top in twenty minutes. He felt good and continued at the same pace through the twentieth, the thirtieth, and finally the fortieth floor, where he began to fall back some, but not enough to worry him.

Two water stations had been set up on the run up, which struck Don as strange. How could you possibly require water in a twelve to twenty minute race? But when Don got to the first water station, his throat felt as though it were lined with cotton, and he gratefully accepted water, swirling it around in his mouth.

He was so focused that he forgot about his cold as he barreled along two steps at a time, pulling on the rail as he passed one of the women somewhere around the fortieth floor. At that point, George Spitz caught up with him, and they were abreast for several floors before George moved to pull ahead. It was at that point Don could see that George was stronger, and not wanting to be a jerk and hold him back, Don gave him the space he needed to step ahead. It would be hard to pass on the stairs if the forerunner wanted to make it difficult, since the stairway was narrow.

Don was glad when he came upon the first cross over area. Here he had relief from the constant climbing as he ran across the flat area for at least one hundred feet before reaching the next set of stairs. He noticed out of the corner of his eye that there were eyes peering from behind the fire door at the landing, maintaining silence as they watched the runners go by.

Coming upon the sixtieth floor, Don started to take some steps one step at a time but still pushed as hard as he could. Somewhere between the seventieth and seventy-fifth floors, he knew he was getting in bad shape, as he took single steps with legs that no longer wished to support him. It was then that he first said firmly, "You've got to show your body who's Boss!" There was no pain or a cramp, which was good, but he was finding it harder to breathe as he admitted to himself this was certainly tougher than a 10K race.

It scared him at first, since he never had trouble with catching his breath, but then he reminded himself he did have a cold and that might be affecting his breathing. This made him feel better as he pushed ahead much slower than before, going one step at a time, but it helped to improve his breathing. Then he was faced with another issue. Foot placement problems happened, which translated to mean that he couldn't judge the height of the step before him. He found himself lifting his foot too high to compensate, because if he fell short he might stumble. He seemed to have lost confidence in the movement of his feet and figured it must be some kind of mental stress. It could be there was not enough blood getting to his brain, since he needed it in his thighs and legs.

Don continued cautiously on his way until finally he was running again, this time to the eighty-sixth floor lobby. He stumbled but didn't fall, and he managed the five steps to the observation base, where he saw his handler just ahead, and the TV crew spotted him. He had finished. Don was pulled away by a tiny attractive Japanese woman, who was there to interview him, and as he spoke he knew he wasn't making much sense.

He tried to stand unsupported but had to lean back against the wall as he gasped for breath. He barely heard them mention he had finished the race in twenty-one minutes, seven seconds, and when he finally grasped what they said, it gave him a boost, but he was still trying to recuperate. The woman who was trying to interview him kept asking if he was all right, and though it was hard to understand her, especially since his brain was trying to recover, his body language was easily translated by her.

Don was allowed some time to catch his breath before the TV crew took him down to the eightieth floor to film. Though he had experienced it many times before, it surprised him now how fast his strength came back. The second time he arrived on the eighty-sixth floor observation deck, he noticed the skyline and how remarkable it was from every direction, but especially looking south. He had missed it the first time.

And now it was time for the award presentation, and with the press gathered in, there was not much space available. The Empire State Run Up, Don realized, was essentially a road race with handrails, and this vertical marathon running was still looked upon as an amateur sport, so there were no cash prizes. The top three received a commemorative medal and a return flight to compete the next year. So when Fred Lebow presented Don with a beautiful silver plate made by Oneida, he took it as indeed an honor.

It was all worthwhile, he thought as he looked out into a sea of flashing cameras shooting his picture at least a hundred times. They took him standing alone, then with each winner, and then with several runners. The winners were young and quite modest as they patiently posed for the camera. There was Jim Ochse, twenty-seven, who finished in eleven minutes and forty seconds, and Mary Beth Evans right behind him in thirteen minutes and thirty-four seconds.

Don heard mention that the prior year's winner fell at the same spot that he'd stumbled near the end, and it was Jim Ochse who had passed that runner to snatch victory at the last moment. Now looking back, Don could only say that it was absolutely a great experience. He had pushed himself every step, making it a very hard three-mile run that he would never forget.

In Japan, a show was produced from the shots done of Don as he performed the Empire State Building Run-up. The show entitled "*The World's No. 1*" aired at 7:00-7:30 p.m. on NTV and YTV. In their coverage, the producer called the run-up a unique annual marathon up the stairway of the Empire State Building in New York. Their coverage made mention that this was a run up of 102 stories (448 meters) high, participated in by thirty-eight men and women ranging in age from twenty-two to sixty-one. Not only the TV show aired, but coverage extended to a report by the *Japan Times* on Tuesday April 6, 1982.

As if that weren't enough, the media coverage reached the ultimate in the United States when it was presented in *Sports Illustrated*, "Faces in the Crowd."

After that first-time experience, Don would enter the DCA Ultra marathon in Louisiana and finish in 5:29:00. That would be followed by the Shamrock Sportsfest in Virginia Beach (4:23:00), the Richmond Ultra marathon in Virginia (9:54:00), the Boston Marathon (4:28:00), the Syracuse Milk Run (4:24:00), the Osborn's Marathon in Waterloo, New York (4:35:00), the Ontario Shore Marathon (4:21:00), and then the Hannibal Ultra marathon (6:04:00).

Don had completed 109 marathons, including sixteen ultra marathons, but he soon realized there was still something he had yet to do, and like before, he was ready to tackle it.

GRTC Hall of Fame 1982

The GRTC Race Committee was formed to develop ideas on how GRTC could help new race directors and foster racing in the Rochester area. The GRTC Hall of Fame consists of American citizens who have shown long-term excellence in long distance running and/or have made outstanding contributions to the sport.

All outstanding sporting events were recorded, and the person who accomplished them did not go unnoticed. Don would become the eleventh inductee into the Greater Rochester Track Club Hall of Fame in 1982; his friend Norm Frank would be inducted in 1981. That recognition made Don feel good, but it also made him want to show he deserved the honor.

Close to his heart was the Strong Children's Hospital located in Rochester, New York. Because he cared about the children and because he believed that this hospital was dedicated to caring for children, Don had set up a special run to raise money for the Children's Hospital wing. Don not only organized a run, he also would run in the event. He would not hesitate to ask his friends and fellow runners to join him, and because they liked Don, they became willing participants.

Figure 13: Neil Bukhardt Don McNelly and Norm Frank before the Strong Children's Hospital run

Cross Country Run

It was on August 15, 1982, when sixteen Rochester men, with an average age of fifty-five met at the Golden Gate Bridge in San Francisco, where they would cross the 1.7 mile-long suspension bridge. The five-lane bridge crosses Golden Gate Strait, which is about 400 feet, or 130 meters, deep. It was there that they began a running odyssey that would take them over 3,200 miles, hopefully bringing them to the already infamous Nathan's Hot Dog Stand in Coney Island by September first.

What had enticed these men to be at the Golden Gate Bridge that day stemmed from hearing about the feat of the RIT students, who had run across the United States. That prompted a local Rochesterian to organize his own group of men to repeat this feat; only the men he would gather would be in their fifties. After putting a bug in the ears of the marathoners he felt sure were crazy enough to join him, the planning began in earnest. The first step was to find a sponsor that would add legitimacy to the event. That's where Don came in, suggesting Strong Children's Hospital as a possible sponsor. Next it was necessary to hire an individual to help raise money, and that job fell to Brenda Babatz, who at the time was the head of development for MCC with a good track record in raising funds for events. Once Brenda was on board, Don put her together with the right contacts at Strong and the sponsorship was sealed. The run was even given a name. It was to be called "Still Going Strong," reflecting its dual purpose to raise money for the Strong Children's Fund of the University of Rochester Medical Center's Department of Pediatrics, and to prove the durability of the human body at any age. Not one of the team of men doubted the group's ability to succeed, and within this group of sixteen was Don

McNelly, who at the time was 61 but wasn't the oldest member of the group.

This was a well thought out run with assistance from Champion Products, Inc., the sportswear manufacturer that furnished all the men's running gear, including red with white trim uniforms. They had also arranged for a Dr. Biro to accompany the runners in case of the need for medical attention. For transporting of the runners there were two recreational vehicles, and each would carry eight runners.

The schematics for the run were designed impeccably. Each runner would complete approximately 5.8 miles during the day and 5.8 miles each night. He would carry a baton (actually a baseball bat's nine-inch handle) and hand it off to the runner who replaced him.

Figure 14: Running from San Francisco's Golden Gate Bridge to Coney Island

This breakdown would allow each runner to run at a good pace, keeping the team on schedule. After the total of forty-six miles was completed by the first van of runners, the second van would meet up with them at a prearranged point, and the baton would then be passed to a runner from the second van. The procedure would then be repeated. This totaled up to require each runner to do five miles per day, which worked out to be a total of 195.6 miles per man by trip's end. Each man would run two miles during the day and three miles at night. The full distance that would be covered during this relay was 3,129 miles, and the aim was to complete the relay in seventeen days. The decision for who ran when was decided by the eight men in each van who randomly volunteered to go first, or second, or third, continuing through the order. Then once the captain of the team marked down the positions, that was the order for the whole run.

Don also took on the arrangements for publicity during the run. He would phone in reports to the *Democrat & Chronicle* newspaper on a frequent basis, so that they knew where the group was and how they were doing. He also alerted the authorities of when they planned to arrive in their cities, providing another avenue for support and advertising the event.

When the day arrived to begin, the runners stood at the first lap in San Francisco at the Golden Gate Bridge. Here, the group of sixteen runners, dressed in red uniforms, climbed out of the two RVs and formed a circle, holding hands as one of them prayed to God to watch over them. The prayer went on until one of the runners had to jump in with an "Amen" so that they could begin the relay. As the hands dropped around the circle, the runners turned and started the relay. It was a sight to see as the group of sixteen men ran the first two miles across the bridge together. That was the start of an unbelievable experience.

On a typical day, someone would wake up and get out, run the assigned miles, come back in the van, cool off, then get back to bed or take a turn driving. Some of the runners read a little and a few kept journals. Mostly, the constant running combined with erratic sleep patterns kept everyone exhausted. The routine and the living arrangements would require adjustments for all of the runners, and after a few difficult days, they were able to settle down and quicken their pace. Actually the easiest part was to run, with the hardest part being in the van. The quarters were cramped, and where one guy slept, the minute he got up to run, another body had to lie down in the same spot. There was no personal space to claim, and the reality of eight sweaty men jammed into a van was not something to write home about.

Even though the quarters were tight and the sleeping arrangements left a lot to desire, they managed by improvising along the way as problems arose. Take for instance the need to shower. The group took one shower in a jail that they came to along the way, and then another when they rented a motel room for three hours, asking for sixteen towels.

Outside the van, there were further impediments to overcome. The biggie was the trucks. When the runners encountered one, the wind tunnel it created would just about blow them off the road. One day the wind gust from a truck actually spun one of the runner's reflector vests completely around.

As the runners headed east, the truck problem was compounded by increased traffic. They came to an area around the Pennsylvania-New Jersey border where runners were out there running on roads with no shoulders, with trucks coming one after the other within a stream of traffic. There were times when for safety the runners had to jump over the wall to keep from getting hit.

Working their relay routine, they ran through California, into Nevada, and on to Utah. They ran through the heat of the western desert. Though the group faced temperatures as high as 110 degrees in Utah, they maintained a seven-minute mile pace. The now-you-are-running, now-you're-not lifestyle during those seventeen days led to occasional confusion. In a shopping center in Utah, one runner was embarrassed to see that he had taken off his running shorts and forgotten to replace them with another pair. But nothing that happened dampened their spirits or slowed their feet. By the time they reached Indiana, the men were in full stride, averaging six minute, forty second miles.

There was much to marvel at during the journey. By day, there were magnificent vistas of winding mountain roads, golden prairies, or rolling farmlands. At nighttime in the west, there were stunning skies with stars, even meteor showers, plus the spectacular sunrises. Then there was Nevada, where one could feel as though he were running on the moon.

When they started out, the early part of the run was marked by desolate landscape and little if any contact with living things, human or otherwise. Once into the Midwest, towns and cities appeared with greater frequency, and many warm receptions greeted the runners. The mayor of Hannibal, Missouri, ran in the rain with them across the Mark Twain Memorial Bridge that spanned the mighty Mississippi. The mayor of Indianapolis presented the runners with a proclamation as they circled the presentation site during the festivities since the relay stopped for nothing. The runners were often met by local officials, accompanied by area track clubs, and occasionally escorted by police as they continued through Colorado, Nebraska, Iowa, Indiana, Illinois, Ohio, and finally into Pennsylvania, where they faced a major problem. They were out of money.

Don was able to come to the rescue again when he realized that they were near the plant he supervised in Pennsylvania. He immediately went to the proper authorities to request funds to help them on their way. And without hesitation, Don was given two thousand dollars. Later, he made a call to Strong Children's Hospital, making them aware of the expense money. The hospital came through for Don by making arrangements to repay the plant for the money Don had borrowed.

When they arrived at Coney Island on September 16, 1982, nearly twelve hours ahead of their original timetable, they admitted proudly that no runners their age had ever tried it. It took sixteen days, twenty-three hours, and seventeen minutes to reach Coney Island in New York City, where they ended the run at the infamous Nathan's Hot Dog stand. The time was around noon on Thursday when they arrived at Nathan's Hot Dog stand—the perfect time for a good hot dog.

Several days after the event, the group of sixteen men staged a phony arrival in Rochester, New York, where they were treated like celebrities with the mayor and county manager putting on a ceremony downtown. The emcee introduced each runner one at a time. Nearing the end of the ceremony, a woman in the audience who turned out to be Doris Robertson, the wife of one of the runners, came on stage and there handed a gift wrapped in Christmas paper to her husband, Paul. Paul began to open the gift and inside was an embroidered map of the United States, outlining the route they had taken during their run across the country. Then she asked the crowd, "Did you notice it was wrapped in Christmas Paper?" Several people nodded, then Doris smiled and said she had done that because if you live with Paul every day is like Christmas.

Throughout the exhausting journey, the men continually thought of the cause for which they ran; the Strong Memorial Children's Fund.

Before the run, the men had visited the children's ward at Strong Memorial Hospital in Rochester, making them aware of the monumental purpose of the funds they collected.

There were stories to share when they reached home. There were tales of vans and runners taking wrong turns; people left behind as they were in the men's room, and items lost but eventually found. Some of the runners fell into a depression for four or five days during the run, partly due to the initial lack of sleep and the desolation of the desert country they were in. There was also the overriding concern for the safety of the runners experienced by those in charge.

The desires to be rid of their omnipresent sweat, for however brief a period, led to some memorable episodes. Just how do you wash sixteen men at once? Easy, find a carwash. At a car wash, the men asked if they could use the big hose and were granted the privilege as they hosed each other down.

Ultimately, the "Still Going Strong" run was defined by one word: performance. Mention this to any of those runners who participated and they take on a glow of pride. This was a practice in precision and clockwork, and no one missed a step along the way. They were able to keep a speedy pace because of the runners' highly competitive natures. All of them were mature businessmen or high-powered type guys, and they didn't leave that at home, especially since they had a worthy cause. Their determination raised donations for the Strong Children's Hospital totaling over thirty thousand dollars after their anticipated expenses.

Don found himself dreaming vividly for the first week or so following the run. He experienced a kind of disorientation. Something seemed to be going on, but he couldn't explain what. He was, he admitted, fascinated by what they were doing right until the end. More than once on their return home he would wake up at night thinking it was his turn to run, feeling as though they were still in the van.

Overall, the runners' capabilities were a pleasant surprise to Dr. Biro, who had come prepared but did not expect the worst since these men were in great shape. Yet, with runners over fifty years of age, Dr. Biro knew that things just don't work quite as well as at twenty-five years of age, especially the reaction time, which goes down as we age. Then there was the other known fact that the heart doesn't pump as efficiently, and there was the reduced capacity of older lungs. The experience for him proved positive in the continuing controversy over the effectiveness of cardiovascular conditioning on the human body. Biro could not deny what he saw during the "Still Going Strong" run, and he expressed hope that this kind of event would prompt others to work exercise into their daily routines.

This was an once-in-a-lifetime experience for each of the sixteen runners, who did not plan a repeat performance. It turned out to be a moment in history that showed age can be a state of mind. The oldest member of the team turned sixty-seven during the cross country run. He celebrated his birthday laboring up the steep slopes of the Colorado Rockies. His explanation of how he felt was mirrored by them all. He said that he knew he was old when he saw his reflection, but otherwise, neither his body nor his mind felt any older.

Proof positive that what they had accomplished was being recognized beyond their environment came when the runners were honored by the receipt of a letter from President Reagan:

THE WHITE HOUSE

WASHINGTON

October 26, 1981

Dear Mr. McNelly:

You and your teammates have my heartiest
congratulations on the successful 200-
mile, 24-hour run you recently completed
at the University of Rochester. This
would be an admirable feat for younger
athletes, and it is highly commendable
that ten men of mature years made this run
and set a record. All of you are obviously
in excellent physical condition. Keep up
the good work!

With best wishes for continued success,

Sincerely,

Ronald Reagan

Mr. Don McNelly
615 Pinegrove Avenue
Rochester, New York   14617

Figure 15: Letter From The White House

By October, Don was on the road again, entering the Columbus
Marathon in Ohio and finishing in 4:54:00. Then on to the Skylon
Marathon in Buffalo (4:02:00), followed by the New York Marathon
(4:02:00), the San Antonio Marathon (3:58:00), the Nickel City 50K ultra
marathon in New York (9:23:00), the JFK fifty miler in Hagerstown,
Maryland (10:49:00), and ending the year at the Rock and Roll Marathon
in Phoenix, Arizona (3:58:00).

Empire State Games

The Empire State Games were a yearly competition for amateur athletes from the state of New York. There were several different Empire State Games competitions that included games for the amateur athletes, the physically challenged, and the senior games, specifically for those ages fifty and older.

Established in 1982, the games were created for the purpose of encouraging fitness as a lifelong activity by organizing competitive recreational opportunities for seniors.

You would think that after making history travelling coast to coast in 1982, Don was good to go for at least a few years before considering any feats of travel on running shoes beyond the distance of a marathon. Well, you would think that, but not Don McNelly, who decided he wanted to take on a New York State tour for the Empire State Games. Don contacted Mike Abernathy and offered their services.

It was 1983 when Don became one of twelve runners, ranging in age from fifty-one to sixty-seven, carrying a torch to light the flame at the opening ceremonies of the sixth Empire State Games held in Syracuse, New York, on August 10. As the coordinator, Don designed the team made up of the same members of the Greater Rochester Track club that had joined him in 1982 on the run from San Francisco's Golden Gate Bridge to New York's Coney Island. There was no doubt in any of their minds that they could make the trip, so they began the preparation.

It was a six-day marathon that began at Shea Stadium's homeplate at 7:15 p.m. on August 3, with the lighting of the official torch that would be carried all over New York State to Syracuse to light the official flame for the games opening ceremonies. Shea Stadium is located on Roosevelt Avenue in Flushing, Queens.

Figure 16: Bringing Home the Torch to Start the NYS Empire Games

After a brief tour on Long Island, the lighted torch was carried to the New York City/Yonkers line for its trip to Syracuse. The team would not take the normal route, but instead a more scenic route that took them through the big cities of New York State and along the mountains and beautiful waterways. Their feet would travel over rolling farmlands, suburban manicured lawns, and roadways as they drew closer to their destination of Syracuse, New York. In total, runners carried the torch through 150 cities, towns, and villages and across thirty-one counties.

The journey was a continuous event, and having experienced the logistics on their coast-to-coast run, Don was able to identify the needs for the group. With two vans used as support vehicles and lighting their way during the evening runs, each runner covered two miles during the daylight hours and three miles at night, relaying the torch to another man before returning to an accompanying recreational vehicle. Doing this during the day was tough enough, but night running posed special problems, and Don took every precaution to ensure the safety of the runner. One support van remained close by, off the road with flashing lights. The runners wore reflective vests and hats, along with glow tape on their shoes. They also carried a blinking flashlight.

The twenty-four-hours-per-day schedule was interrupted only for brief stops in several cities along the route, and they were averaging eight minutes per mile. This allowed them to complete almost 180 miles each day, while depending on fast food outlets for quick nourishment and the heavy carbohydrates their body required. If there was an opportunity along the way, the runners did not hesitate to grab some fresh fruit.

Just as important as eating was, again, the need for showers. The runners were split up in two vans, which meant at any given time there were at least six sweating men resting in the cramped quarters of one of the vans. Without the facilities available in the vans, they found several methods for showering, and as before, they were creative in that they would not hesitate to run through a car wash or spring for one hotel room and request a quantity of towels. To keep on time, they would send one runner up ahead to rent the motel room, and then the two vans would roll into the parking lot and wait while the twelve men took quick showers. Then they hit the road again.

The group was aware that the distance would be 1,040 miles, slightly less than one third of the distance from coast-to-coast, but by no means would it be a snap.

It all went smoothly, and Don would later admit that they hadn't sought advertising and contributions for the torch carrying as they had for the pan-America run. This was not a simple undertaking but more of a rigorous exercise fueled by love for their state. There was no monetary gain, since they were all volunteers and most of them had to take vacation time from their regular jobs. They did it because they loved to run, especially long distances. That and the satisfaction of accomplishing a goal were the factors that kept them going. At the end, Don climbed the platform and lighted the torch to begin the Empire State Olympic Games.

There always seemed to be something unforgettable happening; especially on a run like this, and they were not disappointed. The group entered a down-trodden district in Buffalo; Don came cruising along, and some young black woman yelled out, "Hey, mister, are you running in the Olympics?"

Don replied, "Yes."

The woman replied back, "You won't win shit." As Don continued, he was laughing at the woman's honesty.

Empire State Senior Games

That year, 1982, Don had the privilege of being a part of those first Empire State Senior Games. The more he ran, the more he realized that when you are running, your mind will go blank and it is uninhibited thinking that goes on. You sort of lose control, and your thinking is uncensored so that you may find you come up with some great ideas sometimes and other times some really dumb ones. Don read once that John Foster, then the Secretary of State, said that he always had a pen and paper next to the bed, and if he woke in the middle of the night, he would write down what he had been thinking. It sounded plausible, so Don tried it for awhile, only he found that whatever he was thinking and had written down was definitely not awe inspiring, so he gave it up.

At the fifth Empire State Games, Don had mastered the men's race-walking, as he won in his age group of men between sixty and sixty-four years old. This was the first ever men's twenty kilometer and five kilometer race-walking event in the Empire State Games new masters division. Compared to running long distances, walking a mere twenty kilometers (12.4 miles) was easy for Don.

The Midnight Sun Double Marathon

Don was expanding his travel to marathons and venturing beyond the United States. He entered The Midnight Sun Marathon held in the Arctic Bay, Nunavut, a small town at the top of Baffin Island located some 434 miles (750 kilometers) north of the Arctic Circle, approximately 1,863 miles (3,000 kilometers) north of Toronto. A Midnight Sun Marathon is a marathon run at night in some cities above the Arctic Circle during the period with midnight sun. This was a first for Don, who had entered the ultra marathon that would cover 52.19 miles (84K).

Figure 17: Running In Nanisivik

It's natural to assume there will be ice and snow, igloos, and transportation only by dog sled, but because Nanisivik is too far North and too cold, you see instead mostly barren rocks and hills with a few wildflowers that come out for a few weeks in late June and July when the temperature will get a little above freezing and the sun never goes down. It is indeed a challenge and so very different from other marathons, especially because of the amazing quiet. Views of distant snow-covered rock massifs, cliffs, make for a scenic marathon, but when you are walking up those hills and you see ahead what you hope is the end and you reach that point and find that it continues to curve over and over again, you feel as though it will never end.

Don flew into the Nanisivik Airport, operating as the main airport for the Arctic Bay. He couldn't see a runway when they were going down and could not believe it when they touched down on the top of a relatively flat rock mesa in the middle of nowhere. The flight to Baffin Island left from Ottawa, and as previously explained, he had to be at the Ottawa airport one and a half hours before flight time in order to secure his seat on the flight. Luck was with them, as the weather held out and their flight was not delayed either going to or departing from Nanisivik airport. To get a feel for the place, Nunavut was both the least populated and the largest of the provinces and territories of Canada, which spread over an area the size of maybe Western Europe.

In the town, the runners were put up in a dorm or vacant houses for the five days they were there. The food was fantastic and exotic. For one meal they ate caribou and fern salad, and it surprised Don how hungry he got due to his body converting calories to heat more than normal so Don ate three to four good-sized meals a day, which didn't seem to result in extra pounds. It was July, and the ultra-marathon race would be on a tundra course between the Arctic Bay and Nanisivik.

Don had done ultras before and was confident that the only difference this time was the cold, which was easily handled with tights, hat ear warmers, a long-sleeve under a short-sleeve shirt, gloves, and a nylon pullover. He was tough, as he had proved to himself over and over again, and he knew this was not a marathon for wimps or whiners, so he had to assume that the other runners were of his same caliber. The temperature stayed at thirty-four degrees while he was there, but when the wind came up he was glad he had every part of his body covered against the chill. He remembered being told that the zinc mine in Nanisivik he passed about ten miles east of Arctic Bay on the gravel road promoted the race for recreation, and to keep workers from being bored out of their minds. He could understand that as he continued along the route north of the Arctic

Circle at the end of Baffin Island, where there was only limited population. Strangely, there was not deep ice and snow, as the area was too far North and cold for significant snowfall. The views around him were of a treeless pass with barren hills, except for a few tiny flowers that grew in the cracks of the endless expanse of rock. Distance lost all perspective. A hill that appeared to be just a mile away would be closer to eighteen miles (30K) in the distance.

Silence was endless, except for the wind; there was virtually no sign of life beyond those in the race. The bay during the race week was spotted with icebergs, and Don couldn't get over the amazing quiet and remoteness. It felt as though he were running in another world as he lost all sense of time and perception, only feeling as though he had been moving through timeless emptiness for ever. It did seem endless, and in some ways it was as he crossed the finish line in 12:59:00.

Don's numbers kept increasing as he continued to find more marathons that piqued his interest. By the end of the year of 1983, Don would complete eighteen marathons that included six ultra marathons. He would have run twice in Canada. With so many marathons on his list, Don would run two a month at times. For instance, on January 8, 1983, he would be at the Savannah Marathon in Georgia and then on January 22 at the Orange Bowl Marathon in Florida. Or if necessary it would be days apart. For example on June 6, 1983, he would be at the Lake Ontario Marathon in Greece, New York, and travel on June 11 to finish at the Palos Verdes Marathon in Palos Verdes, California.

The following year was no different, as Don continued his mad path of marathons. Then, as it had always been, he managed something spectacular in 1984.

Race Up Mount Fuji

It was in the early '80s when a sixteen-year-old exchange student came over for several weeks from Nagoya, Japan and stayed with Don's niece, who was a schoolteacher in Ohio. The student's name was Kanae Machida. The following year, Don's niece traveled to Japan to stay with Kanae's family in Japan. It was from this connection that Don would have his chance to experience Japanese hospitality.

Don's traveling was extensive, and he was about to receive an award for the traveling he had done. It came to his attention when he received a letter from the Holiday Inn management, which read something like this, "Congratulations and thank you for staying with us at the Holiday Inn. As a token of our appreciation for the seventy-five nights you have spent with us, please accept these two round-trip tickets to anywhere in the world. We appreciate your patronage."

This was a wonderful, unexpected, bolt from the blue and Don wanted to take full advantage of the tickets, so he sat down with Phyllis to discuss where they should go. They had traveled to many places, and since the tickets were free and had no destination limit, they began thinking about places they had yet to see. They talked about going to Madagascar and other remote locations, but the final decision came down to Tokyo, Japan. It was a place that both Don and Phyllis wanted to experience up close.

With the decision made, the next step was to make sure they could get flights to Tokyo, and onto Osaki and Kyoto, and once that was verified, they went on to learning as much as they could about the country. This would help them design a touring route so that that they could get to see as much as possible during their stay.

It was interesting to learn the origin of the name, Tokyo. It seems that Tokyo was the daughter of a samurai named Oribe Shima who had displeased the emperor and was banished from the kingdom. As a result, Oribe Shima had set up home on a group of islands called the Oki Islands, away from his daughter. Tokyo was miserable and became determined to find her father. Once reaching the island, Tokyo had many adventures until finally finding at the bottom of the ocean, a mighty cave, which housed a statue. The statue was of the emperor who banished her father, and she tied it to herself and began to swim back with it. Before she could leave, a serpentine creature confronted her. Devoid of fear, Tokyo first stabbed it in the eye, blinding it, and then relentlessly attacked it to death. When she arrived at the shore, she was seen as a hero, and ultimately her father was released to return to their home where they would live out their days.

This was but one of the many interesting facts and legends that Don and Phyllis would learn about from their family, friends, and books. Along with learning about customs, historical details, and the topography, it was important to them to take advantage of the opportunity and see Japan the way it was meant to be seen.

It may be true that Don wasn't aware at first of what going to Japan could mean to him, beyond having a good time and, of course, entering a marathon or two. It wasn't until it smacked him in the face that he realize he was about to do something he never thought of doing until now. He could run up Mount Fuji.

There was one big problem, and that was neither Don nor Phyllis spoke a lick of Japanese, but that's where fate stepped in. Don and Phyllis would need a translator, and his niece knew just the person to contact. Don contacted his niece to ask the name of the family of the young exchange student. His niece was only too happy to help out, giving him the information for the Machida family, and soon Don was composing a letter of introduction. When the Machida family received the letter, they responded back graciously, saying that they would indeed be willing to be of service to the McNellys.

Soon the day arrived when Don and Phyllis set out for Japan. It would take a nineteen-hour flight to get them to Tokyo and then another hour flight to Osaka where they were met by the Machida, who assisted them in getting a hotel room for the night.

Osaka is a city in Japan located at the mouth of the Yodo River on Osaka Bay, in the Kansai region of the main island of Honshū. It was often dubbed the second city of Japan, since it was historically the commercial capital of the country. Osaka holds the unique title of being the "nation's kitchen," or the gourmet food capital of the country, and Don did not want to miss out on tasting the food before they had to move on. Osaka's reputation comes from an abundance of quality ingredients that usually includes a stock and light soy sauce: the essence of Osaka cuisine. It is said "Fine food and fine sake: a match made in heaven. For those not living in the area, the food has an acquired taste for some since a dish like Takoyaki will consist of grilled octopus balls topped with katsuobushi (dried bonito flakes), seaweed powder, takoyaki sauce, and mayonnaise.

Home to nearly nine million and powering an economy that exceeds both Hong Kong's and Thailand's, Osaka is an extraordinary place to explore. The stylish city is a shopping hub, with fabulous restaurants and nightlife and for beauty of the area alone there was the aquarium, Osaka Castle, and the futuristic Floating Garden Observatory.

The next day they took a train to Kyoto. Trains were the perfect gateway in Japan, which is known to have the world's most convenient and efficient railway network. It was said that JR (Japanese Rail) trains are so reliable, you can use them to set your watch, plus they are advanced, fast, and safe. Using the JR line, you can travel fairly smoothly. It takes about six hours from Tokyo to Nagoya, eight and a half hours to Kyoto, and nine hours to Osaka. For Don and Phyllis it would be a half-hour trip.

Once in Kyoto, they searched for the perfect gift to present to the Machida family, who would meet them later that day and take them to their home. This was not going to be easy since they did not know the family personally. First they needed to determine exactly what would be a gift that really showed their gratefulness, and then once that was figured out, where they could go to make the purchase. After much discussion, Don and Phyllis decided to do a little window shopping in hopes that something they saw would seem appropriate.

In and out of stores they wandered until finally they saw a beautiful vase that caught their eyes. It was exquisite, a steubin ware vase made by Corning Glass. Steuben Glass is one of America's most cherished producers of collectible crystal. Steuben pieces are always well received gifts and quickly earn their right as family heirlooms. Thought expensive, it was very appropriately matched to the excellent treatment they were receiving from this wonderful family who had offered to house them for four nights at their home in Nagoya.

In Kyoto, there was plenty of things to do. Being that it is a large city, there are plenty of places to shop. Interesting souvenirs can be found at small shops tucked in and around the city. They had read about the

Kinkakuji Temple, or "Golden Pavilion." This temple's upper stories are completely covered in gold. Another temple is Kiyomizudera Temple, which means "Pure Water Temple," is the most heralded temple in all of Kyoto.

Their purchase made, the Machida met up with them in Osaka, and soon they were on their way to Nagoya. Nagoya was the third largest city in Japan and was one of Japan's major ports. It was also the center of Japan's third largest metropolitan region, known as the Chūkyō Metropolitan Area.

At the home of the Machida Don and Phyllis were shown to their rooms so that they could settle in and rest. Later that day at an appropriate time they presented their gift to their hosts. The gift had been spectacularly wrapped by the store owner, and once the outside wrappings were removed, inside the vase had been packed securely within mounds of tissue paper. When the Machida were finally able to remove the gift from the wrappings, to Don and Phyllis's amazement, it had been placed in a zipped leather pouch. The gift was well received.

Words could not do justice to the hospitality of their new friends, who did everything they could to make their guests feel welcomed. As was the tradition, Don and Phyllis slept on futons, and instead of window glass, there were paper panes in the doors and window openings. As their hosts wanted to impress them, one meal that was served during their stay contained forty kinds of sushi, and of course, there was rice. After four nights the family took them to spend the final night at a quaint hotel near Mount Fuji for the next day's race.

They were tired after all the traveling, and that night Don and Phyllis settled in early and rested peacefully until morning. Don was the first one up and went over to the window, opened the curtains of their room, and was faced with a breathtaking view. Outlined in the clear paned window was Mount Fuji, completely filling the window.

Mount Fuji, at 12,285 feet (3,776 meters), is Japan's highest mountain. It is not surprising that the nearly perfectly shaped volcano has been worshipped as a sacred mountain. The volcano last erupted in 1708 and can be seen from Tokyo and Yokohama on clear days. However, clouds and poor visibility often block its view. Visibility tends to be better during the colder seasons of the year than in summer and in the early morning and late evening hours. There are theories, of course, on when the best time to climb is and differing advice on the best way to guarantee success at reaching the summit. To absorb all the beauty, most people try to time their ascent to witness the sunrise from the summit.

Don wanted to not only climb Mount Fuji but enter the race held during the official season of July and August, and this day it was finally happening. During these two months, the mountain was usually free of snow, the weather was relatively mild, access by public transportation was easy, and the mountain huts were open. The Fuji Mountain Race was the most difficult climbing race in Japan. It was an event with two races, both of which began at Fujiyoshida City Hall. The first was a twenty-one kilometer course (13.048 miles) to the summit of Mount Fuji, and the second was a fifteen kilometer course (9.32056 mi) to the Fifth Station of the mountain. The race would start in Fujiyoshida City. Because of the popularity of the race, only three thousand can enter, and the applications are on a first-come, first-serve basis.

Because of the altitude, participants in the Summit Race must be healthy and between the ages of eighteen and sixty years old, and the fifth station competition participants must be healthy and over eighteen years of age. It being August of 1984, Don was sixty-three years old. There were no exceptions for the age limits, but it was no matter to Don, who didn't mind settling for the fifth station competition. As he made it over to the registration table, he prayed that he was in time. He was. After signing the written oath, which stated in Japanese and translated in American, "As I attend to Mt. Fuji Marathon Race, I think highly of the purpose of this race and promise to keep the main points of enforcement. Even if any accident happen by the action without keeping the main points of enforcement."

Don arrived at the base of Mount Fuji, where there were already crowds waiting in anticipation of those who were coming to climb the mountain. When Don moved toward the starting line, there were Japanese swinging the American flag in honor of his presence. Don towered over the spectators as he smiled, feeling uplifted by the wonderful reception, and he wasn't offended that many of the Japanese had brought their children so that they could see the American.

The Japanese say everyone should try to climb Mt. Fuji once in their lives, and it's been one of Don's goals since hearing of the summit race. For the climb, Don wore a fleece jacket and gloves, and carried a flashlight. Japan has a formal society and it sometimes seems impossible to get to know people, but spectators at Mt. Fuji were different. The Fujiyoshida route is the shortest ascent on Mt. Fuji, in terms of the starting elevation. The trail start at about 2400 meters above sea level; higher than all the others. It's almost impossible to see a sunrise from any of the huts on this trail, but for Don this didn't matter. Mt. Fuji is sacred to the Japanese and every citizen is supposed to climb it once in their lifetime and turn to the east to view the rising sun. So to do that one must climb the mountain at night to get in position to see the rising sun and say a little prayer. The path up the mountain is not all that steep since it winds back and forth. You might walk a lot to gain four or five feet in altitude but it is not steep-at least at the 5,000 level. But one could look up the path and see the lights up above all the way to the top. As we progressed upwards the path got a little steeper but what began to bother me was the ditches along the path got deeper and deeper to the extent that one would not want to fall into one. This is where it became obvious that flashlights were required. Next came a little hut built into the mountainside and it had a fairly large, long and narrow patio on the front side so you could look down on the bus parking lot to see where you had been then turn around and look up to see where you were going. Then, after leaving the little hut the path got steeper and the ditches alongside got deeper. Don was not too thrilled with that development.

Finally he arrived at the Fifth Station marking the end of his 15 kilometer race (elevation gain of 1,480 meters) from Fujiyoshida City Hall to the Fifth Station of Mt. Fuji. After the experienced, Don didn't feel that bad but knew the truth of the Japanese proverb that says: "A wise person will climb Mt. Fuji once, but only a fool will climb it twice."

With the official time limit being three hours, Don would complete the race in 2:56.

When it was over and he and Phyllis were making the long journey back home, they both were happy with all they had accomplished and seen during their stay.

Figure 18: Don Prepares For Mt. Fuji Run Up 1984

Sad News & Good News

Many of us have fathers whose death's can be upsetting, because at any age, losing a parent is a critical loss. Sigmund Freud referred to the loss of his father as "the most poignant loss" of his life. Norman Mailer remembered it as similar to "having a hole in your tooth. It's a pain that can never be filled."

It goes without saying that no one can prepare for the death of a parent. You cannot fully accept a father's death; you cannot fully mourn it in advance. And you generally can't predict how you will respond. This was true for Don, whose father would pass in 1984 at the age of eighty-seven. It was a deep loss, softened by the way that he would die. His father was still living his life. He drove his car and was mentally and physically capable right up until the end. There were no warnings or any illness experienced before that evening when his father passed in his sleep. It was a peaceful way to depart this earth.

More of the same marathons were part of the ones Don would enter the next two years to reach a total of 189 by 1986, including forty ultra; and he would bring that total to 210 by the end of 1987, but this did not include the non-certified marthon runs that he did, such as the Empire Games, the Race of the Empire State Building, or the Climb up Mt. Fuji. Don also continued to run in the Boston Marathon eight more times, though he could not reach the qualifying time set and he was now sixty-seven years old. That was okay since he had begun running, it was never about winning, just crossing that finish line. But he had a need to still compete on some level, so he always did his best to cross the finish line in the best time he could manage. You might say he competed against himself.

Long before he began running in the '80s, Don knew this was an addiction that he could not nor wanted to shake. It kept him feeling good, and it didn't interfere with his family life since his family would sometimes run with him and Phyllis loved the travel. It was a good life, and there was no reason to change it.

Number 200

On June 7, 1987, Don would complete his 200th marathon at the Ontario Shore Marathon in Greece, New York, finishing in 5:53:00. The course was not as flat as the elevation graph seemed to indicate, and on this day the temperature was around seventy degrees, and the heat and very strong winds added a lot of time to Don's run. Only one short section of road had any traffic to speak of, and there was lots of farmland on the horizon. As Don ran, he felt the course was easy, with a few gradual ascents, but no real hills to speak of. As he ran, Don remembered the course map and thought it unfortunate that being so close to the lake he couldn't get any good views during the run. The last mile or so of the race track had everyone running passed a spot where the finish line was visible, but then they had to run away from the finish line, down the road, and then U-turn back to the finish line, which was frustrating psychologically.

A new marathon Don would enter and find himself doing twice in one year was the Sri Chinmoy Marathon in Jamaica, New York.

Sri Chinmoy founded the Sri Chinmoy Marathon Team in 1977 as a service to the running community and to help promote spiritual growth through sports. Born in 1931 in the Bengal area of what was then India, but now modern-day Bangladesh, Sri Chinmoy was raised in a traditional Indian family environment, where meditation and inner development featured prominently in daily life. After the death of both his parents, Sri at the age of twelve entered a spiritual community, where he would develop his inner life. From there, history was made that touched all in the marathon community. The Sri Chinmoy Marathon Team became the world's largest sponsor of ultra-distance running. In the early years of the "running boom," the Sri Chinmoy Marathon set standards and levels of service to participants that have now become commonplace: They introduced the regular drink stations, post-race food and prizes, and extended the age groups to seventy-plus years.

Sri had a motto that Don would repeat. "Run and become. Become and run. Run to succeed in the outer world. Become to proceed in the inner world." The marathon Don entered was called the Self-

Transcendence Marathon, held at Rockland Lake State Park on the twenty-seventh of August at 7:00 a.m. Rockland Lake State Park's lake was located on a ridge of Hook Mountain above the west bank of the Hudson River. The marathon was held on the fitness trail around the lake.

This was a beautifully scenic, flat and fast loop that equaled 2.935 miles. The runners did the loop eight times with the final lap marked for a distance of 2.74 miles for the finish of the marathon. There was the marathon and the ultra marathon as well as other categories to enter. Sri was a character, and number twenty-seven was his. So if you were number twenty-seven it meant you were special. Sri had chosen this number because it was his birthday, and for a long time they put on a race every month on the twenty-seventh, regardless of what day of the week the twenty-seventh fell on.

The marathon was held at eight in the morning. Don was working at the time, and it so happened on this Thursday he was due at the Hackensack, New Jersey, plant when he heard that this marathon was being held. So Don went to the airport and rented a car to drive to the race, and when he finished, he went to work in the afternoon. This was possible, since the race was being held just across the river from his Hackensack, New Jersey, plant.

Later, Don would tell his friend Norm Frank about this unique race, and they got together several times to do it. It usually happened that they would take a flight out of Rochester to LaGuardia airport and then rent a car to drive to the marathon, usually arriving ten minutes late but still able to enter the race.

Sri was setting a standard for marathons with this race. Each time he entered, Don received a trophy that was approximately fourteen inches tall for running in his age group. He would enter this marathon so many times and would have a whole collection of these trophies, which he was proud of. For a different flavor, and to eliminate the boredom of running along the same route over and over again, there was a person who sat at different points around the loop, chanting as the runners went by. If you waved, they just kept chanting.

One of the worse things Don ever did in his life, he did at this marathon. As had become the norm, he won a trophy since he was the only runner in his age category, but there came the time when another fellow in the same age group decided to enter. This runner was faster and he would gain on Don, but Don would catch him about fourteen or sixteen miles into the race and not before. By then, his competitor had kept up a fast pace trying to out-distance Don, and by the time they were nearing the end, he would be too tired to fight Don's advance and ate Don's dust as he crossed the finish line. It was as though he had become the "owner" of that trophy since he had received it so many times and he over reacted to the threat that someone esle would take it from him.

Each time that Don entered, he found this runner entering too. One time Don was going along and saw him about a half mile ahead of him, and he seemed to be holding himself back, and so Don held back and didn't try to catch him. Don kept looking at the runner's back. Nearing the end, Don didn't know what to do exactly, but the decision was made when he noticed that the runner had picked up the pace at around the twenty-four mile mark. He was advancing at a pace that Don could see was killing him, but he had a good lead over Don. Don stepped up the pace and ran as fast as he could. Suddenly he was catching up with the runner, and then to his surprise he was passing him. He was in shock because he knew that he might just beat him, and he did. Don was over the finish line first and he won the trophy.

It was after that moment that Don was not proud of happened. When it was all over, Don walked with his prize in hand and passed by a bench where his competitor now sat. The man didn't see Don at first, as he was leaning over the edge of the bench throwing up, and Don paused, but instead of helping, walked on.

Once while running the race along with Norm Frank, it was raining as hard as it could be, but it was a warm rain. The rain was relentless as they ran around the loop, and at the eighteen mile mark, Don turned to Norm and said, "Screw this, let's get out of here."

Back in Rochester, they made a decision to finish the little over eight miles left to the marathon. So Don and Norm set their watches and parted ways. Don went to the Irondequoit Track and finished the marathon, while Norm finished his miles at Cobbs Hill in Rochester, keeping their watches going. It was not an official finish, but it was a finish for them, since they were not used to giving up before the finish line.

The Sri Chimnoy Team put on a more popular ultra marathon. Runners would go out and run for 2,700 miles, and Don would go and watch and do his 26.2 miles. Don became familiar with the runners and soon found himself volunteering after he had finished. He would get the runners dry T-shirts, food, or whatever. It would take weeks to complete the ultra, but Don knew how necessary it was to have people volunteering; especial during the evening hours. So this would be the shift he would do whenever he was available. His reward was the grateful faces. One time he was a little shocked, even though he had learned that modesty had no place at a race of this sort. It happened when he offered a T-shirt to a woman runner, who gave him a grateful look before taking off her old shirt and putting on the new one, giving it no thought at all that he was standing there.

1988 Holds its Own

Recognition is how people express how much they appreciate what you have done for them. With his full schedule, Don still found time to help where needed. He became active in the Strong Children's Center by first organizing a cross-country run. Later, he would become chairman and serve the organization from 1986 until 1988. Don had donated much time and effort over a decade to raise funds for the hospital, including the 1982 run across the United States. He would organize numerous local marathon runs that would result in thousands of dollars donated to the hospital, and even as he stepped down as chairman, he would continue to do volunteer work in one form or another, but the Strong Children's Center chose to have him also chair the Children's Miracle Telethon that was to be held in June of 1988.

To honor Don, a luncheon was held in Rochester, New York, where they knew the man and his heart, and thus presented him with a bronzed running shoe. The incoming chairman, Hart Goldsmith, would explain that it was the same well-worn shoe that Don McNelly had used in the 3,200 mile run across the United States. The plaque would read, "To Don McNelly who gave his heart and sole and is still going Strong, with grateful appreciation from the Strong Children's Medical Center."

Don managed to find time to continue his service to the hospital beyond the time he had to devote to his position as vice president of St. Joe Container Company, which indeed was a demanding job. Don was a shining example of a man who gave fully to his interests, his job, his wife, and his three children.

Figure 19: 1988 Don is honored by Strong Children's Center

Dealing with Cancer

For some, the path of life unfolds clearly so that it is known what to expect, and there are only a few surprises. For others, the path begins and then somewhere along the line something happens that puts in twists and turns. When the path is not as apparent, those who are unsure will panic, while the adventurous welcome the challenge. It can happen to any of us at any age, and can come from the most unlikely experience. For Don it would be unexpected when he faced a new competitor in 1988.

As elusive as the disease is, there is no unanimous opinion in the medical community regarding the benefits of prostate cancer screening. Those who advocate regular screening believe that finding and treating prostate cancer early offers men more treatment options with potentially fewer side effects. Those who recommend against regular screening note that because most prostate cancers grow very slowly, the side effects of treatment likely outweigh any benefit that might be derived from detecting the cancer at a stage when it is unlikely to cause problems.

Prostate cancer usually doesn't produce any noticeable symptoms in its early stages, so many cases of prostate cancer aren't detected until the cancer has spread beyond the prostate. So in 1988 when Don went for his routine physical, there was no reason to suspect anything serious. He felt good and had always had good results on his checkups. When the results came back, the doctor informed him that he had localized prostate cancer, which meant it had not spread beyond his prostrate. To say the least he was surprised by the results, because he felt fine. The doctor told Don that was the usual case for most men, since prostate cancer is first detected during a routine screening. So now it was time to determine what course of action to take.

For most men, the decision rests on a combination of clinical and psychological factors. Men diagnosed with localized prostate cancer can expect full recovery, so careful consideration of the different options is an important first step in deciding on the best treatment course. Don followed the advice of his doctor and had his prostate removed.

It was good to know that since he was in good health, the short-term risks of this surgery were low. The actual surgery had excellent results. At the time of his surgery, Don was sixty-seven years of age, but as a marathoner, he was in better shape than most thirty-year-old men.

The main advantage of surgery was that it offered the most certain treatment. That was, if all of the cancer was removed during surgery, the probability that he would be cancer free was much higher.

Don would not be bed ridden and could get along fine by himself in four or five days. His doctor had told him there would be some pain after surgery, and those days to not be stupid and macho, but instead take the pain meds, which he did. The first few days Don was a little rocky with the first shower, and a lot of that had to do with being weak and having to deal with the urine bag. No doubt, this operation consumed an enormous amount of his stamina. He napped every morning and afternoon. His diet for the first few days was soft and easily digestible foods to eliminate gas or constipation problems. He drank lots of water and followed the restriction of lifting set at no more than ten pounds for the first month.

Walking was the best and only form of exercise Don was allowed for some time following surgery. He was walking over a mile a day with the catheter in. Once it was removed, he quickly got up to five miles a day.

Don experienced post-traumatic shock. Prior to surgery it was all business. He didn't find the surgery to be all that bad, but later, being an active person, he was not happy with the fact that he was tired and seemed to feel more discomfort once he started walking more. Going through this trauma in his life, Don was about to feel the depth of a friendship.

Sy Mah

Sy Mah was as special as he was interesting. Sy was a marathoner who ran 524 marathons during his career. At the time of this accomplishment, it was unheard of for anyone to run that many marathons. To accomplish this, Sy had to run a marathon every weekend for an entire decade; the most ever run by an individual athlete at the time. He was not a superman, and most people he knew were bigger, stronger, or faster than he was, but he lived his life intensely, exploring his limits strenuously. Not only did he run marathons, Sy also established and taught exercise and cardiac rehabilitation classes for most of the last two decades of his life. You can't mention Sy's name without paying the respect of letting everyone know how special this man was to all who came in contact with him. Sy was basically an ordinary runner of ordinary speed, and he never took for granted that come Sunday, he could run another twenty-six miles, 385 yards, but you most certainly would see him out there on the starting line, in another crowd, in another town, at that next Sunday marathon. He also could be depended on to help and give honest advice to his fellow runners. Sy thought nothing of running marathons back to back on weekends when he attempted "triples." He did them entering the same marathons in the same location. This was because back then, there were not as many marathons being held, and to do two or more in a weekend meant he would have to do a lot of driving in between.

Norm Frank and Don McNelly, who were doing around twenty marathons a year, were constantly crossing paths with Sy, and with marathons in common, it was only natural that a friendship would develop. Don counted him as his buddy and confidante. He was a man that Don was proud to have as a friend, and when Sy came to the United States, he stayed at Don's house, and when Don was hesitant about doing his first double, he turned to Sy, asking if he thought he could do it. Don had decided he would do one in Erie, Pennsylvania, and then one in Columbus,

Ohio. Upon being asked his opinion, Sy said, "Prepare for the worst and hope for the best." Don still remembers his advice.

When Don's friend Sy Mah found out that he had prostate cancer, he called Don every week and offered the following advice, "Eat something yellow every day!" Never forgetting the compassion shown by his friend, when Sy Mah developed problems of his own, Don returned the favor and called him every week to support and encourage him. But unlike Don, Sy was going downhill steadily. At the time of his advanced illness, the double was coming up that they had often run together.

Sy was very ill and unable to run or walk a marathon, but he told Don he still wanted to come to the Rochester Marathon. He asked Don to provide him with a chair and a supply of water and cups so he could sit on the edge of the track and hand out water to his fellow runners. But unfortunately, he never made it to Rochester to hand out the water.

Born August 2, 1926, at Bashaw, Alberta, to parents of Chinese ancestry was Thian K. Mah, but everyone called him Sy. Sy died November 7, 1988, at the St. Vincent Medical Centre in Toledo. He was sixty-two. The cause of death was lymphoma, a form of blood cancer that afflicted him following a lingering bout with hepatitis, picked up during a visit to Mexico. The connection between the two illnesses, if any, was not clear. There was no indication running was a factor. Sy was a friend of many runners and very well known. What follows is the tribute given by Don McNelly to his close friend and runner of hundreds of marathons and ultras. Don traveled from his home in Rochester, New York, to attend the dedication and participate in the Twenty-Four-Hour National Championship the next day.

We are gathered here to honor Sy Mah, a distinguished citizen of Toledo, a world record holder, a gentleman, and a mentor for many of his fellow runners, from all over North America.

He started his marathon career with his first in 1967 and was soon caught up in the sport.

He was the most supportive runner I have ever met. I think the word supportive best describes the Sy that I knew. Many times, he would adopt a beginning runner and by his example and encouragement, guide him or her to the finish line. During a race he often sacrificed his finishing time by adding a half hour or longer to his time to see that they achieved their dream of finishing the marathon. By his example, his goals, and most of all by his encouragement, he made me and many others into mega-marathoners. Tonight, we will hear many Sy Mah stories. I have a closet-full. I will limit myself to one that was especially meaningful to me that illustrates the supportive man he was. I organized a number of ultra marathons in Rochester, including a twenty-four-hour on the University track to support our local children's hospital. He came to Rochester and ran all of them.

I had known Sy for maybe fifteen years when I started another 50K race on a Rochester area high school cinder track. Sy ran them. After some time, knowing that Sy was looking to add to his total marathons and ultras, I mentioned to him that I was considering making the 50K a double, and having two ultras, one on Saturday and one on Sunday. He enthusiastically jumped on the idea and suggested that I give the two races two different names and distances so that people would know that there were two legitimate runs. Thus were born the Lilac City 50K and the

Irondequoit 60K. I did it for him, but I and other local runners benefitted. I knew he liked doubles, as he could add two numbers to his already impressive totals over a weekend and cut the average cost in half.

He used to do a triple over Labor Day weekend, by doing a marathon in Port Huron, Michigan, on Saturday, moving on to Waterloo, Ontario, for a 50K on Sunday, and the next day into my home town, Rochester, New York, for our Labor Day marathon. He did this for many years.

And now my meaningful Sy Mah story. I was diagnosed with prostate cancer near the end of 1987. He found out about my problem and phoned me every week to check on how I was doing, keeping up my morale, and advising me what to do—his solution was to eat something yellow every day! I appreciated his support. I was treated successfully and recovered fully.

Soon after that he developed problems of his own. I had to return the favor. I called him every week to support and encourage him. However, he was going downhill steadily. His voice became lower, his speech slower.

We honor a great man, a world-class marathoner recognized by Guinness, and a great friend. I miss him and think of him during every marathon, as I will tomorrow.

Three months after his surgery Don took part in one of his favorite events: the grueling fifty-two mile Midnight Sun Ultra marathon on Baffin Island, Ontario. Don made it halfway, or one complete marathon, and when he told his doctor he cringed. Later after follow-up testing, Don was found to be free of any cancer or related problems since the surgery.

The year was 1989, and Don McNelly had made his decision to retire from the company he had worked at for over thirty-five years. It was a sad time, but a joyful one in that he knew he had done a great job, and it was time for him to move on to the next phase of his life. Don looked forward to retirement with a mix of excitement and anxiety. The anxiety came from knowing he had so much he still wanted to accomplish and retiring meant he was getting older. At least there were no financial or emotional factors to consider. Don and Phyllis had a strong marriage and had faced many changes so one more did not frighten them.

Don had worked hard and, in his estimation, had managed to give his family a good living. Now it was time to prove his theory that if you were successful at raising your children, they won't need you anymore. That was, need your financial support anymore, as they have learned to stand on their own. He knew his children had reached this plateau.

Each one of his children had met with a high level of success in their personal lives and their careers, which made Phyllis and him extremely proud of each one of them.

50 & D.C. Marathon Group

In 1989, Dean Rademaker started the 50 & D.C. Marathon Group. The group shared a goal of completing a marathon in all fifty states and

D.C. To officially join this group, you had to have completed twenty marathons in twenty different states[vii].

Don had run in fourteen states, but overall he had run in a couple hundred marathons. After meeting Dean, Don now knew there was a group of people out to do every state, and it dawned on him that he was doing the same marathons in the same states over and over again. Maybe, he thought, it would be more exciting if he had a purpose, and the purpose could be to conquer the United States's offering of marathons. It was indeed a challenge back when Don attempted this, and it would take him four years to reach his goal. It took four years since a lot of states only had one marathon and because they fell on the same day as that of another state he had yet to add to the collection.

Then he learned that Wally Herman claimed the title of running in a marathon in each state. Wally, a Canadian, had already done all the Canadian provinces and now had done the States. That ignited the fire under Don, and he set out with fervor to meet the challenge. He had done many marathons back to back; only now he had to make snap decisions when he heard of one he had yet to do.

During that year, Don would do Florida, Mississippi, Maryland, Virginia, New York, Massachusetts, Pennsylvania, Oregon, Indiana, Washington D.C., Ohio, Maryland, and Texas. He ran in some of the same marathons as before, and a few new ones to complete the fifty states. By the end of 1989, he had 247 marathons completed with fifty-four ultra marathons. Amongst these were the ones in Canada and Japan, which were yet to be recognized as part of the certified courses, but he was still short for entry.

###

Don had been running and traveling a lot and reached the end of the year feeling good about himself; but he realized that marathons were not an exciting topic for most people. Take the time when Norm Frank, who was one of his best friends, told him a story about his fourteen-year-old daughter. Frank mentioned to her that he was the only one who had done sixty-two miles, thinking that was impressive, but her response was, "Who cares?" Norm thought about that, and he realized that what she said was true. No one cared except another marathoner, but times were changing. Those who had been looked upon as "odd" wanting to do marathons were now being envied for what they could accomplish.

The record of marathons kept growing, and the '80s was impressive on any standard. From 1980 to 1989, Don and completed 180 marathons that were certified by the USATF (USA Track & Field). He had done one in Arizona, two in California, one in Colorado, two in DC, Arizona, fifteen in Florida, one in Georgia, one in Indiana, three in Louisiana, ten in Massachusetts, nineteen in Maryland, one in Mississippi, sixty-nine in New York, sixteen in Ohio, two in Oregon, eleven in Pennsylvania, three in Texas, and eleven in Virginia. Don had also completed eleven marathons in Ontario, Canada. Within the numbers for the decade, he had managed to do forty-eight ultra marathons. September of 1980 Don would be at the Rochester Marathon on the 1st and go to the Gettysburg Marathon in Pennsylvania on the 13th. There would be six days between an Ohio Marathon on November 16 and a JFK Ultra on November 22. The pattern continued whether marathon or ultra marathon and even inside or outside the United States. Don did the Rochester Marathon on September 7, 1981, and turned around to do one in Montreal, Canada on September 13.

Summary of 1980

It had been a good decade of running for Don. He would do his most marathons in 1989 when he completed 26 marathons. He would average around 20 marathons a year with his lowest year being 11 marathons in 1980. The totals were impressive with 185 marathons completed in 1980. His interest in going to out of country marathons was increasing as Don finished in 9 marathons in Canada. His total would include an impressive 48 ultra marathons

With so many marathons one would think his timing would get worse, but it did not. Don's lowest finish time was 3:55:00 at the New York City Marathon and his highest was around 6:00:00 for those 26.2 mile runs. As for ultra marathons his lowest time was 5:27:00 (37 miles) and his highest was 17:45:00. Considering the best timing in 1980 for a marathon was somewhere around 2:10:00 and the best for an ultra was near 6:12:00, Don's were not in the ballpark. But, none of these runners had completed as many marathons as Don or had run as often in a year.

Don completed his 100th Marathon on November 11, 1981 at the JFK Marathon in Hagerstown, Maryland. This was an ultra marathon of 100 miles and Don crossed the finish line in 8:25:00. He would cross the finish line in 5:53:00 at his 200th marathon on June 7, 1987 at the Lake Ontario Marathon in Greece, New York.

His landmarks were not a hoopla yet and they slipped by being done at whatever marathon happened to fall on that marker, with no one taking notice; except Don and his circle of friends.

1990S & NUMBER 500

Don continued to keep the trails of his life connected, which was made easier by an outside source. It all began in 1973, the U.S. Defense Advanced Research Projects Agency (DARPA) initiated a research program to investigate techniques and technologies for interlinking packet networks of various kinds. The objective was to develop communication protocols which would allow networked computers to communicate transparently. This was called the Internetting project and the system of networks which emerged from the research was known as the "Internet." Locating marathons had just started to get easier.

Don had been well-liked during his years on the job, by management and by those he managed. In 1985, the *St. Joe Paper Company* sponsored the Alfred I. DuPont Composer Award that was given each year by the company to an outstanding composer.

The award grew in recognition of the man, Alfred DuPont, who had a grand vision for Northwest Florida that included transforming Port St. Joe into a modern city with a paper mill on the banks of St. Joseph Bay. To achieve this goal, Alfred teamed up with Ed Ball, acting as his agent, buying tens of thousands of acres in the panhandle, including most of the city of Port St. Joe. During Alfred's last years, he focused all his efforts on Port St. Joe becoming a workers' utopia, with a large paper mill and a deep harbor for access to ocean-going ships. But he never realized his dream. Alfred I. DuPont died in Jacksonville in 1935 at the age of seventy-one. His dream did not die, but was continued by his family and a succession of trustees that helped make St. Joe Paper Company a reality.

As ambitious and indeed helpful in keeping DuPont's dream alive, Don McNelly was asked to present the Alfred I. DuPont Composers Award in 1990.

Figure 20: Don was successful and well liked by St. Joe Paper Company

Frankfurt, Germany

On October 28, 1990, Don traveled with Phyllis to Frankfurt, Germany. This being their first trip to Frankfurt, there was much to see and do before and after the marathon, and sightsee they did.

On race day, Don, along with the other marathoners, took to Frankfurt's streets for the annual marathon, a twenty-six mile (40K) run through the city. On that day, the runners lined up at the start/finish line in front of the Frankfurt Messe on Theodor-Heuss-Allee (street). The finish was above the red carpet in the *Festhalle*, which was an arena that was used primarily for indoor sports and music concerts and was absolutely an unusual highlight and quite unique.

The first part of the course led the runners through the city center of Frankfurt, then to the district of Sachsenhausen, which was a part of the city of Frankfurt, Germany and composed of the Sachsenhausen-Nord and Sachsenhausen-Süd districts. The marathon then traveled along the South bank of the Main River, which is one of the significant tributaries of the Rhine that flows through the German states of Bavaria, Baden-Württemberg, and Hesse. Running then into the city center, opposite the Old Town, Don tried not to miss the views, but there were so many to see. The marathon headed toward the residential area of Höchst, Frankfurt's oldest neighborhood, and back along the Mainzer Landstraße through the city center and the trade fair tower into the *Festhalle*. Don finished this marathon in 4:49:00.

Later, Don would escort his wife on a tour before it was time to return to the United States. Frankfurt has a rich 1200-year history.

Don was about to leave the sixties and turn seventy by the end of this century, but he didn't feel like he was turning seventy years old at all. As Don continued to run, he learned from Dr. Kenneth Cooper that he was in the upper one percentile of the men his age for fitness, and he liked hearing that, because it meant that he had succeed in keeping himself in top physical shape. So it would naturally be important to him to know what he could expect as he grew older, so he asked the question. His doctor would tell him that he would eventually slow down and maybe later find that he needed to walk the marathons if he continued to do them. He said that Don could get just as much fitness benefits from walking as from running. It was the distance that counted.

By now, Don was running even more often outside of the United States than he had before, since new marathons were springing up and he wanted the experience of entering them even if they had not yet achieved certification. Even marathons in the United States did not have to be on the certified list for Don to want to enter them, so his count covering only marathons and ultras that were certified did not represent all the marathons that he had acually done.

Everyone Needs a Hobby

Don had marthoning down pat, as far as finding them and entering them. Though it might seem he was either coming or going to one marathon or another with his wife, Phyllis, more often than not, this was not so. It must be understood that marathons were held on Sundays and each marathon only held once a year, so all those days in between Don would keep his training going, but there were many days and many hours of family time. There also was time to take up a hobby or two.

Almost everyone who has appreciated a good glass of wine has considered the notion of creating their own vintage wine. But the vast majority of wine lovers simply leave the process to the professionals. Don had developed an increased interest in home winemaking as a hobby, but he wanted to do it right.

The actual process of winemaking was fairly straightforward. Traditional grape wines can be easily created, as well as those from other fruits, but it would require patience and homemade wines required months and sometimes years to reach their full drinking potential.

The more he read, the more his interest peaked, and soon he was out purchasing the fermentation container and the other equipment he would need if he was really serious about doing this. Step one of course was to organize an area of the basement where he would be able to make his wine and store it, and if that didn't change his mind, then he knew he was indeed serious.

He didn't rush the project but took his time making sure that he was prepared for the first batch attempt. No one tried to discourage him; actually Phyllis was happy to see the basement being organized. His children knew their father was not a stop/start sort of guy, and that if he made a decision, he had thought it through before putting both feet in the rink.

Don started with a simple recipe, and when it had been mastered he moved on. After a year, he was making several different types and was proud of each vintage. There were failures between his successes, but that was okay. He even called upon his computer skills to create his own labels that were simple, but made it easy to determine each type of wine and the date of production.

It wasn't a secret, and soon his friends and church were aware of his latest hobby. It was only a matter of time before Don would find a way to turn this into a way to help, and the church soon accepted his offer to make the communion wine for them.

Number 300

On September 30, 1991, when it came time to mark off the 300th race, Don found himself at the Duke City Marathon in Albuquerque, New Mexico. As the state's premiere running event, the Duke City Marathon was the largest and longest running marathon in the history of the state of New Mexico. The marathon began and ended at the Civic Plaza on 3rd and Tijeras. The scenery was mostly trees, with some views of the Rio Grande River on a very flat course set along the Paseo del Bosque Bike trail that parallels the Rio Grande River. Don had no problems; even the elevation didn't bother him. This was an out and back type course that allowed him to know what to expect, and to his delight, the course was mostly flat with just the heat to contend with. Don completed this marathon in 4:58:00; not a bad showing for number 300.

As for recognition, it was non-existent as there hadn't been a marathon that celebrated the quantity of marathons run. That would come later.

Panama City International Ultra Marathon

Panama was more than just a canal; it was a relatively narrow stretch of land that was said to have at least three extinct volcanoes: Volcán Barú (highest and best known), La Yeguada, and El Valle. Surprisingly, the work of nature was undone when Panama was split in two by the construction of the Panama Canal, with the Pacific Ocean on the south and Caribbean Sea and Atlantic oceans on the north.

Don found it hard to enjoy the scenery that day as he ran in the Panama City International Ultra Marathon because of the heat and the humidity of the day. The temperature was probably at 77 Fahrenheit degrees at 6:00 a.m. and rose to 85 Fahrenheit degrees by 9:00 a.m. With the relative humidity around 80 or 90 percent, Don was sweating profusely and had to constantly hydrate his body, but he finished in 18:06:00.

After that first time, Don had to admit it was worth the effort, and he decided to do it again. Only this time with experience under his belt, Don talked Norm Frank, his son Tom McNelly, and his brother Dick McNelly to give it a try with him, and so they were all there in Panama for the marathon, a year after his first attempt.

At the marathon held in 1991, they all started out together at 10:00 p.m. to avoid the heat. As Don had learned of the tradition, they each dipped their running shoes in the waters of the Caribbean Sea/Atlantic Ocean before they started, and because they would be running all night, every runner hired a driver to stay behind them, so they ran in their headlights. The first twelve kilometers (seven and a half miles) followed Via España with some gentle slopes through several residential and business districts before they entered the rain forest.

Figure 21: Tradition of Dipping The Running Shoe In the Canal

Panamá is where you have the closest contact to a rainforest. It's the only Latin America capital surrounded by rainforest less than ten minutes away from its center, with a variety of flora and fauna. As soon as they entered, they could hear rain, but it was because the humidity was so high. The temperature was around 87 degrees and 86 percent humidity, making it extremely hard on the runners.

The marathon took the runners toward Martyrs' Avenue, which skirted the base of Ancon Hill. It was here that Don ran into a runner who was having trouble with the heat and humidity, and he stopped to help. The man, Dan Newbill, an ear, nose, and throat doctor, was a good runner, but the course and the heat was a factor to deal with and it had Don wanting to catch his breath. Don sat with Dan who soon recovered and was able to continue.

They were now a foursome; Don, his son, and brother, along with Dan Newbill, were running together, until it was necessary for his son and brother to drop back. At that point they told Don to go ahead, and he did, having Dan Newbill as his running buddy. There were pronounced uphill sections and dips along the way that went from Martyrs' Avenue to the Amador Causeway. Formerly a US military base built on an artificial peninsula made of spoil from digging the Panama Canal, the Causeway is practically flat until the course returns to Martyrs' Avenue again, skirting Ancon Hill with its fifteen rises and falls.

They continued along the course as it bared right and plunged through the narrow streets of the Old Quarter, emerging onto Balboa Avenue, which ran along the seaside before it again got a bit hilly. They ran all night, and finally they were nearing the end.

They passed through Panama Viejo, and it was now just a little over three miles before they would arrive at the starting point, the Rommel Fernandez Stadium, where they would take a lap around the track to officially finish the marathon.

Don and Dan were weaving and exhausted as they entered the stadium, completed the lap around the track, and finally were finished. They had been on their feet for 11:59:00 when they finally crossed the finish line.

Later they learned that Don's brother, Dick, and his son Tom had raced together and had quit at thirty-five miles. When Don reached the hotel, he joined Dick and Tom, and they napped for a couple of hours. When they awoke, Don made them pile into the rental car and drove them back to where they had stopped during the race. He told them if they didn't finish, they would regret it the rest of their life, and with that, they climbed out of the car and did the last fifteen miles so that they had officially finished. They all dipped their running shoes into the Pacific Ocean, which was another tradition of the race.

Don had enjoyed the marathon so much that the next year he talked Wally Herman into doing it with him, only this time in reverse. They started early and got the okay to do the marathon in reverse. They did it at their own pace, and because they started so early, at thirty-five miles they merged with the other runners looking fresh and nonetheless for wear. For Don, this marked his first time being one of the first to run across the continental divide in both directions.

Bangkok, Thailand Marathon

Bangkok is to Thailand what London is to England: the metropolis, the hub of business, economic, and political affairs. Although the marathon event attracts plenty of serious runners, there would not be a record time set due to the heat and humidity that makes this one of the toughest races in the world. Don traveled to Thailand in November 1991. The runners would line up along the Sanam Chai Road that runs along the Chai Praya River next to the Grand Palace in Bangkok. From there the course ran along the streets of the capital, passing the Grand Palace, the Temple of the Emerald Buddha, and the National Museum, returning to the starting point for the finish at Sanam Chai Road in front of The Royal Grand Palace. The Grand Palace was a complex of buildings in Bangkok, Thailand and served as the official residence of the kings of Thailand from the eighteenth century onward. Don found Bangkok interesting but was more than ready to return home. He finished the race in 5:50:00.

After returning from Thailand, Don did marathons in Washington, Texas, Mississippi, South Carolina, Florida, and finish up the decade in Greenville, South Carolina.

Don completed nineteen marathons in 1991 and added to his total 312 marathons.

Still working to complete the requirements for the 50 & D.C. Group, Don, who had often done back to back marathons, was faced with an opportunity that he couldn't pass up, an opportunity that would give him entrance into the Group. Phyllis was with him on September 6, 1992, at the Black Hills Marathon in Rapid City, South Dakota, where Don finished in 4:58:26. After the marathon, they should have gone home, only Don heard that in Bismarck, North Dakota, there was a marathon on September 12. They had driven to Rapid City, so there were no flight cancellations to make, only time to kill if Phyllis would go for it. How could she say no, knowing what this meant to Don? So, Don took care of registering for the marathon and making reservations. Don got a map and figured the total distance from North Dakota to South Dakota was 225 miles, which would take them around four to four and a half hours to get there. They had six days to fill either in Rapid City or Bismarck since it would be crazy to go home and come back.

What was there to do in North Dakota? You can hunt, check out the antique shops, and visit the Garrison Dam. Don and Phyllis did it all. The Garrison Dam is a major earth embankment dam on the Missouri River, located in central North Dakota and it is over two miles in length, which makes it the the fifth-largest earthen dam in the world.

By September 10, they were on the road heading toward South Dakota where they checked in and then went sightseeing. They visited Theodore Roosevelt National Park and then it was on to the Black Hills. Don and Phyllis drove from South Dakota's plains into the Black Hills, that are thick with ponderosa pines. The road itself winds upward, through the town of Keystone, once home to miners and now to old stores. Then around a bend they appear: George Washington, Thomas Jefferson, Theodore Roosevelt and Abraham Lincoln, each face some 60 feet high. It was breathtaking and no matter how you describe Mount Rushmore, it is impossible to put it in words. They toured until finally it was time for the marathon. Don was ready. He ran on September 12, 1992, in the Bismark Marathon and finished in 4:56:57.

He had done it. He was now officially eligible for the 50 & D.C. marathon group.

Nothing Went Right in Bangkok

Don had a great trip to the marathon in Bangkok, even though it was his worst marathon ever. He stepped off the plane and was greeted by incredibly warm and rainy weather, and the cab driver told him it was monsoon season. On The first Sunday in December 1992, Don was at the Bangkok Marathon with runners from all over the world. The race started early at 5:30 a.m., taking the runners through the central business district, then turning into the Marina South Park, before making a u-turn back to the city and heading to the east coast, the only place where there is a cool breeze. After another u-turn at the east coast area, the marathon returned to the central business district. The humid weather made it a tough marathon even for the world's elite runners.

Don had just finished the New York City marathon in the rain and gone to Mississippi, where the marathon was cancelled due to rain and floods. Now he was in Bangkok in monsoon season, but the marathon would go on.

Six thousand runners started out in the predawn rain, with temperatures already reaching 75 degrees. Don got to the two-mile mark in about sixteen minutes and had heard that the water stops were every 5K, but he was too thirsty to wait, and seeing a 7 Eleven store didn't help much. He toyed with the idea of buying a drink then decided to keep running.

Finally he could see the water stop ahead, and thirst made him walk slowly past as he consumed two glasses of water and a glass of pseudo Gatorade before he was back running again.

At the 10K mark he was running a nine-minute mile pace, which was a full minute per mile slower than his worst marathon time. He was sweating, which was a good sign, as he approached the second water stop.

Don reached the halfway mark fifteen seconds slower than his usual time. It was getting hotter and more humid than he was used to while running a marathon, and he thought that in this heat, he would be satisfied with just finishing.

Reaching twenty miles in three hours, Don quickly calculated that if he ran at a twenty-minute pace, he still could finish in four hours thirty minutes. It wasn't great, but way better than not finishing at all, which was what he thought might happen if he stayed on his present course and faced the rising temperatures. Right then it had to be in the ninety degree range.

From thoughts of speeding up, he found himself thinking that it wasn't important to finish this marathon. He actually tried to convince himself to stop, but his heart would not listen. And finally he was passing the twenty-five mile mark in four hours and fifty-three minutes and he knew this was to be his worst. Then, just as he crossed the finish line, some guy came barreling passed him as if he were trying to beat the last man across the finish line. Only Don was beyond caring. He finished in 5:04:00 and had only one thought in his mind: to get to the air conditioned hotel.

As he stood waiting for the taxi, he couldn't remember ever feeling so sick after a marathon.

The next morning and the following days, Don felt great. As usual, Phyllis had traveled to the marathon with Don, and now that the marathon was over, it was time for sightseeing. Together they toured

Bangkok, and the one outstanding memory that they both had was how very clean it was there. In the end, he may have had his worst marathon, but he did have a great travel experience.

Paris Marathon

When he was traveling by himself, Don would usually run the marathon and then head straight home, but most times Phyllis would come with him if it was in an interesting place. This time it was to be in several interesting places, as Don did a marathon in Paris, Rotterdam, and London in three consecutive weeks, with his wife, who was not running but traveling with him on March 29, 1992.

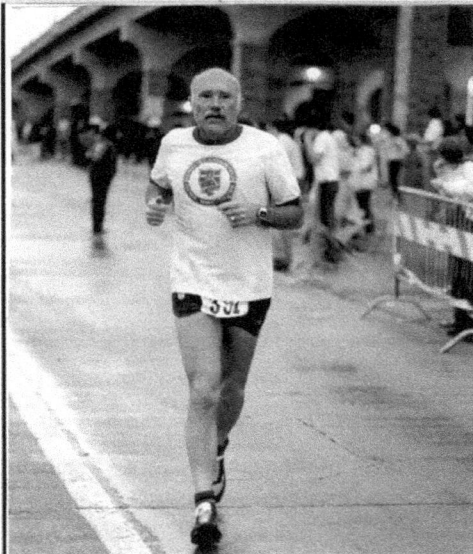

Figure 22: The Paris Marathon

The Paris Marathon was notable for the attractive route through the heart of the city of Paris, France, and for the food and drinks stations, which included wine, beer, cider, and oysters. The race started on the Avenue des Champs-Élysées, going downhill to circle round the Place de la Concorde before turning right onto Rue de Rivoli. The halfway point was reached at Rue de Charenton. The route then went passed the Louvre, around the Place de la Bastille, and down Boulevard Soult to the Bois de Vincennes. From there the race looped back through the Bois de Vincennes to return the runners back through the heart of Paris to finish on the Avenue Foch. Don finished the Paris Marthon in 5:06:45.

Rotterdam Marathon

From Paris, Don and Phyllis traveled to Rotterdam, Netherlands so that Don could enter the Rotterdam Marathon on April 5, 1992. He was looking forward to running in this marathon, as rumor had it the course was very flat and runners were getting faster times in completing the race. That along with the usually ideal weather conditions made for an excellent choice in marathons. At twenty minutes before the start, Don was queued up with the runners ready when a cannon was shot, and the runners began heading down to the waterfront and the rather impressive Erasmus Bridge. There were a few hills that were at least inclines and a headwind that did not take away from the swiftness of the course. Don continued to run with a bunch of other runners and found the experience quite enjoyable. The start and finish were, true to tradition, on the Coolsingel in the very heart of the city. Don crossed the finish line on April 5, 1992, in 4:54:58.

Running In London

After the marathon and a little sightseeing, Don and Phyllis were back on a plane heading for England so that Don could enter the London Marathon on April 12, 1992. The London Marathon began out of the Blackfriars Bridge underpass onto the Victoria Embankment. The course started around Blackheath on the south of the Thames and went through Woolwich, where they passed the Royal Artillery Barracks. The route then went around the Cutty Sark in Greenwich. From there the runners continue through Surrey Quays, Bermondsey, and along Jamaica Road before reaching Tower Bridge at around twelve miles. From there they crossed the Thames, turning east along the highway through Wapping to the Isle of Dogs before returning back along the highway and passing the Tower of London at twenty-two and a half miles.

Almost home, the marathon again followed the Thames along the Embankment up to the Houses of Parliament, where it turned toward St James's Park and Buckingham Palace and finally finished at The Mall. When Don crossed the finish line in 5:30:22 he realized that he had run in two hemispheres, both the East and West, as the full course crossed the Prime Meridian in Greenwich.

It was a full three weeks, and at the end, the McNelly's were both happy to be returning home.

Back in the states, Don traveled nonstop as he did more of the same marathons and then some more new ones that he came upon along the way. He would be in Pennsylvania, New York, Washington, D.C., Ohio, Maryland, Texas, Alabama, South Carolina, Florida, California,

Virginia, Illinois, Minnesota, Vermont, Canada, North Carolina, Indiana, New Hampshire, New Mexico, Utah, Missouri, and repeating some again and again during the year of 1991.

Big Sur

It was in April of 1993 when Don, accompanied by Phyllis, traveled to the Big Sur Marathon. They arrived a few days early so that they could get in some sightseeing.

That first day after arriving they went to see the tall coastal Sequoia trees, also known as redwoods, that stood majestically all around them. As they strolled along, they came to a sign that said "Big Red Woods." They looked at each other and had to laugh. What could be bigger than what they were already seeing? They decided not to find out as they made their way out of the forest and back to the hotel.

It was April 25, 1993, and by race time, the temperature had warmed to the high 40s, and Don was ready as he started out at the rear of the runners. It was easy going during the first five miles or so, running on a gentle downhill through a forest of thick firs. Upon breaking out of the trees, Don was confronted with light, high clouds and almost no wind, with temperatures rapidly climbing toward 60 degrees. As he passed each mile marker, Don was happy to whittle away the time, steadily approaching his projected five-plus hour marathon.

Don wasn't fooling himself, because he knew that the worst of the course was still ahead of him, but he enjoyed the wide open vistas beginning at around mile seven. Because of the road closure there were virtually no spectators on the course for miles, so it was easy to run free and enjoy the beauty of the Pacific Ocean. This continued for the next three miles before reaching Hurricane Point. Taiko drummers serenaded him at the start of the hill to Hurricane Point.

The climb started just before mile ten, at a forty foot elevation, then between miles ten and eleven, the road climbed about 350 feet. It was there that Don began to have Meniscus problems from the strain that is put on the front or back of his knees.

The next mile climbs another 150 feet or so to the summit at 560 feet elevation. He was panting, with his legs tightening up, but in the end he felt he did pretty well up this long climb. At mile thirteen Don felt more spent than he had hoped, and quite hot, as the wind still remained calm. Shortly after crossing the Bixby Bridge, there was entertainment to keep his mind off his pain as he approached mile thirteen where the course drifted gently uphill, and that relatively tough climb sapped his strength. After another short climb above Garrapata Bridge, before mile seventeen, Don stopped running and just walked, his simple desire being to finish.

Somewhere around mile nineteen or twenty, Don gave it a try and was running and walking at intervals and walking most of the time around mile twenty-one or so. When he came to the water stop at mile twenty-three, he was ready for some nourishment and pulled out his last protein bar that he ate as he ran along to what proved to be yet another hill, but it was only fifteen minutes before the end, so he walked and ran up the hill, and at the top Jonathon Lee playing a grand piano on the fantastic cliffs of the Pacific with paramount views kept him going. Then he could see the flags near the finish line and a surprisingly large crowd cheered the runners on. When Don stepped over the finish line, his time was 5:33:06.

It had taken him four years to seek out the states to total up to twenty, and now he was done. He made his application and was accepted.

On June 19, 1993, Don was officially noted as member number twenty-four in the 50 & D.C. group.

As the group of marathoners eligible to join grew, it was felt that there was a need for some common guidelines. It would be Don McNelly, along with Wally Herman, Norm Frank, and a few others who would sit down and develop the rules. Those official rules evolved and became known as the North American Rules.

North American Rules

To be accepted as a valid marathon or ultra, each run must meet the definitions listed below:

For credit as a marathon, the runner must complete the full distance of 26.2 miles or 42.125K. An ultra must be 31.1 miles or 50K or more. Both marathons and ultras count to arrive at the lifetime or yearly total.

Completion of at least one 26.2-mile portion of an ultra may be counted as a marathon, if the race director so designates this as such. Similarly, if permitted by the race director, completion of a minimum distance of 31.1 miles (50K) in any ultra event may be considered as an ultra. However, if the race director and race rules do not accept those shorter distances as an event, then it cannot be counted as such.

Each event shall count as one run, that is, a six-day race is one run, even though 26.2 miles or more has been run each day; an ultra of more than 52.4 miles shall count as one run, not two. Organized stage races, however, may be counted as one event completed for each segment of at least 26.2 miles when held on separate days. Only one event per day may be counted.

For a marathon/ultra to count, it must have had advance publicity, preferably in a running publication such as one or more of the national, international, or regional running magazines.

The event must be announced as a marathon or ultra. Running a 10K race four times plus 2.125k does not qualify as a marathon event, nor does running a half-marathon twice. A marathon must be a marathon.

The event shall have an announced race director or running club who supervises and takes responsibility for the event, and is available to certify the runners' completion of the marathon.

The event shall have a minimum of five starters and three finishers going the marathon or ultra distance.

A marathon shall be run without interruption, except for natural events, such as a thunderstorm on the established course. In example, it is not acceptable to run five miles a day for five plus days. A marathon/ultra distance completed during an ultra shall be counted even though the runner may not have run for a period during the total period of time. A run temporarily interrupted by natural events, etc., can be counted if at least 26.2 miles has been completed, and it was allowed by the race director as stated above.

Each member shall retain information to substantiate the run, such as certificates, running numbers, entry blanks, names of other runners participating or witnessing their run, signature of the race director, etc. (Also a log of events providing date, name, location, finishing time, distance, participants, finishers, comments on the event such as weather, is optional.)

A marathon that has a route that runs into two states cannot be counted as two states. It counts as one. It is recommended that the second state be run in another marathon rather than running it twice and counting the other state. The run must either start or finish in the state being counted.

In an advertised triathlon, in which the run was 26.2 miles, this marathon run was considered valid and countable.

Completion of an officially certified distance of at least 26.2 miles in a time-specified event, such as a twelve or twenty-four-hour run, will be accepted. Regardless of the actual distance covered, this event will be counted as a marathon—either regular marathon or ultra, depending on the distance certified.

Lisbon Portugal Marathon

Don traveled to Lisbon, Portugal with Wally Herman to complete his 384th marathon. This was a new location for Don, and it would prove to be an interesting city to visit. Situated on the Tagus River estuary, Lisbon is the capital, largest city, and the chief seaport of Portugal. It lays on the river's entrance into the Atlantic Ocean.

The Lisbon Marathon starts at the Praça do Comércio, the square commonly known as The Palace Square, since it was the location of the Royal Palace until it was destroyed by the great 1755 Lisbon Earthquake. After the earthquake, the square was completely remodeled.

The route took the runners down the seafront, finishing in the Praça do Comércio. The course was mainly flat, apart from around four kilometers of uphill running in the middle, and a heart-breaking steep bridge, which murdered Don's legs. Both legs locked up for thirty seconds, and he could not move either of them without shifting his weight from side to side. Don quickly found this to be a dull course, and there were practically no supporters. The entire course looped back on itself, so runners had the disheartening sight of watching the faster runners coming toward them all the time. Then there was the heat, which even in November was cruel, making it worse as Don went through the first circuit of the race that took him back to The Praça do Comércio, only to begin the second circuit along the same route and seeing the same sights as before.

Figure 23: *Don in Lisbon, Portugal.*

On May 22, 1994, Don was at the Sugarloaf Marathon in Kingsfield, Maine, where he met Dean Rademaker, the founder of the 50 & D.C. Marathon Group. They had a lot in common. Dean was a farm boy, had served in World War II, and his running career started in 1979 at the age of fifty-four. The meeting took place at, no less, a marathon.

The Sugarloaf Marathon was Maine's oldest continuously run marathon, in a beautiful setting that follows the Maine Highway of Route 27, meandering through the mountains of Western Maine. The course starts in Eustis, travels through Carrabassett Valley, and ends in Kingfield, with the weather usually in the forties at the start and reaching around seventy by noon. Despite the mountainous surroundings, the Sugarloaf's course had been ranked high as a marathon to enter and Don found it a comfortable run. The first five miles were flat; miles five through ten were rolling hills, with a gradual two-mile climb at mile eight. The last sixteen miles were downhill and flat. Don crossed the finish line in 5:25:46.

Figure 24: Don At The Wild West Marathon

On May 1, 1994, Don was at the Wild West Marathon in Lone Pine, California. This is a challenging point to point course starting in the foothills outside of Lone Pine, California to the eastern Sierra foothills. There were several steady climbs and moderate declines at altitudes between 3,700 and 6,600 feet with temperatures reaching 90 degrees by noon. Don reached mile marker eight with his legs feeling heavy and making it hard to put one foot in front of the other. The course to that point was mostly uphill on fairly steep roads and trails contouring and climbing to the highest point at 6,600 feet at the intersection of Whitney Portal Road and Hogback Road. At nine miles he was on a long, winding descent on a wide graded dirt road that led to the north end of the famed Alabama Hills. Winding and rolling, the road took him southbound through a geological formation of huge rounded oblong rocks. By now he could feel the painful blisters and the cracking of toenails as he pressed on. Around mile twenty the marathon began a moderate elevation gain on a single track trail followed by a five-mile descent. Don crossed the finish line in 7:20:55. At the end, Don's grandson, Nick, took a picture of his bare foot, which was black and blue.

Showing Respect Gains Rewards

It was July of 1994 when Don hit another landmark. He would run his 400th at the Midnight Sun Double Marathon in Nanisivik, Ontario, Canada. He had done this marathon eleven times before and knew what to expect, but still wanted this to be the one for this extraordinary count. Don had already done eighty-four ultra marathons, and as he flew on a charter out of Montreal to the Great White North, he slept until they landed in the middle of nowhere, five hundred miles north of the Arctic Circle. As had been prearranged, Don was driven to the mining town of Nanisivik and was graciously put up in the home of a local mining family. It would be then, since McNelly was presumably a Scottish surname, that Don had his picture taken in kilts. He rented the outfit but purchased the socks to go with it, wanting it to be as official as possible. Don had a buddy who was the president of a zinc mine in Canada, who as a favor to Don, set up his photographer to take a picture of Don in his kilts. Don had spent just a lot of time putting together an official Scot dress, which he found that depending on the occasion, a kilt was normally worn with accessories such as a belt, a Prince Charles Jacket, black tie, sporran (a type of pouch), Ghillie Brogue Kilt Shoe, Kilt Socks, Flashes (pockets worn on socks), and following tradition, a Sgian Dubh, pronounced *Skeen' Doo*, literally translated as "black knife." This Sgian Dubh was originally hidden in the folds of the tartan, but now is usually worn inserted in the top of the right kilt hose. All of this detail Don painstakingly duplicated. Now there is a tie-in for this story, but bear with me as it comes a bit later on.

The photographer spent quite a bit of time taking many pictures so that Don would have the best shot possible. Finally, to make sure the photo had emotion, the photographer had Don say, "For the Clan!" as he raised his right arm up, bent at the elbow.

This year the group was very international, with runners from England, Germany, Australia, Canada, and the USA, and among them were many runners he had met before. On race day, the temperature was around forty degrees, and there was a tail wind all the way to Arctic Bay before turning around and heading back.

Starting back, everything changed. The strong tailwind became a stronger headwind. The temperature dropped and it started snowing sideways. To make any headway, the runners had to lean forward about ten degrees or risk being blown backwards. To make matters worse, any attempt to look ahead would be met with tiny ice particles stinging your face. Sky and ground appeared as one, since it was totally white. By mile thirty-five, the total white-out condition and Don's inability to sense his position was unsettling. Approaching the forty-mile mark, Don tried to occupy his mind with thoughts to make the distance pass quickly.

Somehow, despite the final precipitous drop down to sea level and brutal climb back into town, called the "Crunch," Don managed to finish in one piece in a place that looks like no other place on the planet. Don would finish in 8:28:56.

Now to unveil the purpose of all the earlier pomp and circumstance; this year he planned to do the marathon and was aware that he would be recognized by the director as having completed his 400th here. This photo was to be added to a plaque that was presented to Don on the completion of his 400th marathon. At the conclusion of his 400th marathon, there was a ceremony held in his honor where he was given a wooden plaque with the picture of him in kilts. The plaque was engraved with all the dates, distances, and times, along with a commemorative statement saying, "a great companion and a role model for us all."

Not one to quietly go on his way, Don became best friends with Graham, the fellow who operated the mine, and they would travel together pretty much all over the world. Another Canadian friend, Laurie Dexter, who was a minister of Scottish descent and who translated the Bible into Inuit, would also become one of his dear friends.

Later, Don realized that he had made a miscalculation on his part. He had actually done his 400th at Randalls Island at the Sri Chinmoy Marathon, and the one at the Midnight Sun had actually been his 401st marathon. Yet, in his mind and that of the marathon, it was and would remain his 400th to all of them who were there on that day. On the same day, Horst Priesler of Germany would complete his 500th.

Figure 25: Receiving the 400th Trophy at Nanisivik. On the left Joe Wormersley and Graham Farquahrson on Don's right

Venice Marathon

October 9, 1994, Don McNelly was a challenge taker, and so much so that he had by now become one of North America's three most prolific marathon runners, and he believed that challenges were what made life interesting, the person who stepped up to the plate became his own hero. That was the reason Don was interviewed so much and why his notoriety extended throughout the United States and beyond. He has experienced more than the average person can hope to experience in a lifetime, like the time when he was asked by a friend of his to go with him to the Venice Marathon.

The marathon began in Stra, a small town west of Venice, and the beginning of "Riviera del Brenta," the riverside area famous for the rich mansions. From there, Don would see the countryside as the route took him along the river at the "Riviera del Brenta" before going through the center of the boroughs of Marghera and Mestre. Then it was on to San Giuliano's Park and into Venice via the Liberty Bridge, which luckily was flat. Then Don headed toward the Venice port area and the city center before going to the Giudecca Canal to Punta della Dogana, where he crossed the Grand Canal on a pontoon bridge, especially built for the race. The course was basically flat, making the going much easier as they passed by the Piazza San Marco and the Palazzo Ducale on the way to the finish line, where he ran mainly on large rectangular stone slabs until reaching the picturesque waterfront of St. Mark's Basin at Riva Sette Martiri. Throughout the course, there had been only four short slopes to master, and though adding to the difficulty, the view as Don ran over the fourteen little bridges crossing the canals was made easier by the wooden ramps placed over the steps. An interesting change from the norm was that each runner was given two personal sponges in their race packet, and they were encouraged to carry them with them during the race. These sponges were to be soaked in the fresh water tanks that were set up every five kilometers.

Don's friend, who lived in Ottawa, was born thirty miles from Venice and spoke the language, so he was able to show Don around Venice and point out different things along the marathon route.

Later, after the marathon, at one point a motorcycle policeman gave them a ride through Venice, and later Don learned this was his friend's nephew. It was indeed an experience of a lifetime, as Don was introduced to the real Venice and the real Italian restaurants, along with having the best type of tour guide, a friend.

Tim Horton's Valley Harvest Marathon

In 1994, Don, at the age of seventy-four, entered the Tim Horton's Valley Harvest Marathon in Kentville, Canada. Kentville is approximately sixty-four miles (103K) from Halifax and was the most populous and fastest growing town in all of the Annapolis Valley. Many dykes had been built to keep the high Bay of Fundy tides out of farmland. Kentville has the added distinction of being at the junction of seven roads, turning it into a commercial center, serving agricultural villages throughout the Annapolis Valley. The town was originally known as Horton's Corner but was named Kentville after Prince Edward Augustus, Duke of Kent.

You might think that since the town was known as Horton's Corner, this was the base for naming the marathon, but that's not so. It was named after Tim Horton, who was born Miles Gilbert and who was a Canadian professional hockey defenseman from Cochrane, Ontario. He played twenty-four seasons in the National Hockey League for the Toronto Maple Leafs, the New York Rangers, the Pittsburgh Penguins, and the Buffalo Sabers. He was also the co-founder of Tim Horton's, the Canadian equivalent to Starbuck's, and Canada's largest coffee and doughnut store chain. He died in a car accident in 1974.

By the time Don entered this marathon, he had a total of 436 certified course marathons and ultra marathons completed and had finished all but two provinces across the Canadian map. He had yet to do Prince Edward Island and Saskatchewan. He had run in all temperatures, in towns, in cities, and rural areas. He had run on pavement, dirt roads, uphill, and flat surfaces, eliminating most surprises that he might encounter doing a marathon. By now, his time to complete a marathon was up to 5:30 from his personal best of 3:50 done in 1971. There were other changes as well.

Instead of forty-two marathons a year, from 1990 on he was averaging twenty-four marathons in a year. Yet Don was rated third among "mega-marathoners."

With temperatures in the mid 50s to 60 degrees Farenheit, Don completed the marathon course, which was run on public roads that normally had minimal traffic, but for safety reasons, traffic was restricted. The runners started on Main St., then went west of the Kentville Fire Hall, where they did one loop in downtown Kentville before crossing the Cornwallis River. Then it was on to Brooklyn Street, followed by Somerset, where the runners turned around to return to Kentville. Here, the finish was a direct route from Brooklyn Street to Cornwallis Street to Aberdeen Street to Main Street and into Centre Square in Downtown Kentville. Runners refer to this type of course as an "out and back." It was also relatively flat, with some rolling terrain and no major hills.

In an interview following this marathon, Don was asked what he would do when he completed the last two provinces, and he replied that he would start on countries. He had two continents to go at this point, and they were Africa and Australia.

Don was glad to be running in Nova Scotia, and like many of his other marathons, he ran into friends or "passing" acquaintances. This marathon was no different. Here in Canada, he had run at last fifteen times with the Canadian ultra marathoner Ashley Evans. Whenever their paths crossed, she would wave as she passed him by.

1995 The Last Marathon

On February 6, 1995 Don was in Antartica. Every winter, alone in the merciless ice deserts of Antarctica, deep in the most unwelcoming terrain on Earth, a truly remarkable journey takes place. Emperor penguins in thousands leave their ocean home, scrambling onto the frozen ice to begin their long journey into a region that supports no other wildlife at this time of year. They march in single file, fighting blinding blizzards and gales of wind. They have no choice, as they are guided by instinct to this breeding ground, where they perform a ritual courtship, pair off, and mate.

Figure 26: Finishing In Antartica

Just as determined as those penguins, though not driven by instinct or performed in a line, there is a human need to conquer this land where you come face to face with icebergs, penguins, seals, and whales while exploring the most pristine corner of the planet. It is a different need that drives the flock of marathoners to this remote area. It is the peak interest in running on the darkest, windiest, and most remote continent on earth, and it is held every year at an expense of around five thousand dollars per person, requiring eighty runners to hold the marathon.

Don understood the need, as he had been drawn long before this marathon made the yearly change. Don had the distinction of having run in the first ever offering of this marathon.

Most entrants in the Third Antarctica Marathon (also dubbed the "Last Marathon"), rated the course as the most difficult they've ever run. The course, a double out and back held in early February on King George Island just off the coast of the Antarctic continent, began on a beach strewn with fist-size rocks, followed by a mile each way up and down a glacier, then ten miles along dirt paths with now-and-then streams, shoe-sucking mud, and severe hills. Some runners reported being dive-bombed by skuas, a seagull-sized predatory bird.

With all this to contend with, a wind that sometimes approached gale force lowered the wind-chill factor to a single digit and forced most runners to wear several layers of clothing.

Runners huddled by the start line, shielded from the wind in the lee of a Russian research base before bursting out along the rugged, hilly course. Up and down three quarters of a mile of glacier, twice, and looping through three more Antarctic research stations. Along with the demanding course, to run in this marathon, one must complete about a seven-thousand-mile travel that, usually, was done with an eleven-hour flight from JFK to Buenos Aires, followed by a three-and-a-half-hour flight to Ushuaia in Tierra del Fuego, Argentina, the southernmost city in the hemisphere.

Don recalled it was in February that they held their first ever marathon in Antartica and the course was torturous. He ran part of it on a glacier, and it was freezing. When he reached the muddy hills, he had a hard time making it up, his feet slipping every inch of the way. There also weren't any paved roads, none whatsoever, and the only civilization there was research centers with rough dirt paths between them, but Don said he'd do it again in a minute.

He completed the race in 7:30:00 and was among eighty finishers in the event, which had been set up as a tour.

On November 18, 1995, Don marked his eighteenth time finishing the John F. Kennedy (JFK) ultramarathon. As he reviewed his marathon table, he noted that it was in 1974 that he recorded his best time, finishing the JFK in 10:49:12.

That and much more made him proud of his accomplishments to this point in his life.

As a fan of running in the High Arctic, Don participated in the First Musk Ox Marathon with eight other runners in August of 1995. Six runners were from the fifty states club, who were concentrating on getting each of the twelve Canadian provinces/territories added to their marathon collection. Several had finished adding these but were there just for the sheer joy of it.

Then in the hamlet of Cambridge Bay, with a population of 1,300, situated on Victoria island in Canada's northwest territories, 183 miles north of the arctic circle, he was there at the Cambridge Bay Marathon, which combined a scenic rolling course interaction with local Inuit people, and the opportunity to see native arctic wildlife about as far north as you can get without charting a private expedition. After eighteen hours and four different flights, Don arrived from Rochester, New York, and spent the next day charting the course. Conditions at the start were mild in the area of 38 to 42 degrees, but with a twenty-five mile-per-hour wind.

Don had made this trip to Cambridge Bay to run the 26.2 miles on a gravel road out of the village to the Passage, then back through the DEW line installation. Cambridge Bay was the site of the Royal Canadian Mounted Police and the Hudson's Bay Company outposts that were established during the 1920s. Following World War II, a LORAN tower was built near the previous location of Cambridge Bay and a DEW Line site[viii] established in 1955. For Don, his goal was to finish the 26.2 mile race and not dwell on how long it would take him.

While completing a lap around the bay, he stopped to observe a herd of eight musk oxen with their thick undercoats of soft brown fleece and thick overcoats of shaggy, long straight hair that hung to the ground. He had read somewhere that if the musk oxen sense danger, they form a defensive circle around their young and face their enemies. They may even charge and try to gore the enemy with their horns, but Don was tt far away to be seen as a threat, so he stood and looked. He had read somewhere that their name came about because they gave off a musky smell when excited. He could hear them snort loudly as he stood and watched them put on a show. The herd ran together, stopped, and ran in the other direction, then stopped again. That was when it finally dawned on Don that he wasn't doing the most sensible thing standing there. These were not zoo animals that had limited territory. These were wild animals and he cautiously went on his way.

In 1996, Don would be at the Kilauea Volcano Marathon, which had been rated as one of the ten roughest marathons in the USA, mainly due to the first twelve miles on a rough lava flow, followed by a second half done in the rain forest. You really had to concentrate on the first half of the course, which was marked by piles of rocks every fifty yards, so as not to get lost or fall into a steaming vent that went a long way down. Some runners wore knee and arm pads, so as not to get cut up by the lava if they fell, which seemed sensible. This was the first time that Don thought of doing a marathon as dangerous beyond the scope of the torture it can do physically on the body. Yes, he had been on terrain before that made it critical for placing his feet, but for some reason this seemed worse.

This marathon stood out in other ways, too. Runners' shoes were scrubbed by volunteers at the start to ensure that no foreign seeds accidentally got planted, which could screw up the ecology.

The start was usually cool, between 60 and 70 degrees, given that the altitude was four thousand feet and typically cloud covered. It could get into the high 70s or low 80s though, and some humidity by 10:00 a.m. in the rain forest. There were plenty of aid stations spaced every three miles, but it was best to carry one bottle just in case. The first eight miles on the lava fields were downhill, dropping a thousand feet. Then the course turned left, going by sulfur-smelling splatter cones and deep sand and ash areas. Just before mile fourteen, runners reached some pavement that lasted for about five miles before turning into a rough road that paralleled the Escape Road, where there were a series of tough hills.

Then they were on their way past the Thurston Lava Tubes and entered the ledge trail along the top of one of the active volcano, Kilauea Caldera, and then finally Don was crossing the finish line at the Kilauea Military Camp.

On August 18, 1996, Don completed the Cambridge Bay Marathon held in Cambridge Bay, Canada; only the marathon would not add to his count, as it was not considered official since there were not enough participants entering that year.

Last Chance, First Chance Marathon

It was December 1996, and like an elite athlete, Don McNelly was given his own police escort as he made his way toward the finish line of the Last Chance First Chance Marathon. Shuffling south along the powdery sand of Daytona Beach under blue skies, McNelly's eyes were burning and so was his desire to finish the 26.2 miles that were trying to best him.

He was tired, but kept going because he knew that somewhere down the world's most famous beach was a double-decker scaffold and the narrow shoots that mark the end of the race. As he checked his timer, he figured he had just two more miles to go. After that there would be a comfortable hotel room and a nice relaxing shower with his name on it.

From the beginning of the race Don was separated from the field except for a good friend who matched him step for step the entire distance. After following a course that took them up the beach, over a bridge, along a river, through a nature preserve, and back to the beach, Don and his friend were almost alone. Almost, because there was a lone Volusia county Sheriff's car with lights spinning as they made their approach to the finish line. Unlike the other eight lead cars, this vehicle didn't have to pull over to let Don break the finishing tape. That's because Don was finishing last. That Sheriff's car was what runners affectionately called the "Sag Wagon."

By the time Don made it to the finish, he had been on his feet for almost seven hours. While he was out on the course, a chilly morning had evolved into a mild afternoon, but all that mattered was that he made it and crossed the finish line in 6:41:54

The Most Unforgettable Marathon Experience

It was September of 1997 when, in the middle of the night, somewhere over the Atlantic, Don turned to his two fellow runners, Wally Herman and Dan Newbill, and asked, "How do you feel about having to carry a rifle during this marathon?"

Wally Herman, at the time, was a seventy-four-year-old retired civil servant from Ottawa. He had completed 565 marathons and ultras on all seven continents and was the first to finish marathons in each Canadian province and territory as well as in all fifty states and D.C.

Don Newbill was sixty-nine at the time, a micro surgeon from Honolulu with similar accomplishments, having completed 150-plus marathons and ultras, including Sahara, Everest, Western States, and Comrades.

They joined Don McNelly, who was then seventy-nine and had completed 560 marathons and ultras, including all fifty states, each Canadian province and territory, and twenty countries.

The three were together on their way to participate in the third Spitsbergen, Norway Marathon on September 6, 1997. The run was held in Svalbard, a group of Norwegian islands midway between the top of mainland Norway and the North Pole with Spitsbergen being the main island in the archipelago. This marathon represented the northernmost organized marathon in the world.

Don and his fellow runners had already completed marathons in Bangkok, Panama, Lisbon, Nanisivik, Buenos Aires, Kilauea, and Cyprus, to name a few, and this would be one more shared experience.

Having his eye on running in Spitsbergen for some time, Don originally signed up for the 1996 Marathon, but a Russian plane crashed near the Longyearbyen Airport, killing 141 passengers and crew, leading to the rescheduling of the marathon in 1997.

In gathering details on the Spitsbergen Marathon, Don discovered that there was a marathon in Oslo, Sweden on the following Saturday and talked Wally and Dan into running with him. They met in Boston, Massachusetts, and left together for Oslo. After a lengthy layover, they caught a small jet with some seats blocked out for freight, medicines, mail, and food to Svalbard.

In checking the preliminary entry list, they found that they were in the sixty-five-plus age group, which turned out to be the largest group of runners. On race day, time went fast. The sun was up at 2:00 a.m., Don was up and dressed by 7:00 a.m., and had picked up his *startnummerutdeling* (racing number) at the starting line by 11:00 a.m.

The course was fifty-fifty gravel and pavement laid out in the town and on the roads along the fjord to the airport in one direction, and to one of the coal mines in the other. Mud and coal were used as gravel along the route, which rose 275 feet or more in several spots. The views were spectacular. Everywhere he looked there was a postcard scene of mountains, glaciers, fjords, blue sky, and several glacier-fed streams flowing swiftly from the mountain.

Staying together for the first eleven miles, Don, Wally, and Dan cruised up the main street, passed the only church in the small town, and were on their way to the airport. The course was not extremely punishing, except for the gravel and the very strong winds that blew up to forty miles per hour. The temperature was forty-five to fifty degrees Fahrenheit, and in 6:53:54, Don managed to cross the finish line.

Figure 27: From the left, Wally Herman, Dan Newbill, and Don McNelly prepare to run Svalbard Marathon in Norway

After a quick shower, it was time to attend the awards ceremony, where they were served reindeer stew and Norwegian beer as they watched the winners collect their prizes before calling it a night. As previously arranged, after leaving Svalbard, Don flew with his friends Wally and Dan to Oslo, Norway to run in the next marathon.

The first part of the Oslo Marathon course was two times around a nearly five-mile loop through downtown Oslo, past the harbor, and on to the main street. They ran through the university and cultural areas, which included the old fort that once guarded the city and a park filled with the life's work of the Norwegian sculptor Vigeland. There were rolling but fair hills and another strong wind off the fjord that had whitecaps and waves crashing against the seawall. The final leg ended on the best track Don had ever encountered. It had been the site of the Bislett-Mobil games, similar to the Olympics, which had been held several months before. Don crossed the finish line in 6:26:27. Though he really enjoyed it, tThis would be his first and last time doing this marathon.

Don McNelly sat back, reviewing. He had run in all fifty states plus D.C., every Canadian province (twelve), seventeen countries, and Antarctica. That put him at third in the country and around eighth in the world in terms of number of completed races. He would say that in Greenland he hobnobbed with the native Inuit's. Antarctica, he said, was pristine and cold. In London he recalled, Big Ben was striking as he crossed the finish line, but what it really meant was there was something special beyond the marathon that Don had gained in each location that he had the chance to visit.

First Global Autumn Marathon

On October 11, 1997, Don entered a marathon put on by the Full Hyaku Club in Japan and of which he was a member. Held in Kokyo Japan, a place he had visited during his first trip to the country, Don found the course to be easier than the feat of climbing Mount Fuji. Most of the path carried the runners along the Yura River catchment, or drainage basin, which represents 40 percent of the area of Kyoto Prefecture . Don finished in 6:23:36.

In October of 1997, Don McNelly had managed to find another first, as he would run the Twin Cities Marathon for the first time. Wearing number 402, this was one that he felt he needed to do since it had been ranked the third most competitive marathon for American runners by *Running Times* magazine.

It was unseasonably warm for the Twin Cities; in fact, it was hot! The sky was pitch black when he left the hotel, so there was no way of knowing it was cloudless and that later he would find himself baking in the sun. Finally, the gun went off, and it took Don almost two minutes to get to the start. It felt great running through Minneapolis, on the wonderful scenic route. It was very winding and crowded; it was still cool and shaded until mile fourteen, then heat hit hard. The part of the course that goes over Highway 55 was hot, open, and really formidable. The course wound around all the lakes in Minneapolis then traveled parallel to the Mississippi on West River Road. The whole course was lined with spectators, and it was very scenic; truly, a beautiful urban landscape. Don felt excellent and was running easy, over the bridge, to the water stop at mile twenty. There were hundreds of people; music was blaring, and an announcer urged runners on. Then the hills began. The course traveled up Summit Boulevard and gained two hundred feet from river level at mile twenty up to mile twenty-three where it flattened out and continued up to the old cathedral of St. Paul, the highest point in the city. Though it wasn't quite as steep, the rolling hills were still a struggle. At mile twenty-four it got really hard, and Don had to suck it up, focus, and dig in. Then he was around the bend and heading down the hill with the State capitol building in view. Don crossed the finish line.

Since 1963 there had been a marathon in Minneapolis, but the name had changed several times before being called Twin Cities. It was a challenge, but it rounded out that decade nicely.

Number 500

On February 1, 1998, Don was in Ocala, Florida, for his next marathon. It would be his 500th. The course went through gentle rolling hills on rural roads, with some nice views of farms and small-town Ocala with beautiful horses dotting the countryside. There was a cooling fog, and even though it was a bit challenging, it was fun and Don was glad he chose this marathon to mark his 500th. Even on his flight to the marathon, he had a memorable experience. First, his coach ticket was upgraded to first class, and then in first class he was seated next to a pleasant woman.

That woman turned out to be Mrs. Theresa Castro, who owned the Castro convertible sofa stores. Being the friendly guy that he was Don struck up a conversation. Her husband, Bernard Castro, had not only sold but invented more than five million Castro Convertible sofas and had passed away in August of 1991 at the age of eighty-seven. As they talked, Don mentioned that he recalled the little girl who opened the sofa in commercials during the early days of television and commented on it being a great sales method, and Mrs. Castro shared that the little girl was their daughter, Bernadette.

All in all, this would be something to remember when he thought about his 500th marathon.

Before the end of the year, Don would do a Marathon in Greenland and another marathon in Japan.

Nuuk Marathon

This was a fairly new marathon, having started in 1990, but Don did not enter until July 25, 1998. No one denies a marathon being a challenge, but the Nuuk Marathon was particularly challenging, as it would have Don going up lots of inclines. Nuuk, the capital of Greenland, has much to offer, but Don could only remember the wind, rain, and single-figure temperatures that were just as challenging as the topography. Runners were informed upfront that their finishing times here were much slower than that of other marathons.

The marathon route took Don past beautiful old homes along the colonial harbor before leaving Nuuk and heading past the airport and out to the turning point of the district of Qinngorput, which was framed by mountains. Then it was the run back to the starting point again. The Nuuk Marathon's route is 13 miles 192.5 yards and thus two circuits have to be completed by the marathon runners. Don crossed the finish line in 6:45:19

Pafos Marathon (Cyprus Marathon)

On February 28, 1999 Don was in Cyprus. Sometimes called the Cyprus Marathon, this was not only a place to go for a marathon, but also a place to be to just enjoy the small charming harbor town of Pafos, located on the west side of the island of Cyprus. Of course, the interesting tale is that this was the birthplace of Aphrodite, the Goddess of Love.

Don would say that Cyprus was the perfect location for runners trying to get away from winter! The Cyprus Marathon began at *Petra tou Romiou*, the legendary birthplace of Aphrodite, and continued on an almost flat course along the Pafos seafront to finish at the Pafos Medieval Fort square. It was an experience worth doing at least once. Don crossed the finish line in 7:34:01.

Changes at Home

Around 1999, Don was feeling under the weather and decided to have a checkup. He had been quite busy with marathons, volunteering as well as visiting the children, and planning outings with Phyllis. He figured the doctor was going to tell him to slow down, but it was not the case. Instead, after reading test results, his doctor informed him that he had chronic lymphocytic leukemia, or for short, CLL. Unfamiliar with the term, Don asked what exactly was CLL, and should he be worried?

It was explained to him that chronic lymphocytic leukemia (CLL) is a type of cancer of the blood and bone marrow, and no, he should not worry. CLL is called chronic leukemia because it progresses more slowly than acute leukemia. It's called lymphocytic leukemia because it affects a group of white blood cells called lymphocytes, which typically fight infection. When these cells grow old, they die naturally and are replaced by new cells, but in patients with CLL, this process goes awry. Over time, they accumulate in large numbers and eventually crowd out other healthy cells, leaving people with chronic lymphocytic leukemia vulnerable to infection.

A decade ago, doctors thought CLL always affected older adults and rarely posed enough risk to warrant cancer treatments, so "watchful waiting" was the treatment of choice. Today, new laboratory tests, new medications, and a new understanding of chronic lymphocytic leukemia have dramatically changed the rules for treatment of this type of leukemia. Doctors now know that chronic lymphocytic leukemia can behave aggressively in some people. Although watchful waiting is still the best option for some people, new medications are helping people diagnosed with a more aggressive form of chronic lymphocytic leukemia at a younger age. In Don's case, his CLL was not aggressive enough to warrant more than keeping tabs on it.

In a few days, Don was feeling like his old self again and ready to get his life back in full swing. Nothing seemed to get Don down, as he faced all obstacles as minor impositions, for Don had a secret, and that was: regardless of the circumstances, most bad patches soon pass. Only there was something yet to come to test his theory.

Back when Don and Phyllis had moved to their home in Irondequoit, they had planted trees on their property, and over the years, these trees had become more than just trees to the McNellys. They had become a timeline measuring the growth of their family.

Phyllis had planted a maple tree in the front and one in the back of the house, which had now become too big for the lot as the limbs spread out and had branches over the house. When they moved there, Don and Phyllis would watch the sunset from the window, but now they couldn't see the sunset anymore. The house was darkened by the shade, and so they decided to have the tree in the front of the house taken down.

They were in agreement that something had to be done about the tree on the front lawn, but it was hard to think of cutting it down. The year was 1999, and the issue became the topic of conversation as they discussed what they could do until finally coming up with a solution.

Phyllis and Don decided to have a carving put on the tree, so they went to see a chain saw carver named John Dempsey. With John's talent and the McNellys' vision, on the three branch bases that remained after the tree was cut down, two were to have carved blue jays, and on the remaining was carved a nest, holding three baby birds, to symbolize their three children. Later, a neighbor down the street said that to make it more realistic, they should have a worm in one of the adult bird's beaks to appear as though she is feeding her babies, and so a rubber snake was substituted, matching the size of the carved birds.

Summary of 1990

Since the start of the '90s, Don was making his own history as he passed the four hundred marathon mark and continued on. His record was astounding with thirty marathons in 1990, thirty-three in 1991, thirty-six in 1992, thirty-seven in 1993, twenty-five in 1994, twenty-six in 1995, twenty-seven in 1996, twenty-four in 1997, thirty in 1998, and twenty-four in 1999. Within the total were fifty-six ultra marathons completed. Don had done extensive traveling to complete fifty-one marathons in foreign countries including, Antartica, Argentina, Canada, Cyprus, England, France,Germany, Greenland, Holland, Italy, Japan, Norway, Panama, Portugal, and Thailand. Don would cross the finish line with his best time of 4:20:00 on October 6, 1990, at the St. George Marathon in New York. He managed to keep his longest time in the five-hour range and his ultra marathons running not far off for the less than fifty milers, and on the mark for two to three times the average time it takes to do the marathon for those ultras that ran closer to one hundred miles.

With his travel to so many marathons across the world, his expenses had grown tremendously, but only if thought of in terms of a marathon. Don and Phyllis used the travel as vacation spots where they stayed and enjoyed the sites around them, and in some areas they visited friends whom they had met at other marathons.

By the end of the '90s, Don had seen new marathons and ultra marathons appear on the scene. At the age of seventy-nine, he had also witnessed marathons that he had entered and enjoyed disappear or have their name changed. The sport was growing by leaps and bounds and attracting more and more players each year, but he had experiences that none would master.

It was not always simple or painless. In 1994, when Don found he was doing better with his time, he faced a setback. He had several serious injuries during the years that followed. In 1995 he developed foot problems, plantar facieties, and an inflamed metatarsal. In 1996 Don broke a rib falling off a ladder, and then in 1997 it was discovered that he had a heart blockage, leading to his doing fifty percent more walking. It would be easy to just stop doing marathons if Don wasn't a victim of self-determination. Webster defines self-determination as free choice of one's own acts without external compulsion, which is exactly what drove Don. It was his choice to continue doing marathons, though he could have used many excuses. Cancer didn't stop him, leukemia hadn't either, so a few ailments didn't stand a chance. As the author Claude M. Bristol said, "It's the constant and determined effort that breaks down all resistance and sweeps away all obstacles." At this point Don thought it could only get better.

2000 AND BEYOND

The new century began on an up note. During the year 2000, Don would turn eighty, and that meant he would run in a whole new age category. Truthfully, this was the first time the word "win" entered his mind. The fact that he was running marathons had been enough, because he made the choice to only compete against himself and not others. Each marathon he continuously tried to improve on his time and compete against his own recorded finish. When he first started running, he may have had a star or two in his eye, but early on as he heard the finishing times, he knew there was no star low enough to carry him over the finish line. Besides, it was fun when the objective was to beat his best.

Only now a possibility had presented itself. This was uplifting, since being the oldest in the seventy age group category made it hard to seek any reward for his effort, but now he was definitely part of an elite group that had very few members. Not ready to admit it outloud, Don did some research. He figured it out one day that on the average, if there were a thousand runners in the race, only ten would be eighty years of age. But more than likely, the odds were that he would be the only one in that age category at a marathon. From that point of view, getting older increased his odds of winning.

Don was excited as he looked forward to another year of running and the possibility of soon being able to place in the marathon. So much had changed over the years since he began doing marathons. Where he had to make phone calls and hear word of mouth what was happening in other states, he now just had to log on. The magic of the Internet could not be overestimated for obtaining information and as he was quickly learning, producing publicity.[ix]

Don was more than ready to start the year with a bang. He made it interesting for those who interviewed him by saying that he would hit six hundred marathons by 2002. Don made such an assumption because he knew how to play the publicity game. If you know how to answer why would readers/listeners/viewers be interested in learning about you, they will be happy to use your story to fill up their air time or column space. A reporter once said "The media are a hungry animal that needs to be constantly fed." So the trick is to feed them an angle on you that their audience will perceive as news, entertainment or useful information.

Freescale Austin Marathon

Don was off to Austin, Texas, to run with his son Tom on February 20, 2000. Sponsored by Tom's employer, Motorola, Don's son was the only employee who had competed every year, so he was given free entry and special treatment. Don was also given a free entry because he was Tom's father, a nice perk for fathering his son.

The Freescale Austin Marathon, which was formerly known as the Motorola Austin Marathon, follows a loop course that starts and finishes at Congress Avenue between the Texas State Capitol building and the Sixth Street entertainment district. Racers head south across Town Lake into the South Congress Avenue district, go back north and run along Town Lake, and through the Tarrytown neighborhood and up into North Central Austin, then head south through Brentwood and down Red River before returning to the starting point. This marathon fit perfectly into Don's marathon schedule, since in February there were three marathons in three consecutive weekends: Surfside, Austin, and Cowtown in Fort Worth, and Don did them all. Being able to do this with his son, the Austin Motorola

Marathon held special meaning, and Don would cross the finish line in 6:47:37.

The Oklahoma Marathon

On November 17, 2001, Don was in Tulsa, Oklahoma. Marathons were in Don's blood, but along with the desire to do marathon was the desire to help others, so running in the Oklahoma City Marathon was important to Don. This marathon was run as a tribute to those who lost their lives in the tragedy that occurred in Oklahoma City in April of 1995, and to show love, compassion, and generosity. Throughout the course, 168 banners flew to commemorate each individual who gave their life that day, and starting at the Oklahoma City National Memorial deepened the meaning in Don's heart. This was where the race started and finished and Don would finish in 7:59:34.

The course ran through the streets of Oklahoma City, starting near the memorial and running in a generally counter-clockwise direction through the city. There were no difficult hills to speak of, and that made it easy to complete the marathon in the seventy degree weather.

At the Oklahoma Marathon held in Tulsa in 2001, a special announcement was made at the pre-race dinner. The emcee acknowledged the top mega marathoners and the foreign visitors, stating:

Norm Frank, seventy, is one of the world leaders with 760 marathons/ultras. Wally Herman, seventy-six, from Ottawa was the first person to complete the fifty states and D.C. cycle and has run 590 marathons. Don McNelly, eighty-one, has run 590 marathons. KG Nystrom of Sweden has run 553. Rick Worley ran 200 marathons in 156 consecutive weekends. During that time span, he ran three Fifty States and D.C. cycles, including one with the thirteen Canadian provinces.

###

600th Lifetime Marathon

Don had predicted that he would complete his 600th marathon by 2002 and he did. On June 7, 2002 at the Spencerport AmCan Marathon in Spencerport, New York, Don would cross the finish line in 8:38:34.

Each year, across the nation, one event brings together entire communities to take part in the fight against cancer. That event was the American Cancer Society Relay for Life. The relay was held at a time and place where people come to celebrate those who have survived cancer, remember those they've lost, and fight back against a disease that touches too many lives.

Relay for Life was an overnight event designed to celebrate survivorship and raise money for ACS research and programs. During the event, teams of people gather and take turns walking or running laps. Each team tries to keep at least one team member on the track at all times. Don ran with the team of Charlie's Angels, as the Charlie's Angels star Farrah Fawcett had been diagnosed with cancer. She had done a public service poster and commercial for the American Cancer Society, which led many of the teams across the United States to take on this team name. The relay took fifteen hours to complete, and after it was over, on that Friday in June, Don reached his goal of six hundred marathons, but just as important was that Don, like the other runners, entered the race by getting pledges to raise money for cancer research. The money could be for each mile or per lap that the sponsored individual completed. That year, when Don did the marathon, he raised thirty-five dollars per lap he completed, which equaled slightly over nine hundred dollars.

Along the edge of the track were paper bags with votive candles in each, and written on the outside were the name of someone who had died or had beaten cancer. As a cancer survivor himself, Don was happy to mark this as his 600th marathon. On June 7, 2002 at the Spencerport AmCan Marathon in Spencerport, New York, Don would cross the finish line in 8:38:34.

As the day grew dark, Boy Scouts walked around the perimeter, lighting the candles that served as a border beacon for all the runners, while giving hope to many now and in the future.

In November of 2002 The Seneca Park Zoo held a celebration for Don's eightieth birthday that was well attended by his friends and family, along with many mammals, reptiles, and birds. Built in 1997, the Rocky Coasts exhibit has an observation room below the water level outside where the polar bears and seals can be viewed during the warmer months. It was here that the guests were taken that evening from the main entrance of the zoo in the open air zoo carts. It was a chilly evening, but once inside, the atmosphere was warm and inviting. There was all kinds of food and entertainment, mostly provided by the animals that were circulated through the group by zoo personnel. It was a night that Don McNelly would always remember. Over his years of service to the zoo, his group of friends embodied the animals, staff, and visitors. His name had become legendary in Irondequoit, just as it had throughout the marathon world.

Figure 28: Don being interviewed as he stands amongst the elephants at the Seneca Zoo Society

Just as memorable was the inauguration of a bench with a plaque commemorating his years of continuing dedication to the zoo.

I was lucky enough to be able to be part of the birthday party and was impressed by the feelings of everyone at the zoo when it came to Don. Amy Zastrocky, who had met Don at the Jungle Jog in 2002, told how she soon realized that no one was a stranger to this man; he treated everyone as though he had known them for some time. She said he was protective when he needed to be, and he was a teacher always. He had so much he wanted to share with everyone around him, and all one needed to do was stop and listen.

Wineglass Marathon

This would be Don's 607th marathon that he would run on October 6, 2002 at the Wineglass Marathon in Corning, New York. There was not much that Don McNelly did these days that wasn't considered newsworthy. He was becoming a celebrity of sorts in the marathon arena. In 2002, when a pair of thirty-eight-year-old out-of-staters, Mark Hoon (2:33:28) and Branford, Connecticut's Kerry Arsenault (2:55:05), were tops among their gender in a field of seven hundred, it would be reported that despite running on a chilly, overcast day with brisk winds and enduring an occasional hail storm, eighty-two-year-old Don McNelly added another marathon to his prolific running. Don finished in 8:24:16.

Running in Japan in 2003

The marathon life continued for Don, with a close connection to Japan where his physique stood out whether walking around or running. His height had him towering over his peers, but it was those size fifteen running shoes that drew their attention more. Though his coloring and size may have set him apart, his heart and personality made him many friends who honored him by making him a part of their Full Hyaku Club and invited Don and his wife into their homes.

Figure 29: Don McNelly and fellow members of the Full Hyaku Club

Located in the center of Tokyo, where once stood the Edo Castle, the Imperial Palace in Tokyo was the residence of the Japanese emperor and it was called Koukyo. Some of the original gates, moats, and stone walls remain in the area even after the Meiji Restoration, when Emperor Meiji moved to Tokyo from Kyoto. The palace was surrounded by moats, and some of the original gates and stone walls remain in the grounds, including the large Sakuradamon Gate. The size of the grounds was close to that of Central Park's three miles (5K). The marathon trail as it loops through doesn't cross any streets. This plus a three-mile loop on the sidewalk around the gate makes a full loop of six miles, done eight times.

[Note to Layout: Photo 28; caption below in italics]

Figure 30: Don runs in Tokyo around the Imperial Palace. Left to Right: Yasu Enomoto, Don McNelly, Junko Okazoe, Akihiko Tayeda (president of the Full Hyaku Club), and Takashi Yoshino (secretary).

Another favorite marathon for Don was done from the Tokyo Metropolitan Government building in Shinjuku, also referred to as Tokyo City Hall. The route took him around the Imperial Palace, Tokyo Tower, Shinagawa, Ginza, Asakusa, and Tsukiji before ending at Tokyo Big Sight, the popular nickname for the Tokyo International Exhibition Center located in Odaiba of Tokyo Bay.

It was during a race in Hirosaki, Amori, Japan that Don first crossed paths with his friend Hiroyasu Enomoto. Hiroyasu Enomoto (Yasu) was the spokesperson for the Japanese Marathon club known as "Full Hyaku." When Don heard of the club, he approached Yasu, who with his impressive use of English and obvious passion for marathon running, described the group Hyaku as a club, the Japanese name being "Furu

Hyakkai Rakusokai." Yasu would go on to explain that in Japan, people called all road races marathons and in translation *Furu Hyakkai Rakusokai*, taking the words separately translated as follows: *furu* means "only the full 26.2 miles or 42K." *Hyaku* means "one hundred," and the word *Hyakkai* means "one hundred times." *Raku* means "enjoyable." To become a member you must have completed a hundred marathons.

Don was honored to be a member and would become one of approximately 280 members, of which only six were Americans, with Don holding the distinction of being the oldest in the group. *Hyaku* members run marathons for their health primarily, but veteran members enjoy running a marathon for its own sake.

So special was this Japanese connection that during spring break in 2003, Don took his eighteen-year-old grandson, Nicholas, to Japan. By this time, Don had been there seven times before and wanted to show his grandson around and introduce him to some of his Japanese friends.

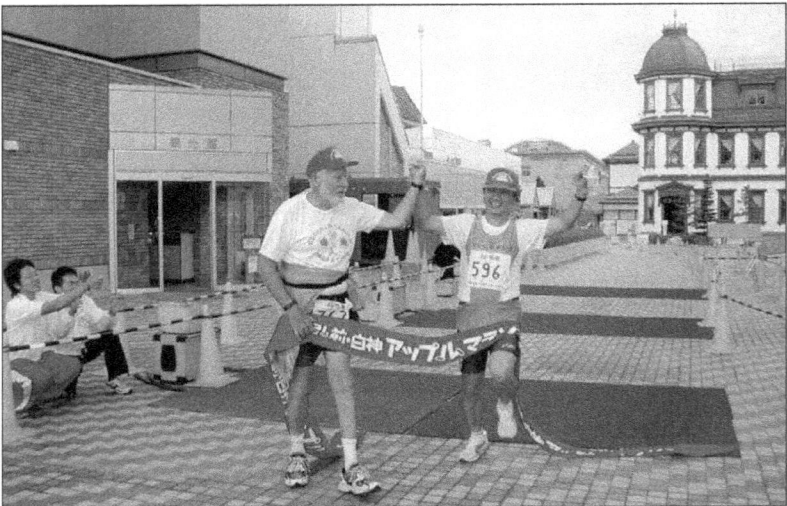

Figure 31: Running In Japan

While they were there, the club organized a run called the Nara Heijo-kyo Marathon. It was named for *Heijo-kyo*, which was the capital of Japan from 710 to 784. The course was a 1.63-mile loop in a park, where the capital's castle once stood. Don and his grandson did the marathon together, with Don running half the marathon and his grandson completing the other half. This was an experience that Don would never forget.

To add to the specialness of that day, Don got to watch his friend Noriko Sakota, who at the age of fifty-seven, finished her forty-seventh and last prefecture, the Japanese equivalent of finishing the fifty states. For Noriko Sakota, it meant she would be the first woman to do so.

Of all his marathons the thought of this one done with his grandson ranked it as superior in comparison to others of the same kind.

100 Mile Roadrunning Championship

It was September of 2003 that the American Ultrarunning Association joined forces with the Toledo Road Runners to host the 2003 USA 100 Mile Roadrunning Championship at Olander Park in Sylvania, Ohio. This would be the first USA Championship longer than fifty miles. The event was hosted by the New York Road Runners Club and was conducted on a loop in and around Shea Stadium in Queens, New York. The pancake-flat, traffic-free, shaded 1.09-mile loop in Olander Park had resurrected a great but almost forgotten chapter of national championship history, the ultra runners. Don, who by then was eighty-two years old and had walked or run sixty thousand miles, was not about to pass up this opportunity, so he submitted his entry.

The ultra marathon committee was not new to the marathon world, so they knew who Don McNelly was and gave him the No. 82 to match his age. On race day, Don arrived ready to compete in his fashion, which was to make it across the finish line, but once he had entered and realized he was the only entry in his age group of 80-84, he decided to go as long and as far as he could within the time restrictions. Don completed thirty-two laps, going 34.540 miles in 23:16:08. He finished ninetieth overall out of a field of ninety-five participants.

Later being interviewed, Don said, "You have to work at getting old. You can sit on the couch and say, I've worked all my life and now the world can serve me. You can take the remote in your hand and watch TV, maybe drink a little beer, go to the golf course and get in a cart for nine or eighteen holes. But it's just not for me."

Rekyjavik Marathon

Having lived in the Snow Belt, Don admitted that he didn't especially seek out the marathons done in the cold. However, he had fallen in love with running marathons in the far north in the high Arctic. The proof of this was that by 2003 Don had completed marathons and ultra marathons fifteen times north of the Arctic Circle in four locations and once in Antarctica.

Don had always had Reykjavik on his list and decided to enter the August 2003 marathon. He signed up with Marathon Tours for their four-day visit to Iceland, planning to travel with several friends, of whom four were fifty staters (had run in fifty states), one being Walt Boltech. They flew to Baltimore and then on to Reykjavik on Icelandic Airlines. It was a five and a half hour overnight flight.

After checking in at their hotel, Don and Walt went on a short city tour to see the sights. It was easy to see that Reykjavik had the best of both worlds. There were the qualities of a modern society complemented by a close connection to beautiful and unspoiled nature near the city. This northernmost capital was framed by the majestic Mt. Esja, and the blue waters of Faxafloi Bay. Their sightseeing tour over, Don and Walt returned to their hotel tired from their long trip and soon fell into a deep sleep.

The next day, they picked up their numbers and T-shirts and had the traditional spaghetti dinner, which, as prearranged, would be where they would meet up with another friend, Dan Newbill, who had also received permission to start early. At the age of eighty-two, Don was now walking every step of his marathons and shooting for an eight-hour finish.

The marathon, being one of the city's major events, had been combined with the Culture Night in Reykjavik, which was held the evening of the marathon. In celebration, businesses stayed open longer, and this event, along with the Reykjavik Marathon, drew thousands of participants and spectators.

On race day, Don, Walt, and Dan were at the start point in City Center. Shortly after daylight, it had begun to rain, and to add to this there was a 30 miles per hour wind with a temperature around 50 degrees Fahrenheit. Since Don had experienced conditional changes here before, he and his friends were dressed appropriately and figured they would have no problem.

The course was a double loop, keeping them always near the water as they walked on bike paths or city streets along the shore, so that traffic was not too much of a concern. The course took them past the building where Gorbachev and Reagan met in 1986 for their summit meeting to discuss disarmament and Star Wars, the anti-missile defense that Reagan supported.

Don trudged along with conversation at a minimum and the weather taking its toll by the time he crossed the finish line in 9:03:04. The cooler temperatures did not provide the warmth for the wind to help keep their clothing dry, and as a result it was like carrying extra weight on their shoulders. Walt and Don kept to the same pace and finished together in last place.

This was the twentieth edition of the race, and it attracted 3,236 runners to enter in different distance categories. A record total of 283 finished the marathon. Hungry, they decided to dine at Tveir Fiskar (Two Fishes). Don had researched the menu on the internet and was looking forward to having lundi, the breast of puffin, which is a pigeon-like bird. There were whale steaks and *hakart*, which is a putrefied shark fin that has been buried for six months, and other strange concoctions not seen in America. The experience was memorable not only because he had finished the marathon, but because he had shared the experience with his friends.

Life Changes

It is hard to keep friends in the loop when your life has you traveling from state to state at one marathon or another. The only constants in his life were having his wife travel with him and spending time with his children, either out for a run or seated at a dining room table for dinner. New friendships developed, and old friendships, in most cases, become pleasant memories, and the importance of family became even more significant. Don developed a best friend philosophy that began by stating that you can't have more than five best friends. Since he had moved around a lot, he began to define a best friend as someone who shares history with you; which made Phyllis, his wife, his first best friend.

Then over time there was work, family commitments, and coming from a big family to start, Don would soon be consumed with nieces and nephews, along with all his brothers and sisters. Don realized that he had a special closeness to his siblings and saw them as his best friends after his wife, Phyllis.

To Don, family was everything, and the same feeling was there amongst his brothers and sisters. Whenever there was a dispute among them, they tried to settle the issue right away, without holding any grudges or feuding with each other. Just as important as his relationship to his siblings was the relationship he promoted with his own children. Perhaps the most challenging adventure of our lives is parenting, since it requires all of our skill and lots of patience. But oh, what rewards! From the beginning, Don wanted to teach his children self-esteem, self-motivation, and self-confidence. He didn't lecture or hammer away at this, but tried to instill this message by setting an example, and it worked. He was proud of his children, whom he saw as his legacy, evidence that his life mattered and that he made a difference in the world and in the lives of those he cared about. It's something that parents seem to take for granted.

Nancy Ann Filbrun McNelly

She had used her mind, her heart, and her soul in furthering knowledge, but keeping so busy, Nancy never married. In 2002, Nancy moved from her long-time Cambridge, Massachusetts, home to live at home with Don and Phyllis in Rochester, New York. On December 16, 2004, Nancy Ann Filbrun McNelly died at the age of fifty-five.

Figure 32: Don With Daughter Nancy In Nanisivik

This was a very devastating time for the family, as they went through the different phases and symptoms of grief. The grief consumed Don, and though he responded to what was going on around him, it felt as though he were watching someone else rather than it being him. It was hard to imagine that the tragedy that had befallen his family had really happened, and that he would not wake up and discover it was all just a nightmare.

Don couldn't help feeling enraged and was sure he would never get over the loss of his precious daughter, but the living adjust and accept what they cannot change. As Don and Phyllis prepared to say goodbye to their only daughter, they tried to make it as special as possible, and by all accounts they succeeded.

Each day brought memories, and eventually the memories were what helped to let Nancy rest in peace. She had lived a full and inspirational life doing what she had wanted to do. She had left her mark through her work and the interests that had grown during her life time, such as her interest in the Mayan Culture. How many parents can look back and say, "She had done all she was meant to do," and really mean it?

When death comes without warning, the shock and disbelief can be overwhelming. It is never in the natural order of things for a child to die before his or her parents, and this can be especially intense when the death is sudden. It was not known beforehand that Nancy had a bad heart valve, and they would learn that even in serious cases there may not be evidence for a long time. There may be no symptoms, even though the heart is already under strain. But because of not knowing or expecting to have no more time with Nancy, it was not only a shock, but there was not a chance to even say goodbye.

Don would enter the American 100 Mile National Championship in September 10, 2005, an ultra marathon held in Sylvania, Ohio. As was quickly becoming the norm, Don would be the only one in his age group. He would finish in 8:36:59. At mile fifty or so, Don found he could not go the remaining half of the marathon because his heart wasn't in it. For so long he had used his time doing those lonely stretches to think, and now those thoughts were of his daughter. This was the first time that he felt a change as a result of her death. The reality of the death had finally settled in, and intense anger at the injustice and deep anguish at the realization that she was gone forever hurt him deeply.

Later he would admit that complete recovery was a myth. Phyllis and Don, along with their sons, would gradually put their lives back together again, but they would never truly "get over it." They would never totally have the same lives they had before. The family "unit" was changed forever, and there would always be a place at the table forever unfilled.

Even at that moment of discovery, he did not doubt that he would continue to run and continue at his unbelievable pace set from the start of his running career.

2006 Austin Marathon

Don had set a tradition with this marathon that continued year after year, and it did not go unnoticed. Since 1992, he had run in this marathon 12 times (12 years) missing only 1994, 2002, and 2003. The local station, KXAN, had Shannon Wolfson speaking with three runners. Shannon covered the fact that Don's son, Tom McNelly, had crossed the finish line at the Austin Marathon fifteen times previously, and that his goal was to just finish it, since he felt he did not train nearly enough to accomplish more than that.

Shannon would then interview Don McNelly and learn that this would be his thirteenth time running in the Austin Marathon with his son. Don would share with Shannon that he was flattered, proud, and felt lucky to be able to still enter marathons. Don was now eighty-six years old and would be the marathon's oldest participant. He would say, "My motto was quantity not quality," then add, "I'm very slow, as I do a lot of walking, which I can get away with because I'm eighty-six!" When asked by Shannon how to keep motivated to cross the finish line, Don would reply, "Just keep moving forward," Don said. "Simple."

Surfside Marathon

The Surfside Beach Marathon in Surfside, Texas, starts at the spectacular moment when the sun rises over the gulf. The runners follow the public beach to San Luis pass before they double back. The entire course is on sand, beginning and ending at the Stahlman Park pavilion. On February 10, 2006, along with 120 or so other runners, Don began the marathon on the level beach along the Gulf of Mexico, which always seemed to add very strong winds, up to at least thirty miles per hour, to the challenge of doing a marathon. Since it was an out and back, the runners had a head wind going out and a tail wind coming back. This marathon was convenient for Don, since it was located about forty miles west of Galveston, Texas, where Don vacationed so that he could be near his son who lives in Austin, Texas. Don had done the Surfside Marathon for the first time in 1999 and thought the winds had been strong enough to pepper his face with the spiraling sand; he had a desire to do it again.

Don had begun this year walking his marathons, and being a well known marathoner, was able to get compensation in many ways, but mainly allowing him to start out earlier than the scheduled start time. At this marathon he started out by himself in the dark at 5:00 a.m., wearing a headlight that illuminated the path to follow.

It was peaceful at that time of the morning, with the darkness enveloping his body and the wind blowing gently, as if making him aware of its presence. Don was able to see a sight that his comrades would not, and that was the sunrise, but this time it was greeted by a cloud-covered sky.

As he made his way walking quickly along the route, by the nine-mile point, he began to hear runners in the distance gaining on him. The silence was gone, and Don welcomed the new sounds of footsteps muffled by the sand and stirred by the quick pounding of feet as they gained and passed him by, but not all of them. A long-time running buddy, Jim Reeves, caught up with Don and decided to walk the rest of the way with him.

Another point in favor of walking was being able to talk, and Don and Jim did just that, making the distance go faster until reaching the finish line in 9:10:00. When he finally crossed the finish line, he was exhausted, but fortunate. He won in his age group, and was awarded a finishers medal and an unusual plaque reading "First Place, Age 80 and Up." The plaque was a spiral shell, native to the area. Don's win had been secure, since he was the only one in his age to enter the marathon, but in his defense, there was nothing stopping other eighty-year-olds from entering, except they had decided to stay home.

2007: Another Battle to Defeat

His old enemy, prostate cancer, came back. He had gone for surgery and had the cancer removed, but it had come back. As suggested by his doctor, he had PSA (prostate-specific antigen) blood tests every six months for five years, and then once every year after his initial bout with the cancer. With a PSA level of twenty-seven in October of 2006, Don was placed on Casodex in July 2007 and had thirty-eight radiation treatments to the prostrate. After the radiation, the PSA dropped to 01.1 and remained at that level.

Don knew he wasn't alone, as prostate cancer affects nearly two hundred thousand men in the United States every year. Don had chosen radiation over chemotherapy since radiation is a local treatment and the side effects were confined to the area being treated. The worst part of his recovery was feeling so tired after a few weeks of radiation therapy, and the fatigue got worse. It was stressful making the daily trips for treatment, and he was thankful that part was behind him. But he was an energetic person, and the fatigue sapped his energy to do the things he normally did, let alone what he most wanted to do—marathons. But he knew that soon this, too, would pass.

For several weeks, Don was out of the running business and too tired to do more than just think. His doctor had told him often that he was physically stronger than most men his age because of his running and he had no doubt that Don would be back 100 percent. Those words gave him hope and dreams of putting on his running shoes once again.

Don, exhausted by the treatments, spent his time recuperating from the effects, until finally he was given a clean bill of health.

Soon he was back at the West Irondequoit High School track getting his body in shape for the next marathon. He walked around the track over and over again until he completed five miles. Each day he would continue.

The Columbus Marathon

It was October 15, 2006, and Don was at the Columbus Marathon surprised to find that there was one other eighty-five-year-old entered, plus an eighty-year-old who qualified for his age group. It was a rarity to have someone in his age category, making him stand out from the crowd. Most times he was the focus of attention by the marathon and by the news media, but not just because of his age. Don knew that, and as he signed in he was given his number, V24, which presented him as an honored veteran of the Columbus Marathon, only this time he would share the honor with another veteran, Jack McClain, 85, of Granville, Ohio, given the number V16. John McCormac, at the tender age of 80, from Worthington, Ohio, would have the number V25. Don had met these runners before, but they were merely acquaintances. Back around 1986, Don and other veteran runners had join the Ohio Veterans Club, an organization set up with the assumption that it would grow. Though the Ohio Veterans Club still exists, it is more or less a email now and then type club with members changing constantly as runners either stop running or have died.

That Sunday morning as prearranged, Don readied himself for his pre-dawn start, since the course would close at 3:00 p.m. and he needed the extra time. The morning air was bitter with the temperature registering 29 degrees, so Don dressed as warmly as possible without donning items of clothing that would hamper his stride. In most cases, this meant the basics of a sweatshirt over a long-sleeved shirt, tights under loose-fitting, long-legged shorts, sweat socks, and running shoes. The weatherman was calling for a warm up to 52 degrees later in the day, which Don saw as ideal marathon temperature.

As Don set out early that morning along the familiar route that he had traveled many times before, he was alone with the music of his headset playing his favorite songs. As each rhythmic beat of the classical music filled his head, he started out on the deserted, flat street of downtown Columbus. His mind began to drift.

He was only eighty miles away from his hometown of Brookville, Ohio. He could head west on West Broad, which would take him to South Wall Street and on to I-70. Then a few more turns and he would be there. His whole self had been molded in the small community of Brookville.

The people of the village lived a simple life, then and still to this day as they linger through the major floods that come with such frequency to Englewood, washing away the crops and their very existence. Just like the earthquakes of California continue to be a part of the area, residents remained. It was the 1913 flood in Englewood that took the life of his great uncle, who drowned rescuing people caught in the fast-moving water.

The course was basically flat as Don walked alone on the deserted streets of downtown. Then he came to the first turn that would have him heading east through Bexley, the music from his earphones keeping him company and pulling his mind back to a time when earphones hadn't existed. Men and women born in a world without airplanes, radios, automobiles, or x-rays were given the first chance to relate to the scientific revolution, and the upsurge of technology.

Don imagined his parents on their farm in Ohio, their roots firmly planted in the soil, not wanting anything more than they had. That indeed was the life.

Don recognized the Governor's Mansion in Bexley up ahead and knew that those runners who would start later that day would be seeing the governor as he cheered them on from his driveway. Only now there was still silence as he passed.

Over the sound of Johannes Sebastian Bach's "Brandenburg Concerto No. 1 Allegro," Don could now hear the first of the pack of runners coming up behind him. The first runner passed wearing his short shorts and sleeveless shirt, which he would have worn even if the temperature remained in the thirties. Less was best. Behind him was another male runner similarly attired, focusing straight ahead as if he could already see the finish line, some twenty odd miles ahead.

For the next few minutes there were more passersby until finally the field thickened with runners who were working on twelve-minute miles. Don checked his watch, happy to see he was still doing around eighteen to nineteen minute miles.

Slowly the last of the runners were followed by the start of the walkers, who surrounded Don. There were light conversations and laughter as the group continued along the route just having a good time.

Then he was alone again, greeted by Mozart, "Piano Concerto #20 In D Minor, K 466 – 1 Allegro."

Don could see the twenty-mile marker just up ahead, which meant that he had less than seven miles to cover before reaching the finish line. A glance at his watch verified that he was right on schedule. Around him now were a sparse selection of stragglers, keeping at his pace with the same ambition in mind—stepping over the finish line.

This was the point where Don got excited, but there was no amount of excitement that would make the pain in his legs go away. They felt like Jell-O, boneless and shaky, making him wonder how he was still picking up his feet. His hands were numb, his legs begged him to stop, but he could not; he had to keep walking.

It always hurt. Every muscle in his body hurt, but experience had taught him how to ignore the pain and push onward. The streets were lined with people cheering him on now. He was less than a mile from the finish line and could see runners hanging around, some stretching, others taking on nutrition. With a smile on his face, he stepped over the finish line, ignoring the pain while feeding on the attention that was given so freely. The attention he had earned because of his age, and because this marathon done in 8:37:37 marked his 713th completed. That made him stand out from the crowd, even though John and Jack had completed the marathon two hours before him. After being interviewed and chatting with a few of the regulars, Don excused himself. He had a plane to catch.

The Portland Marathon

Don entered the Portland Marathon in October 2007. He had done this marathon in 1986 and again in 2005 and found it quite enjoyable. The musicians and entertainers who perform annually for the Portland Marathon were part of a long tradition. The Portland Marathon was a pioneer in having music entertainment and had perfected the performance over more than twenty years, having classical and jazz whistlers, an all-women's jug band, and every kind of rock, blues, and jazz. The music was top rate, and the performers were Portland citizens who played for the marathon, volunteering their time and accepting a T-shirt as a thank you. But then six years earlier something happened.

Figure 33: The Portland Marathon

Some other nationally recognized marathons jumped on the entertainment bandwagon, and Portland had to face reality. It had always been way out in front in the amount, variety, and quality of the groups it offered, but now the competition was catching up. T-shirts alone would no longer suffice as compensation.

After setting a goal of at least one music stop per mile, the financially compensated musicians included sixty-eight groups spread over fifty-three locations. Unless one lists every single group, it really isn't possible to convey the breadth of this. But consider at least the following: the race has a drum corps, a hand bell choir, two eighteen-piece big bands, a world champion baton twirler, cheerleaders, bagpipes, salsa, Christian rock, blues, jazz, rock, classical, mariachi, folk, calypso, harps, belly dancing, bluegrass, accordions, Dixieland, and many others.

Because of the distance and the fact that most marathons try to set up routes that have wonderful scenery, Don loved this special attraction.

At the Portland Marathon this year, as he came around the bend, he heard a band playing a piece by Bach, and from his upbringing with music, he knew it was one of the four Brandenburg concerti. The Brandenburg concerti were originally titled "Six Concerts by Johann Sebastian Bach" and were widely regarded as among the finest musical compositions of the Baroque era.

Don had to pause, listen, and then whisper to the conductor that he was familiar with this concerto. The conductor was impressed, even though Don did not know exactly which of the Brandenburg concerti they played. As he went on his way, he had a smile on his face, knowing he had just made an impression on that man. He crossed the finish line in 8:32:57.

Giving Something Back

No matter how many times he experienced it, it still amazed Don how quickly the body recovered after completing a marathon. It was as though the body needed to be pushed hard every now and then so that it could rebuild itself.

Don was a volunteer, and he enjoyed volunteering at the zoo. Just as he had done the run across the country to raise funds for the Strong

Children's center, he also gave of his heart and time to serve as Santa Claus at the zoo. He had watched his children marvel at Santa, and when he saw the opportunity to give back to the community, he took it. The zoo needed a Santa Claus, and he could easily fit the role, and he did so with fervor; his hair and beard were gray, so all he needed to do was let it grow longer than he usually wore it. He wanted to be the best Santa possible, and he was. He was invited back each year to participate in the "Breakfast with Santa" event at the zoo.

When the Seneca Park Zoo Society evolved into a non-profit organization holding special events for fundraising, Don was the one who suggested and managed the Jungle Jog to raise funds. He also lent collections from his travels for display at the zoo, such as the soapstone carvings done by Inuit[x], that he had purchased during his many marathons in the arctic.

Figure 34: Don starts the Jungle Jog 5K Race

The Niagara-Fallsview Marathon

So we come back around and find ourselves where we started out, the marathon that Don had me enter with him for research. On that Sunday of October 22, 2006, it was not only the weather that deterred tourists from going to Canada. The border crossings between the US and Canada had tightened since the September 11 terrorist attacks, so that even with three bridges to choose from, traffic was backed up. For Don, there was no alternative, since he needed to get into Canada to do the marathon. This was my marathon initiation.

While Don moved about the country, I was busy getting ready. I had purchased a great little digital voice recorder and packed our Kodak digital camera and my Compaq Presario laptop so I could immediately record my observations and pertinent details. From our past experiences, I knew that Don was a talker and the most interesting stories came up unannounced.

Take, for instance, the time I asked him about marathons. If there had been any conversation that had led to us deciding to write his life story, I think this could have been one of them, because Don is a man who never conserves words. At the time, we were working out a problem on his computer. His system was slow, and it took quite some time to come back up once we restarted it. Only it didn't matter, since I knew that once Don returned with the coffee, I was about to be told a story.

If you are like me, your knowledge of marathons comes down to people running and winning prizes for their accomplishments. You probably have no idea that individuals who are non-runners enter marathons as well, and that most marathons have more than just the full marathon distance as part of their contribution. There are ultra-marathons, which consist of any running event longer than the traditional length (26 miles, 385 yards, or 42.195 kilometers), half-marathons (13, 193 yards, or 21.0975 kilometers), 10K (6.2 miles), 5K (3.1 miles), and even categories for walkers.

Having seen the event during the Olympics, I had witnessed only the competitive runners. Not all marathoners pull on their running shoes to run for the prize; some run just for the joy of running, and others just for the companionship.

But Don knew more. He was the type of person who read, asked questions, or did research on anything that piqued his interest, so he was a wealth of information.

I was interested in learning more, and Don knew that he had my full attention. I could not imagine anyone better to tell me about marathons, and once he did I was hooked.

The revival of the marathon happened in the 1896 Olympics when it was run as the final track-and-field event in Athens, Greece. It was included at the suggestion of a man named Michel Breal, and the length of the event was 40K (24.8 miles). This marathon added local interest to the games, commemorating the run of Pheidippides from Marathon, a city in Greece, to Athens in 490 B.C.

It was all about war, really. The Persians went to conquer the Cyclades islands in the Aegean Sea. According to legend, at the end of the battle, Pheidippides, a Greek soldier and champion runner in the ancient Olympics, had been chosen as the courier to announce the surprise Greek victory over the invading Persians on the plains of Marathon. Pheidippides was determined to not let his country down, and though exhausted, ran the full 24.8-mile distance from Marathon to Athens. He ran, ignoring his body's signals of physical exhaustion, not allowing himself to sleep or eat. He paid the price when he arrived in Athens, shouting, *"Nenikikamen!"* ("We are victorious!") He only managed to get the words out before he dropped to the ground and died.

I waited, knowing there was more. As I said, Don was not a man of few words. Don took a sip of his coffee and then began again.

Then there were the Olympic Games in Athens. History states that Georgios Averoff, a philanthropist who financed the rebuilding of the Olympic stadium, offered his daughter's hand in marriage and a dowry of one million drachma, about two million in today's dollars, to the Greek marathoner declared the winner. Following suit, a doctor offered a barrel of vintage wine, a tailor offered clothing for life, and still others donated prizes such as food for life, two thousand pounds of candy, free shaves, haircuts, cattle, sheep, and jewelry.

A Greek victory seemed assured, since twenty-one of the twenty-five entrants were Greek. The other four runners were from France, Australia, Hungary, and the United States. As the race began, the three leaders were not Greeks, running full out and keeping in front at a fast pace that challenged the field of runners, until they reached Athens. They say that was when the tides turned. First the American, then the Frenchman, and finally the Australian collapsed; it was the steady pace of a Greek runner named Spiridon Louis that prevailed. As he staggered into the stadium, covered with perspiration and dust, he was seven minutes ahead of the second-place finisher.

Don paused for emphasis and took another sip of coffee while I attentively waited.

The Greeks were cheering, and you could even hear sobbing as women threw their jewelry at Louis's feet as he rounded the track. That day, only nine runners crossed the finish line and eight were Greek. The winner, Louis, was greeted by Prince George and Prince Constantine, who carried him on their shoulders to the royal box of their father, King George. Spiridon Louis had saved the day, but who was this man? No one really knew which of the many legends told were true. Some say Spiridon Louis was a poor shepherd who trained for his Olympic marathon debut by praying in front of holy icons and fasting for two days and two nights before the race.

I would accept that as probable, but Don wasn't finished.

What was known was that Louis was earning his living at that time by selling water to the Athenians, who did not have good water sources in the city. Twice a day, Louis was seen with his load of two barrels of water on his mule, running beside the animal the 14K (8.6 miles) from the water supply in the village of Amarousi to Athens. Although unknown at the time, Louis's routine of running shorter-than-racing distances with periods of rest in between was not unlike current training methods, giving him an advantage over the other marathoners.

Just as mysterious was the legend of the gifts that Louis accepted after the games. Some sources say he accepted nothing. Others say that after the marathon Louis became a wealthy man. What is known, however, was that the gift of the philanthropist's daughter's hand in marriage was not accepted, since Spiridon Louis was already married!

By then the computer was up and running, only I was puzzled. Don had said the Olympic marathon distance was 25.8 miles, but I knew marathons were 26.2 miles. So I asked for clarification, and Don was more than willing to explain as he told me that at the 1908 Olympic Games in London, the distance was changed to twenty-six miles to cover the ground from Windsor Castle to White City stadium, and an additional 385 yards were added so the race could finish in front of King Edward VII's royal box.

Don never ceased to amaze me. We had met first when he took a computer class with me. Then over the years I became his system support person, fixing minor problems with his computer or printers, and all the time learning more and more about the man. He was incredible. To me, just doing one marathon was an accomplishment, but Don had done a lifetime total of 102 ultra-marathons included in the total of his many marathons completed. He made me laugh when he said that he used to say when asked how he could accomplish such a feat, "Oh, I eat those up." Only now, he added, those words no longer came out of his mouth and his running shoes no longer went that distance, because he was sticking with just the standard length of a marathon.

If there was one thing I have learned over my years of writing, it is that research can supply dry facts, but hearing it said by those who know from experience and reading, the words get colorful. In this case, I would have the opportunity to physically experience what marathons were all about, and I knew that no matter how much I suffered, the results would be more than worth it.

So it was that I did the Niagara Fallsview Marathon with Don and learned that it takes more than just walking or running. It takes stamina of the mind and the soul to make it over the finish line, especially when there will be no prize beyond your prize of accomplishment. Yes, before I found Don fascinating, but after learning more about him, my fascination was deeper and not so easily summed up in that one word.

Summary of Don's Marathon Career

From his first marathon in 1969 to his last record marathon at the end of this writing, Don has had an unbelieveable "second" career. His marathon experience to date covers thirty-six years—longer than some marriages will last. When he went to his high school reunion for the class of '38, he was the only guy there. It was him and six women, which didn't bother Phyllis, who by then had been his wife for sixty-three years, but for Don it was a signal that living right had paid off.

Someday it will all come to an end, but Don plans on walking those marathons for as long as he can. Unlike most, Don has never been happier and feels lucky to be able to say that he doesn't have a single problem worth mentioning.

As far as it's known, there are four ultra marathoners in the Rochester, New York, area who have completed ultra distances of fifty miles. Joining Don McNelly are Norm Frank, Ed Cohn, and Tim Avinney. But more important to note is that Don is the oldest of the ultra marathoners.

By the end of 2006, Don completed 150 marathons with twenty-nine marathons completed each year from 2004 to 2006, remarkable, as Don turned eighty-four years old in 2004. He would complete marker 600 at Spencerport AmCam Marathon in Spencerport, New York, on June 7, 2002. Then on June 4, 2006, he would cross the finish line at the San

Diego Rock And Roll Marathon in San Diego, California. Still going strong, Don would complete six ultra maratons in this period of time.

A Family Affair

The McNelly sons get together at races about three times a year. They compete in a 26 mile, 385 yard race that starts at noon. The brothers meet at the 50-mile ultra marathon in Hagerstown, Maryland, and also get together in Toledo, Ohio, in June. They have been doing this since their youngest brother, Dick, started running in 1975. The brothers like to do a relay together and make up a five-member team.

Don and Phyllis had three children who were influenced by their father's "hobby." Tom, the oldest, works in Austin, Texas, and he ran in the Motorola Marathon each year with his father and later walked at his side. Tom also once ran the JFK 50 with Don. Then there is his other son, Dan, who runs in a lot of 5K and 10K races. Dan has a foot problem that has impeded him from running another marathon, but he still hopes for that day when he will be physically ready to experience the thrill of crossing the finish line in a marathon once again. Lastly, there was their daughter, Nancy, who had a knee problem that kept her from running during her lifetime, but it didn't keep her from being on those sidelines to hand out water or yell out encouraging words to keep them going.

Running for the McNelly family was like an epidemic, with his grandson taking up running by the age of thirteen and Don's brothers running in marathons, some of which they have run together. Even Phyllis has participated and set a 10K age-group record at Nanisivik as well as ran a quarter-marathon in Canton, Ohio. It was in their blood to run, or at least try. And it is no wonder that their circles of friends are runners too.

The One That Got Away

The Pikes Peak Marathon begins at the base of Pikes Peak, in Manitou Springs, Colorado, and climbs over 7,700 feet (2,347 meters) to the top of the 14,110 foot (4,300 meter) tall peak. The race takes place in late summer and involves a day for the round-trip race (full marathon). Underfoot are dirt trails, rock, and other natural obstacles, which along with the high altitude make this marathon the most difficult marathon ever. Even the completion time for those who have succeeded is much longer than the average marathon completion time.

The race bills itself as "America's Ultimate Challenge," and for Don McNelly, who went one-third of the way and quit, it was.

It has not all been a success story crossing the finish line, however, which has been Don McNelly's trademark. There was one marathon that defeated him. The Pikes Peak marathon Don tried one time without success, and never tried again. If he had managed to make it to the finish line, it probably would have been his most difficult. The temperature can drop fifty degrees from the start in Manitou Springs, to the summit at 14,110 feet, and on the upper reaches of the mountain, weather can be cold rain, snow, or sleet, all powered by high winds.

Today, Don admits that he is getting slower, but he's not the only one who is slowing down, as it seems for everyone once you reach seventy, your running time begins to slide further away from the qualifying time.

Nowadays, Don, at the age of eighty-six, must save his energy, and so he does very little training during the week. Usually there will be a brisk walk and some light jogging as he averages one marathon every week and a half. He is hurting a little bit more after a marathon, and that probably has a lot to do with his advancing years. There was indeed a time when Don was able to run a Saturday-Sunday back-to-back marathon, but that time has come and gone.

Yet he has memories to last him a lifetime. There was the time in the early eighties when he was about to go out for a run down Pinegrove, where he lived, when he looked out and saw a man and woman jogging together past his house. On closer observation, he realized that the woman was Audrey Hepburn, who at the time was dating a man who lived down his street. The man sold movie film for Eastman Kodak company.

Yes, sightings and sounds are all part of running. Howard William Cosell, born Howard William Cohen, was an American sports journalist Don had the chance to meet at a marathon that he ran with his brother Byron and his son Tom. They were just standing around at the time when they noticed Cosell was interviewing some of the hot runners. It was 1972 and Don was not one to let an opportunity pass, so he went up and asked Howard Cosell if he would take a picture with him and his son. Howard didn't hesitate, and Tom managed to hold the camera steady as he snapped the picture. That year, in time for Christmas, Don had the picture blown up into a poster and gave one to his nieces and nephews, who got brag time out of it. Not many could say that their uncle was a buddy of Howard Cosell.

And don't forget the travel. Don has seen places that he normally would never have seen, and all because of a marathon. Depending on where the marathon was held, he either flew or drove.

He sometimes found himself driving from point to point as he went to marathon after marathon. For example, he would sometimes drive to Washington, and then the following week he might fly to Osaka, Japan, and then return, only to find himself behind the wheel and driving to Columbus, Ohio. Imagine this being all for the sake of marathons.

Every day he thanks God for such an understanding and supportive wife, because without that, he could not have accomplished what he set out to do. Marathons were his only vice, and spending money to participate in a marathon was money well spent. Not that he goes first class. No, he doesn't stay at the elaborate hotels the marathon committee will recommend. Instead he finds a more reasonable one. And when he must fly, he searches for the bargains, because entrance fees to marathons can add up. For example, Don has this T-shirt that he wears, and on the back is a slogan that says, "I'm a 50 States finisher." It catches people's eye and many will comment, saying it is a nice T-shirt, and when they do, his comeback is, "It sure was. It cost me $30,000."

Of course, it dribbles out, but Don started keeping a record of his expenditures and found that for every marathon for the past six years, he spent an average of $10,000 and $14,000 a year for the marathons that were close to Rochester, New York. As you can imagine, that changes when he traveled to one in Europe or Japan. Just the travel cost to Antarctica alone was around $3,000.

Don couldn't have done it with out his wife, Phyllis. Phyllis had experienced having Don away for weeks when he traveled for business, so now having him gone for a weekend was not a big deal. Besides, she got to travel too. She had the opportunity to not only see different places, she saw them with people who felt privileged to point out the sights or take them to dinner. Don had never lived a simple life after marriage; it had always been exciting with one experience after the other, and the family was always involved. Financially, Don had earned a great living and had provided for retirement so that they were not limited by money.

Don is a Public Figure

Week after week and year after year, Don had made his mark. He had become a public figure in the sporting world, and news on his accomplishments are printed in books as well as on the internet.

Jeff Galloway wrote in his book *Running Until You're 100*, published in October 2006, that Don McNelly was the picture of health. Later, when Jeff was interviewed on "House Call with Dr. Sanjay Gupta," he mentioned Don McNelly.

The Ottawa Marathon of June 2006 featured Don McNelly on the CD distributed as a promotional for their marathon.

The Shamrock Marathon printed an interview with Don McNelly at the age of eighty-six. His face appeared in the article on the Mega-Marathoners that were at the Portland Marathon in 2007. Local coverage appeared often, including in May 2006, the *Rochester Healthy Living* magazine showed Don on the cover, along with an article on his accomplishments. Don McNelly had become a public figure who stressed what one could do if they only tried.

The Florida Gulf Beaches Marathon publicized Don in an article entitled, "Running for Their Lives" by Pete Young of the *St. Petersburg Times*:

###

Last week, McNelly, 79, and Herman, who were good friends, did marathon No. 552 in New Port Richey (a 50K race at Starkey Park). Though he has been an avid marathoner since the 1970s, McNelly has picked it up since he retired and reached age 70. As a septuagenarian, McNelly has completed more than 300 marathons... "He's addicted," said his daughter, Nancy McNelly. "It's become so much a part of his life, I couldn't imagine him not doing it."

The Ocala Marathon would do an interview with Don and call him a running legend. Don would respond to questions they asked, and one interesting point printed was the following:

I have been keeping a detailed record of my costs since 1990. Since then I have spent $127,068 for my 399 marathons since then, averaging $317.46 per run. Projecting at the same rate for my 646 runs would total $205,729 and worth every penny. (However, do not tell my wife.)

After his friend Sy Mah died, Don McNelly would be asked to speak at his statute dedication. He would be mentioned in the *Los Angeles Times* May 2000 article by Ben Dobbin entitled, "Senior Marathoners Haven't Run Down Yet." The Cowtown Marathon in a February 22, 2008, human interest story noted the fact that Don McNelly, at eighty-seven, would be up against Gene Brock, eighty, at that year's marathon.

Don McNelly appeared in an article by *Roadrunner Sports* on his marathon accomplishments, and The 100 Marathon Club North America, Newsletter Number Three, September 27, 2002, reported "Don McNelly was one of the three members in their 80's who were still active marathoners."

The Quad Cities Marathon reported, "Don McNelly was the world record holder for number of marathons completed over the age of 80. This year he's 85 and will be coming to the Quad Cities again to participate in the marathon." The 50 States & D.C. Marathon Group U.S.A. accolades stated, "Don McNelly holds the record for the most marathons ran after the age of 70." Even the popular magazines wrote articles, such as the one by Adrian Brune of the *Chicago Tribune*, and the book *Second Wind-The Rise of the Ageless Athlete* by Lee Bergquist, in which a section highlighted Don McNelly.

Each time Don McNelly became the topic of a news article, there would be interesting ways to state the accomplishments. In "Marathon Men," by Phil Jurik, reporting on the Brookville Reunion Marathon, stated that at the August marathon there would be two Brookville High School alumni, Denny Fryman and Don McNelly, No. 2 and No. 3 in career marathons in North America. At the time, Fryman had done 760 marathons by his sixtieth birthday; Don McNelly had 725 to his credit and along with Jerry Herndon, West Virginia's all-time leader with 600-plus marathons, who also was there, the accomplishment in marathons equaled out to 55,000 miles, or better than twice around the equator. Another interesting point was that Don and Phyllis McNelly had been married sixty-five years. Between them and Denny and Dorann Fryman, there were about one hundred years of marriage.

The Need to Know about Running

Running begins with the mind. Starting a new habit can feel overwhelming to a beginner whether it's running or exercising. It's scary to start something new that is long term because it seems impossible to stay with. That is the number one excuse why people fail at keeping fit. It begins with strong legs, strong lungs, strong will. Such is the portrait of a typical distance runner.

It's not hard and it's not impossible if you start your running by first learning some basic information. If you are new to running, make sure to stretch before and after every run. Walk briskly for at least five minutes at the beginning of each run. Once you feel your body starting to warm up, do some gentle stretching exercises. Focus on steady, continuous stretches and avoid bouncing through the stretch. Running can be stressful on your body, particularly on your leg muscles and knees.

Begin by walking at a brisk pace for thirty minutes and keep doing this until your body and your breathing adjust to the routine. Once you master the walk, try running at a slow pace until you become short of breath. But don't stop. Instead walk briskly until you feel like you can run again. Continue this routine over and over again. Once you feel comfortable and in control, you can challenge yourself by timing these intervals and working toward longer intervals. For example, maybe the first day you will run for thirty seconds and walk for two minutes. As your endurance increases, run longer and walk for shorter distances.

Once you are running for a full thirty minutes, try running at your normal pace and then speed it up for thirty seconds or one minute.

It helps to keep going if you can picture the results. On the average for every mile you run, you will burn 100 calories. But other factors play into the equation such as your running speed and your body weight. Generally, a 135-pound person will burn about 100 calories per mile. A 200-pound person, running at the same speed, may burn 150. Obviously, the faster you run, the more calories you will burn.

When you have mastered this feat you are on your way, but before you go any further you need to invest in a good pair of running shoes for comfort and to reduce the risk of injury You need to get in the habit of hydrating you body every ten minutes during your run.

The best places to run are smooth dirt roads or paths, which are not as hard as asphalt and concrete, but if you plan on running a marathon you need to practice on all surfaces.

On really cold days, make sure you monitor your fingers, toes, ears, and nose. They may feel numb at first, but they should warm up a few minutes into your run. If you notice a patch of hard, pale, cold skin, you may have frostbite. When this happens, get out of the cold immediately and seek emergency care.

You will need to take precautions if the wind is strong, because it penetrates your clothes and removes the insulating layer of warm air around you. Your movement also creates wind chill because it increases air movement past your body. If the temperature dips below zero or the wind chill is below minus 20, hit the treadmill instead.

You will need a good pair of gloves as well. You can lose 30 percent of your body heat through your hands and feet. On mild days, wear gloves; on colder days wear mittens because your fingers will share their body heat. You can also tuck disposable heat packets into your mittens and look for something called a wick sock liner that you can wear under a warm polar fleece or wool sock, but make sure you have enough room in your running shoes to accommodate these thicker socks.

For the rest of your body, start with a thin layer of synthetic material such as polypropylene, which absorbs sweat from your body. Stay away from cotton because it holds the moisture and will keep you wet. An outer, breathable layer of nylon or Gore-Tex will help protect you against wind and precipitation, while still letting out heat and moisture to prevent overheating and chilling. If it's really cold out, you'll need a middle layer, such as polar fleece, for added insulation.

Just as important is to not overdress. You're going to warm up once you get moving, so you should feel a little bit chilly when you start your run. A good rule of thumb: dress as if it's 20 degrees warmer outside than it really is. The act of running also produces heat at a level that is far more than the body needs. Lucky for us, as soon as the body senses a rise in temperature, it signals the brain.

Another important step to take is to wear a hat when it's cold because you will lose about 40 percent of your body heat through your head. When it's really cold, wear a face mask or a scarf over your mouth to warm the air you breathe and protect your face. You should also have polarized lens shades to eliminate glare

Once you are into running, maintaining your motivation will be easy; you just need to remember to not over push yourself and keep your goal simply to finish the 26.2-mile race.

You can see why it was said that running begins with the mind. With the exception of involuntary muscles, the body will not do what the mind does not will it to do. As we begin training to run, we begin strengthening our mind. Running day after day in good weather and in bad, we teach our body self-discipline. That is why sticking to a training program is the best way of ensuring individual improvement.

A study in *Circulation: Journal of the American Heart Association* has shown that the blood vessels of older athletes behave like those of people half their age. The research studied both young and old inactive individuals and athletes. The athletes were long-distance runners, cyclists, and triathletes, who combined running, cycling, and swimming. The study found that the older athletes' blood vessels functioned as well as those of the participants in either of the two younger groups.

"This study demonstrates that regular physical activity can protect aging blood vessels," says the study's lead author, Stefano Taddei, M.D., an associate professor of internal medicine at the University of Pisa in Italy. "Long-term exercise protects the inner lining of the blood vessels from age-related changes and makes them behave more like those of a young person," he says.

Summarizing His Experiences

It must be said that Don McNelly doesn't have a need for speed. He considers his style to be more cruising than running nowadays. "I'm a Mac truck, not a race car," he jokes. "I have terrible times—always have." But it hasn't always been that way, as his personal record is somewhere around 3:51.

He has so many distinctions in his career, such as running in the northernmost and southernmost organized marathons and being at the first-ever marathon in Antarctica, where he traveled south and took an ice pick. Then on the opposite side of the world from Antarctica, he ran in Spitsbergen, the largest in a chain of Norwegian islands in the Arctic Ocean.

The climate never gets to him, he says. And he's never been put out of commission with an injury, which he says supports his motto, "You gotta show your body who's boss."

Not that he hadn't faced a physical problem. In 1988, after having surgery for prostate cancer, he did curtail his running a bit. While in recovery, he still competed in marathons, but began walking them.

These days he walks every race. To the very end, with no shortcuts, no cheating (because you only cheat yourself, he says).

As for family, his children think he may be a little mad for running as much as he does, but his wife understands it is a big part of her husband. And so he'll keep going until he no longer can.

Don McNelly is truly an outstanding marathoner, with 657 marathons run in the United States, sixty-six in Canada, four in Japan, three in Panama, two in Norway, two in Greenland, and one in Antarctica, Argentina, Cyprus, England, France, Germany, Holland, Iceland, Italy, Mexico, Portugal, and Thailand. He has run in 117 ultra marathons, which have been of varying lengths up to and including 100 miles. His shortest time was 5:15:27 and his longest was 18:06:00.

Don is motivated by wanting to keep in shape, which will help him reach his ultimate goal of living forever. A big part of it remains to be that he is a competiive person and is really proud of being number three in North America in completed marathons. But he holds no ill feelings against the number one, Norm Frank, who has been his friend for forty years. Two years ago, Norm had a stroke that ended his running career, but not the friendship. Norm lives in an assisted living facility now and said to Don, who visits with him every few weeks, "You're going to live forever."

At his age, it feels good because it's better than the altenative would be. Having to start walking after running for so many years was not an easy change, even though it happened slowly. First he ran, then he ran and walked, and the walking became more and more until finally he was just walking the marathons. As he considers this, it comes to him that it might have been easier for him to make the change than it would be for someone younger and focused on winning rather than just finishing.

Don has run just in marathons and ultras, and he has put over 31,000 miles in running shoes that were ones he found on sale. Being an engineer at heart, the next thought that comes to mind would be how many running shoes does it take to go the distance? Well, if you follow the measure of running shoe companies, they say five hundred miles in one pair, so we are talking a little more than fifty pairs of running shoes for just the certified miles covered in marathons. There are many more marathons and ultra marathons that were not done on certified courses but have been covered in this book. There are also the ones that he would use for training. Don considers this for a moment and feels that he has gone through at least sixty pairs of running shoes.

Talking about shoes, Don recalls that after running across the country, the Strong children at the Strong Children's center wanted to thank Don by giving him some kind of trophy, and they called Phyllis and told her what they planned to do and asked for one of Don's running shoes that he had worn. Phyllis liked the idea and gave them the shoe, and managed keep it a secret from Don so that it would be a surprise.

The Children's Center took his shoe to a place that specialized in bronzing baby shoes and would later tell Don that in bronzing his size 15 running shoe they ran out of bronzing material and had to get more. After the bronzing, the shoe was mounted on a board so that it could be hung on the wall.

When the day came to present the plaque to Don, it was done at an awards luncheon attended by over six hundred people who had an interest in supporting the wonderful work of the Strong Children's Center.

Don was touched and almost speechless that day because what he had done was from his heart, a heart that so many people have seen and know that even though his marathon record is that of a madman, his heart is that of a saint.

Sometimes you need inside information to trace a marathon through all of the changes; the Maui Marathon, for instance, was first known as the AAU Hawaiian Marathon, and the Niagara Fallsview Marathon was originally known as the Skylon Marathon. Then other races have divided into two marathons, holding each one at different months during the year. Then there is the fate of some marathons to just end and no longer exist. At other times, races fuse together, so it is impossible to provide a hard copy of marathons. For those who are interested, you can obtain an updated listing of North American races at http://www.marathonguide.com/races/races.cfm. For marathons in other countries try going to: http://www.geocities.com/schoenmaeker/marathon.html.

2017 - SAYING GOODBYE

Don McNelly was known for his many acts of kindness, his sense of humor and his insatiable thirst for learning and living life to its fullest.

His advice to men was "Marry the right woman," and he could point to himself. He and Phyllis would have been married 75 years in April.

Family and friends was always Don's Mr. NcNelly's No. 1 priority and he was most proud of his three children. Each earned advanced degrees and went on to successful careers in medicine and science. He also bragged about Phyllis obtaining two degrees from the University of Rochester at age 50.

"He was ebullient — a man of real character," his son Dan McNelly would say.

And Don had stamina.

Don's self-confessed positive addiction seemed to work well for him. When Runner's World last contacted him 18 months ago, he told them, "I've lived longer than any of my relatives, and I haven't noticed any mental slippage. I'm very happy and content. I feel very fortunate."

Don and Phyllis spent their 'golden years' at the Highlands at Pittsford, but my husband and I continued to meet them for dinner—at first bringing them to Irondequoit to their favorite place and later dining with them at the Highlands. When Don became too ill to go out to dinner, we would have a meal with them in their apartment. Later as I saw he was not getting better, I contacted a number of his old running buddies, including a Japanese marathoner Don had befriended somewhere along the road. "Yasu came immediately from Japan to visit Don," It was great to see him brighten up again, seeing his old pal.

On February 5, 2017 Don died at the age of 96. He leaves behind his wife, Phyllis, two sons, Tom and Dan, and one grandson, Nick. He was predeceased by daughter Nancy.

A funeral service was held on February 11, 2017 at Bethlehem Lutheran Church.

As he lived his life, he continued in his passing by asking for donations to the Golisano Children's Hospital and the Seneca Park Zoo Societyin lieu of flowers.

On September 16 at the Irondequoit Cemetary a military service was held for Don McNelly.

Rest well my friend. You will be missed.

LIST OF MARATHONS

No	Date	Marathon Name	Location	State	Time	Country	Ultra
1	04/21/69	Boston	Boston	MA	5:01:00		
2	04/20/70	Boston	Boston	MA	4:50:00		
3	10/25/70	Ohio River RRC	Xenia	OH	5:08:00		
4	04/19/71	Boston	Boston	MA	4:41:00		
5	10/10/71	Akron-Canton	Canton	OH	3:59:00		
6	10/24/71	Ohio River RRC	Xenia	OH	3:51:00		
7	04/17/72	Boston	Boston	MA	4:18:00		
8	05/21/72	Milk Run	Syracuse	NY	4:44:00		
9	06/12/72	Glass City	Toledo	OH	4:19:00		
10	09/24/72	First Rochester	Rochester	NY	4:48:00		
11	03/18/73	Earth Day	Earth Day	NY	4:31:00		
12	04/16/73	Boston	Boston	MA	4:56:00		
13	05/06/73	Hike for Hope	Rochester	NY	4:21:00		
14	05/12/73	Plattsburgh	Plattsburgh	NY	3:58:00		
15	05/20/73	Yonkers	Yonkers	NY	4:14:00		
16	06/17/73	Glass City	Toledo	OH	4:25:00		
17	10/06/73	Oktoberfest	Kitchener	Ont	4:14:00	Canada	
18	10/21/73	Ohio River RRC	Xenia	OH	4:39:00		
19	03/16/74	Shamrock Sportsfest	Virginia Beach	VA	4:14:00		
20	03/31/74	JFK	Hagerstown	MD	10:44:00		1
21	04/15/74	Boston	Boston	MA	4:06:00		
22	05/19/74	Milk Run	Syracuse	NY	4:18:00		
23	06/02/74	Yonkers	Yonkers	NY	4:07:00		
24	06/16/74	Glass City	Toledo	OH	4:06:00		
25	09/02/74	Rochester	Rochester	NY	4:01:00		
26	10/20/74	Ohio River RRC	Monroe	OH	4:23:00		
27	10/26/74	Buffalo	Buffalo	NY	4:14:00		

No	Date	Marathon Name	Location	State	Time	Country	Ultra
28	02/16/75	Washington Birthday	Beltsville	MD	4:30:00		
29	03/03/75	Earth Day	Earth Day	NY	4:11:00		
30	04/21/75	Boston	Boston	MA	3:57:00		
31	05/18/75	Syracuse Milk Run	Syracuse	NY	4:37:00		
32	06/15/75	Glass City	Toledo	OH	4:33:00		
33	09/01/75	Rochester	Rochester	NY	4:24:00		
34	09/28/75	New York City, Central Park	NYC	NY	4:36:00		
35	10/25/75	Skylon	Buffalo	NY	4:19:00		
36	11/15/75	JFK	Hagerstown	MD	13:34:00		2
37	04/19/76	Boston	Boston	MA	4:40:00		
38	05/23/76	Yonkers	Yonkers	NY	4:49:00		
39	06/09/76	Rochester	Rochester	NY	4:28:00		
40	11/20/76	JFK	Hagerstown	MD	12:42:00		3
41	03/19/77	Shamrock Sportsfest	Virginia Beach	VA	4:20:00		
42	04/18/77	Boston	Boston	MA	4:20:00		
43	05/15/77	Syracuse Milk Run	Syracuse	NY	4:10:00		
44	06/18/77	Glass City	Toledo	OH	4:36:00		
45	09/05/77	Rochester	Rochester	NY	4:39:00		
46	10/22/77	Skylon	Buffalo	NY	4:25:00		
47	11/19/77	JFK	Hagerstown	MD	11:53:00		4
48	12/26/77	Orange Bowl	Miami	FL	4:13:00		
49	03/18/78	Shamrock Sportsfest	Virginia Beach	VA	4:18:00		
50	04/17/78	Boston	Boston	MA	4:21:00		
51	05/14/78	Syracuse Milk Run	Syracuse	NY	4:12:00		
52	06/18/78	Glass City	Toledo	OH	4:46:00		
53	09/03/78	Rochester	Rochester	NMY	4:14:00		
54	10/22/78	New York	New York	NY	4:24:00		
55	10/29/78	Panama City Internat	Panama City	FL	4:47:00	Panama	

No	Date	Marathon Name	Location	State	Time	Country	Ultra
56	11/18/78	JFK	Hagerstown	MD	15:53:00		5
57	12/02/78	White Rock	Dallas	TX	4:27:00		
58	03/17/79	Shamrock Sportsfest	Virginia Beach	VA	4:13:00		
59	04/16/79	Boston	Boston	MA	4:15:00		
60	05/20/79	Syracuse Milk Run	Syracuse	NY	4:28:00		
61	03/06/79	Lake Ontario	Greece	NY	4:31:00		
62	06/17/79	Glass City	Toledo	OH	4:30:00		
63	03/09/79	Rochester	Rochester	NY	4:28:00		
64	10/13/79	Skylon	Buffalo	NY	4:19:00		
65	10/21/79	New York	New York	NY	4:39:00		
66	11/17/79	JFK 50 km	Hagerstown	MD	13:13:00		6
67	12/29/79	Atlanta	Atlanta	GA	4:30:00		
68	02/10/80	Mardi Gras	New Orleans	LA	4:14:00		
69	03/15/80	Shamrock Sportsfest	Virginia Beach	VA	4:31:00		
70	04/21/80	Boston	Boston	MA	4:23:00		
71	05/18/80	Syracuse Milk Run	Syracuse	NY	4:30:00		
72	06/01/80	Lake Ontario	Greece	NY	3:59:00		
73	06/15/80	Glass City	Toledo	OH	4:18:00		
74	07/05/80	Hannibal 50km/50 miles	Hannibal	NY	9:54:00		7
75	09/01/80	Rochester	Rochester	NY	4:27:00		
76	09/13/80	Gettysburg	Gettysburg	PA	4:37:00		
77	10/18/80	Skylon	Buffalo	NY	4:02:00		
78	10/26/80	New York City	New York	NY	3:55:00		
79	11/16/80	Columbus	Columbus	OH	4:08:00		
80	11/22/80	JFK	Hagerstown	MD	11:32:00		8
81	12/07/80	Baltimore	Baltimore	MD	4:27:00		
82	01/15/81	Orange Bowl	Miami	FL	3:57:00		
83	02/01/81	Mardi Gras	New Orleans	LA	4:45:00		

No	Date	Marathon Name	Location	State	Time	Country	Ultra
84	02/15/81	Beltsville	Beltsville	MD	4:22:00		
85	03/14/81	Shamrock Sportsfest	Virginia Beach	VA	4:07:00		
86	03/29/81	Monroe Community College	Rochester	NY	5:24:00		
87	04/20/81	Boston	Boston	MA	3:59:00		
88	05/17/81	Syracuse Milk Run	Syracuse	NY	4:09:00		
89	06/01/81	Cleveland	Cleveland	OH	4:30:00		
90	06/07/81	Lake Ontario	Greece	NY	4:09:00		
91	06/27/81	Hannibal 50km/50 miles	Hannibal	NY	8:58:00		9
92	08/01/81	Adirondack, Star Lake	Star Lake	NY	4:27:00		
93	08/29/81	Laurel 50 miles	Laurel	PA	9:52:00		10
94	09/07/81	Rochester	Rochester	NY	4:29:00		
95	09/13/81	Montreal	Montreal		4:16:00	Canada	
96	10/11/81	Columbus	Columbus	OH	4:12:00		
97	10/17/81	Skylon	Buffalo	NY	4:16:00		
98	11/01/81	Lilac City 50k	Rochester	NY	5:18:00		11
99	11/15/81	Nickle City 50km	Nickle City	NY	9:40:00		12
100	**11/21/81**	**JFK**	**Hagerstown**	**MD**	**8:25:00**		**13**
101	01/16/82	Orange Bowl	Miami	FL	4:24:00		
102	03/13/82	DCA 50km	DCA	LA	5:29:00		14
103	03/20/82	Shamrock Sportsfest	Virginia Beach	VA	4:23:00		
104	04/03/82	Richmond 50 miles	Richmond	VA	9:54:00		15
105	04/19/82	Boston	Boston	MA	4:28:00		
106	05/16/82	Syracuse Milk Run	Syracuse	NY	4:24:00		
107	05/29/82	Osborn's	Waterloo	NY	4:35:00		
108	06/06/82	Lake Ontario	Greece	NY	4:21:00		
109	07/10/82	Hannibal 50km/50	Hannibal	NY	6:04:00		16

No	Date	Marathon Name	Location	State	Time	Country	Ultra
		miles					
110	10/10/82	Columbus	Columbus	OH	4:54:00		
111	10/16/82	Skylon	Buffalo	NY	4:02:00		
112	10/24/82	New York	New York	NY	4:02:00		
113	11/06/82	San Antonio	San Antonio	TX	3:58:00		
114	11/14/82	Nickle City 50km	Nickel City	NY	9:23:00		17
115	11/20/82	JFK 50 miler	Hagerstown	MD	10:49:00		18
116	12/04/82	Rock and Roll	Phoenix	AZ	3:58:00		
117	01/08/83	Savannah	Savannah	GA	4:22:00		
118	01/22/83	Orange Bowl	Miami	FL	4:26:00		
119	02/20/83	Beltsville	Beltsville	MD	4:19:00		
120	03/06/83	Ohio River RRC	Xenia	OH	4:45:00		
121	03/19/83	Shamrock Sportsfest	Virginia Beach	VA	4:35:00		
122	04/02/83	Richmond 50 miles	Richmond	VA	10:21:00		19
123	04/18/83	Boston	Boston	MA	5:58:00		
124	05/28/83	Osborn's	Waterloo	NY	4:54:00		
125	06/05/83	Lake Ontario	Greece	NY	5:08:00		
126	06/11/83	Palos Verdes	Palos Verdes	CA	4:51:00		
127	07/05/83	Midnight Sun Double	Nanisivik	ON	12:59:00	Canada	20
128	09/05/83	Rochester	Rochester	NY	5:01:00		
129	10/15/83	Skylon	Buffalo	NY	4:12:00		
130	10/16/83	Columbus	Columbus	OH	4:50:00		
131	11/05/83	Lilac City 50k	Rochester	NY	5:17:00		21
132	11/13/83	Nickle City 50km	Buffalo	NY	5:59:00		22
133	11/19/83	JFK 50 miles	Hagerstown	MD	13:11:00		23
134	12/17/83	Tallahassee Ultra	Tallahassee	FL	5:27:00		24
135	01/07/84	Orange Bowl	Miami	FL	4:51:00		
136	02/19/84	Beltsville	Beltsville	MD	4:27:00		

No	Date	Marathon Name	Location	State	Time	Country	Ultra
137	04/16/84	Boston	Boston	MA	4:27:00		
138	06/03/84	Lake Ontario	Greece	NY	5:44:00		
139	06/09/84	Strong 24 Hr Run	Rochester	NY	6:10:00		25
140	07/01/84	Midnight Sun Double	Nanisivik	ON	11:50:00	Canada	26
141	07/19/84	Empire State Games	Syracuse	NY	5:05:00		
142	10/06/84	Eriesistible	Erie	PA	4:27:00		
143	10/07/84	Columbus	Columbus	OH	4:56:00		
144	10/13/84	Skylon	Buffalo	NY	4:26:00		
145	10/22/84	Richmond	Richmond	VA	5:27:00		
146	11/04/84	Lilac City 50km	Rochester	NY	5:31:00		27
147	11/18/84	JFK	Hagerstown	MD	13:22:00		28
148	12/15/84	Tallahassee Ultra	Tallahassee	FL	7:03:00		29
149	01/05/85	Orange Bowl	Miami	FL	4:57:00		
150	01/17/85	Beltsville	Beltsville	MD	4:51:00		
151	03/16/85	Shamrock Sportsfest	Virginia Beach	VA	4:43:00		
152	03/31/85	Wolfpack	Columbus	OH	8:11:00		30
153	04/15/85	Boston	Boston	MA	4:56:00		
154	04/27/85	Strong 24 Hr	Rochester	NY	16:39:00		31
155	05/05/85	Mile High City	Denver	CO	4:53:01		
156	06/02/85	Lake Ontario	Greece	NY	6:00:00		
157	06/07/85	New York City 100 miles	NYC	NY	6:30:00		32
158	06/30/85	Midnight Sun Double	Nanisivik	ON	13:19:00	Canada	33
159	08/11/85	Empire State Games	Syracuse	NY	4:46:00		
160	09/03/85	Rochester	Rochester	NY	4:33:00		
161	09/21/85	Skylon	Buffalo	NY	4:41:00		
162	10/05/85	Eriesistible	Erie	PA	4:18:00		
163	10/13/85	Columbus	Columbus	OH	4:35:00		
164	10/20/85	Richmond	Richmond	VA	4:40:00		

No	Date	Marathon Name	Location	State	Time	Country	Ultra
165	10/27/85	New York City	NYC	NY	4:56:00		
166	11/03/85	Lilac City 50k	Rochester	NY	5:31:00		34
167	11/23/85	JFK 50 miles	Hagerstown	MD	17:45:00		35
168	12/14/85	Tallahassee Ultra	Tallahassee	FL	5:50:00		36
169	01/04/86	Gulf Beaches	Jacksonville	FL	4:43:00		
170	01/11/86	Orange Bowl	Miami	FL	4:31:00		
171	02/15/86	Beltsville	Beltsville	MD	5:02:00		
172	03/15/86	Shamrock Sportsfest	Virginia Beach	VA	4:49:00		
173	03/27/86	Jim Thorpe	Carlisle	PA	4:37:00		
174	04/21/86	Boston	Boston	MA	4:36:00		
175	06/01/86	Lake Ontario	Greece	NY	6:07:00		
176	06/08/86	Hamilton	Hamilton	ON	5:11:00	Canada	
177	06/14/86	Gods Country	Coudersport	PA	5:08:00		
178	06/29/86	Midnight Sun Double	Nanisivik	ON	12:24:00	Canada	37
179	07/03/86	Dublin	Dublin	OH	5:45:00		
180	08/10/86	Empire State Games	Syracuse	NY	4:54:00		
181	09/01/86	Rochester	Rochester	NY	4:49:00		
182	09/08/86	Portland	Portland	OR	4:33:00		
183	10/04/86	Eriesistible	Erie	PA	4:38:00		
184	10/18/86	Richmond	Richmond	VA	5:06:00		
185	11/02/86	New York City	NYC	NY	4:42:00		
186	11/09/86	Lilac City	Rochester	NY	5:55:00		38
187	11/16/86	Columbus	Columbus	OH	4:57:00		
188	11/22/86	JFK	Hagerstown	MD	12:49:00		39
189	12/13/86	Tallahassee Ultra	Tallahassee	FL	6:14:00		40
190	01/10/87	Orange Bowl	Miami	FL	5:17:00		
191	02/25/87	Beltsville	Beltsville	MD	5:03:00		
192	02/28/87	Cow Town	Ft Worth	TX	4:48:00		

No	Date	Marathon Name	Location	State	Time	Country	Ultra
193	03/16/87	Ohio River RRC	Xenia	OH	4:51:00		
194	03/21/87	Shamrock Sportsfest	Virginia Beach	VA	4:21:00		
195	03/27/87	Sri Chinmoy	Jamaica	NY	4:40:00		
196	04/20/87	Boston	Boston	MA	5:32:00		
197	05/03/87	Pittsburgh	Pittsburgh	PA	4:38:00		
198	05/16/87	Strong 24 Hr	Rochester	NY	13:25:00		41
199	05/27/87	Sri Chinmoy	Jamaica	NY	4:26:00		
200	**06/07/87**	**Lake Ontario**	**Greece**	**NY**	**5:53:00**		
201	06/13/87	Gods Country	Coudersport	PA	5:24:00		
202	07/05/87	Midnight Sun Double	Nanisivik		13:06:00	Canada	42
203	07/20/87	San Francisco	San Francisco	CA	4:54:00		
204	08/13/87	Sri Chinmoy	Jamaica	NY	4:41:00		
205	09/07/87	Rochester	Rochester	NY	5:10:00		
206	10/27/87	Sri Chinmoy	Jamaica	NY	4:22:00		
207	11/01/87	New York	New York	NY	5:17:00		
208	11/08/87	Columbus	Columbus	OH	6:13:00		
209	11/14/87	Lilac City	Rochester	NY	6:33:00		43
210	11/21/87	JFK 50 miles	Hagerstown	MD	9:56:00		44
211	12/06/87	Tallahassee Ultra	Tallahassee	FL	6:33:00		45
212	01/02/88	Charlotte	Charlotte	MD	4:58:00		
213	02/14/88	Washington Birthday	Beltsville	MD	5:12:00		
214	03/18/88	Shamrock Sportsfest	Virginia Beach	VA	6:00:00		
215	07/10/88	Midnight Sun Double	Nanisivik		6:10:00	Canada	46
216	09/27/88	Sri Chinmoy	Jamaica	NY	5:14:00		
217	10/02/88	Rochester	Rochester	NY	5:00:00		
218	10/22/88	Lilac City	Rochester	NY	6:11:00		47
219	11/06/88	Marine Corps	Washington	DC	5:02:00		
220	11/13/88	Columbus	Columbus	OH	5:19:00		

No	Date	Marathon Name	Location	State	Time	Country	Ultra
221	12/10/88	Tallahassee Ultra	Tallahassee	FL	6:43:00		48
222	01/07/89	Jackson	Jackson	MS	5:09:00		
223	02/19/89	Washington Birthday	Beltsville	MD	5:07:00		
224	03/16/89	Shamrock Sportsfest	Virginia Beach	VA	5:30:00		
225	03/27/89	Sri Chinmoy	Jamaica	NY	5:30:00		
226	04/15/89	Boston (for '88)	Boston	MA	5:14:00		
227	04/17/89	Boston	Boston	MA	6:06:00		
228	04/27/89	Sri Chinmoy	Jamaica	NY	5:56:00		
229	06/07/89	Pittsburgh	Pittsburgh	PA	5:00:00		
230	06/27/89	Sri Chinmoy	Jamaica	NY	9:38:00		
231	06/04/89	Strong 24 Hr	Rochester	NY	10:34:00		49
232	06/27/89	Sri Chinmoy	Jamaica	NY	6:15:00		
233	07/02/89	Midnight Sun Double	Nanisivik	ON	13:31:00	Canada	50
234	07/27/89	Sri Chinmoy	Jamaica	NY	5:27:00		
235	08/06/89	Empire State Games	Syracuse	NY	5:28:00		
236	08/12/89	Crater Lake	Crater Lake	OR	5:23:00		
237	09/10/89	Eriesistible	Erie	PA	4:41:00		
238	09/27/89	Sri Chinmoy	Jamaica	NY	4:37:00		
239	10/01/89	Rochester	Rochester	NY	4:31:00		
240	10/15/89	Lilac City Double Ultra	Irondequoit	NY	6:21:00		51
241	10/16/89	Lilac City Double Ultra	Irondequoit	NY	6:35:00		52
242	10/21/89	Muncie	Muncie	IN	4:42:00		
243	11/05/89	Marine Corps	Washington	DC	4:46:00		
244	11/12/89	Columbus	Columbus	OH	4:23:00		
245	11/18/89	JFK	Hagerstown	MD	12;38:00		53
246	12/03/89	White Rock	Ft Worth	TX	4:36:00		
247	12/08/89	Tallahassee Ultra	Tallahassee	FL	5:28:00		54

No	Date	Marathon Name	Location	State	Time	Country	Ultra
248	01/06/90	Charlotte	Charlotte	NC	4:58:00		
249	02/03/90	Las Vegas	Las Vegas	NY	4:36:00		
250	02/19/90	Washington Birthday	Beltsville	MD	4:36:00		
251	02/24/90	Smokey Mountain	Townsend	TN	4:51:00		
252	03/17/90	Shamrock Sportsfest	Virginia Beach	VA	5:05:00		
253	03/27/90	Sri Chinmoy	Jamaica	NY	4:31:00		
254	04/07/90	Hogeye	Fayetteville	AR	4:54:00		
255	04/16/90	Boston	Boston	MA	5:14:00		
256	04/27/90	Sri Chinmoy	Jamaica	NY	5:07:00		
257	05/06/90	Lincoln Nebraska	Lincoln	NB	4:25:00		
258	05/26/90	Andy Payne s	Oklahoma City	OK	4:45:00		
259	06/27/90	Sri Chinmoy	Jamaica	NY	4:56:50		
260	07/01/90	Midnight Sun Double	Nanisivik	NY	12:45:00	Canada	55
261	07/27/90	Sri Chinmoy	Jamaica	NY	4:45:00		
262	08/06/90	Empire State Games	New York	NY	4:53:00		
263	08/11/90	Crater Lake Rim Run	Crater Lake	OR	5:15:00		
264	09/01/90	Across the Isthmus 50m	Panama City	Pan	18:06:00	Panama	56
265	09/09/90	Toronto	Toronto	)N	4:48:00	Ontario	
266	09/16/90	Eriesistible	Erie	PA	4:54:00		
267	09/27/90	Sri Chinmoy	Sri Chinmoy	NY	5:55:00		
268	10/06/90	St George	St. George	NY	4:20:00		
269	10/13/90	Lilac City 50k	Rochester	NY	6:58:00		57
270	10/28/90	Frankfurt	Frankfurt	GR	4:49:00	Germany	
271	11/04/90	Marine Corps	Washington	DC	4:42:00		
272	11/11/90	Columbus	Columbus	OH	4:43:00		
273	11/17/90	JFK 50 miler	Hagerstown	MD	13:09:00		58
274	11/27/90	Sri Chinmoy	Jamaica	NY	4:44:00		

No	Date	Marathon Name	Location	State	Time	Country	Ultra
275	12/02/90	White Rock	Dallas	TX	4:45:00		
276	12/08/90	Rocket City	Huntsville	AL	4:37:00		
277	12/29/90	Greenville	Greenville	SC	4:59:00		
278	01/05/91	Jacksonville	Jacksonville	FL	4:57:00		
279	01/20/91	Miami Dade	Miami	FL	4:55:00		
280	02/09/91	Jed Smith Ultra Classic	Sacramento	CA	6:23:00		59
281	02/17/91	Washington Birthday	Beltsville	MD	4:47:00		
282	03/03/91	Ohio River RRC	Dayton	OH	4:59:00		
283	03/16/91	Shamrock Sportsfest	Virginia Beach	VA	5:11:00		
284	04/15/91	Boston	Boston	MA	5:53:00		
285	04/28/91	Lake Country, Zion	Waukegan	IL	4:47:00		
286	05/06/91	Brockport MCC	Brockport	NY	5:33:00		
287	05/19/91	Bud light Kingsfield	Kingsfield	MN	4:58:00		
288	05/25/91	Key Bank Vermont City	Burlington	VT	4:58:00		
289	06/23/91	Yukon Gold	Whitehorse	YK	5:22:00	Canada	
290	06/30/91	Midnight Sun Double	Nanisivik	Nun	6:17:00	Canada	60
291	07/21/91	Voyageur	Massey	ON	4:53:00	Canada	
292	07/28/91	Empire State Games	Albany	NY	5:09:00		
293	08/17/07	Lake Junaluska Ridge Run	Lake Junaluska	NC	6:21:00		
294	08/18/91	Lake Junaluska Ridge Run	Lake Junaluska	NC	5:55:00		
295	08/19/91	Lake Junaluska Ridge Run	Lake Junaluska	NC	6:58:00		
296	08/31/91	Ultra Adidas De Panama	Panama City		11:59:00	Panama	61
297	09/07/91	Stride Around the	Indianapolis	IN	7:30:00		

No	Date	Marathon Name	Location	State	Time	Country	Ultra
		Clock					
298	09/15/91	Eriesistible	Erie	PA	5:45:00		
299	09/22/91	Clarence deMar	Keene	NH	4:53:00		
300	**09/30/91**	**Duke City**	**Albuquerque**	**NM**	**4:58:00**		
301	05/10/91	St George	St. George	UT	4:46:16		
302	10/12/91	Lilac City 50k	Irondequoit	NY	6:37:17		62
303	10/20/91	Hilton	Rochester	NY	4:42:50		
304	10/27/91	Kansas City	Kansas City	MO	4:49:40		
305	11/03/91	Marine Corps	Washington	DC	5:05:50		
306	11/10/91	Columbus	Columbus	OH	4:47:24		
307	11/11/91	Lake Junaluska Ridge Run	Lake Junaluska	NC	7:50:00		
308	11/24/91	Bangkok	Bangkok	Thai	5:50:00	Thailand	
309	11/30/91	Seattle	Seattle	WA	5:40:00		
310	12/07/91	Sunmart Texas Trail	Huntsville	TX	K6:50:22		63
311	12/14/91	Mississippi	Clinton	MS	4:50:22		
312	12/29/91	Greenville	Greenville	SC	5:28:56		
313	01/05/92	Miami Dade	Miami	FL	5:10:37		
314	01/11/92	Jacksonville	Jacksonville	FL	4:59:02		
315	02/03/92	Lake Junaluska Ridge Run	Lake Junaluska	NC	7:27:44		
316	02/08/92	Jed Smith Ultra Classic	Sacramento	CA	6:17:00		64
317	02/16/92	Washington Birthday	Beltsville	MD	5:11:00		
318	02/23/92	Ohio River RRC	Dayton	OH	5:11:58		
319	03/15/92	Motorola	Austin	TX	5:16:32		
320	03/21/92	Shamrock Sportsfest	Virginia Beach	VA	5:00:08		
321	03/29/92	Paris	Paris		5:06:45	France	

No	Date	Marathon Name	Location	State	Time	Country	Ultra
322	04/05/92	Rotterdam	Rotterdam		4:54:58	Holland	
323	04/12/92	London	London		5:30:22	England	
324	04/20/92	Boston	Boston	MA	5:58:00		
325	05/03/92	Pittsburgh	Pittsburgh	PA	5:11:44		
326	05/30/92	Strong 24 Hr	Rochester	NY	7:30:00		65
327	06/06/92	Governors' Cup	Helena	MT	5:35:45		
328	06/20/92	Grandma's	Duluth	MN	5:17:38		
329	06/27/92	Ridge Runner	Cairo	WV	5:51:00		
330	07/05/92	Midnight Sun Double	Nanisivik	Nun	14:00:52	Canada	66
331	07/19/92	Voyageur	Massey	ON	5:27:23	Canada	
332	07/25/92	Delaware Shufflers	Wilmington	DE	5:23:54		
333	08/08/92	Paavo Nurmi	Hurley	WI	5:31:47		
334	08/23/92	Waterloo 12 Hour	Waterloo	NY	6:58:27		
335	09/06/92	Black Hills	Rapid City	SD	4:58:26		
336	09/12/92	Bismarck	Bismarck	ND	4:56:57		
337	09/20/92	Eriesistible	Erie	PA	4:52:21		
338	09/27/92	Mystic Places	East Lyme	CT	5:14:04		
339	10/03/92	Lilac City 50k	Rochester	NY	7:14:00		67
340	10/04/92	Irondequoit 60km	Irondequoit	NY	6:58:00		68
341	10/11/92	Columbus	Columbus	OH	5:15:09		
342	10/18/92	Louisville	Louisville	KY	5:02:06		
343	10/24/92	KAKE-TV Wichita	Wichita	KS	4:58:06		
344	11/01/92	Blue Cross of Rhode Island	Rhode Island	RI	4:51:47		
345	11/07/92	Heritage Trail 50	Durango	IA	6:49:38		69
346	12/06/92	White Rock	Dallas	TX	5:24:01		
347	12/13/92	Honolulu	Honolulu	HI	6:26:40		
348	12/19/92	Sunmart Texas Trail	Huntsville	TX	6:05:57		

No	Date	Marathon Name	Location	State	Time	Country	Ultra
349	12/27/92	Last Chance 50 mile	Lakeland	FL	7:34:06		70
350	01/09/93	Jacksonville	Jacksonville	FL	5:17:16		
351	01/17/93	Miami Dade	Miami	FL	4:56:30		
352	01/24/93	Raritan Valley	Raritan	NO	5:42:25		
353	02/14/93	Washington Birthday	Beltsville	MD	5:28:52		
354	02/27/93	NY Nat.Championship	New York	NY	5:20:00		71
355	03/07/93	Motorola Austin	Austin	TX	4:51:04		
356	03/10/93	Shamrock Sportsfest	Virginia Beach	VA	5:13:21		
357	03/28/93	Wolfpack Festival of Miles	Columbus	OH	5:28:35		
358	04/19/93	Boston	Boston	MA	6:28:30		
359	04/25/93	Big Sur International	Carmel	CA	5:33:06		
360	05/02/93	Michigan Trail	Pinckney	MI	7:23:00		
361	05/08/93	Great Potato	Boise	ID	5:10:12		
362	05/16/93	Cleveland Revco	Cleveland	OH	4:46:23		
363	05/21/93	Monroe Louisiana 12 Hour	Monroe Mainline	LA	6:54:18		72
364	05/30/93	Rocky Mountain 50km	Laramie	WY	6:36:17		73
365	06/05/93	Team Up/Children's Health	Rochester	NY	7:30:00		74
366	06/19/93	Anchorage Midnight Sun	Anchorage	AK	5:24:00		
367	07/14/93	Midnight Sun Double	Nanisivik		7:04:00	Canada	75
368	07/18/93	Voyageur	Massey		5:21:10	Canada	
369	07/24/93	NUUK	Nuuk		5:07:39	Greenland	
370	08/08/93	Empire State Games	Rochester	NY	5:16:59		

No	Date	Marathon Name	Location	State	Time	Country	Ultra
371	08/13/93	American Cancer 24 Hour	East Rochester	NY	7:00:00		
372	09/04/93	Scotty Hanson	Port Huron	MT	5:24:37		
373	09/12/93	Duke City	Albuquerque	NM	5:36:14		
374	09/19/93	Eriesistible	Erie	PA	5:08:02		
375	09/27/93	Sri Chinmoy	Jamaica	NY	6:43:50		
376	10/02/93	Lilac City 50k	Irondequoit	NY	6:25:00		76
377	10/03/93	Irondequoit 60km	Irondequoit	NY	7:07:00		77
378	10/10/93	Wineglass	Corning	NY	5:15:41		
379	10/16/93	Bay State	Lowell	MA	5:09:59		
380	10/24/93	Columbus	Columbus	OH	4:58:04		
381	10/31/93	Chicago	Chicago	IL	5:02:06		
382	11/06/93	Andrew Jackson	Jackson	TN	5:11:29		
383	11/20/93	JFK Double	Hagerstown	MD	7:11:00		78
384	11/28/93	Lisbon	Lisbon	Port	5:11:17	Portugal	
385	12/05/93	White Rock	Dallas	TX	5:04:43		
386	12/11/93	Tallahassee	Tallahassee	FL	5:15:27		79
387	12/18/93	Texas Trail	Huntsville	TX	6:40:00		80
388	01/22/94	Mardi Gras	New Orleans	LA	5:28:07		
389	02/05/94	Tallahassee Ultra	Tallahassee	FL	5:28:00		81
390	02/20/94	Washington Birthday	Beltsville	MD	5:45:06		
391	02/27/94	Ohio River RRC	Oxford	OH	6:27:31		
392	03/20/94	Shamrock Sportsfest	Virginia Beach	VA	6:19:00		
393	03/27/94	Wolfpack Festival of Miles	Columbus	OH	6:26:17		82
394	04/09/94	Hogeye	Fayetteville	AR	6:27:21		
395	04/18/94	Boston	Boston	MA	6:06:00		
396	05/01/94	Wild Wild West	Lone Pine	CA	7:20:55		

No	Date	Marathon Name	Location	State	Time	Country	Ultra
397	05/15/94	Toronto	Toronto		5:28:32	Canada	
398	05/22/94	Bud Light , Sugarloaf	Kingsfield	ME	5:25:46		
399	06/04/94	Team Up for Children's Health	Rochester	NY	6:18:00		83
400	**06/26/94**	**Sri Chinmoy**	**Randall's Island**	**NY**	**5:57:32**		
401	07/03/94	Midnight Sun Double	Nanisivik		8:28:56	Canada	84
402	08/12/94	American Cancer 24hr	Rochester	NY	7:10:00		
403	09/11/94	Yellowknife	Yellow Knife		5:21:00	Canada	
404	10/02/94	Finger Lakes	Ithaca	NY	6:00:50		
405	10/09/94	Venice	Venice		5:47:00	Italy	
406	10/16/94	Bay State	Lowell	MA	5:16:43		
407	10/30/94	Chicago	Chicago	IL	5:11:17		
408	11/05/94	Heritage Trail	Dubuque	IO	5:17:00		
409	11/13/94	Columbus	Columbus	OH	5:45:00		
410	11/20/94	Nifty Fifty	Coventry	RI	5:59:31		
411	12/04/94	White Rock	Dallas	TX	5:22:02		
412	12/10/94	Tallahassee Ultra	Tallahassee	FL	5:55:08		
413	12/17/94	Texas Trail	Huntsville	TX	6:15:00		
414	01/08/95	Walt Disney World	Orlando	FL	5:34:28		
415	01/29/95	Yours Truly	Buenos Aires		7:07:52	Argentina	85
416	02/06/95	Last	Antarctica		7:31:51	Antarctic	
417	02/26/95	Ohio River RRC	Oxford	OH	6 10 42		
418	03/05/95	Motorola	Austin	TX	5:28:19		
419	03/18/95	Shamrock Sportsfest	Virginia Beach	VA	5:03:44		
420	04/09/95	Hogeye	Fayetteville	AR	5:59:14		
421	04/17/95	Boston	Boston	MA	5:49:05		

No	Date	Marathon Name	Location	State	Time	Country	Ultra
422	04/23/95	Glass City	Toledo	OH	5:14:43		
423	04/30/95	Michigan Trail	Pinckney	MI	7:18:46		
424	05/07/95	New Brunswick	Frederickson		5:28:25	Canada	
425	05/27/95	Bayshore	Traverse City	MI	5:58:05		
426	06/03/95	Team Up/Children's Health	Rochester	TN	7:50:00		86
427	06/11/95	Hoosier	Ft Wayne	IN	5:27:03		
428	06/18/95	Manitoba	Winnipeg		6:29:32	Canada	
429	07/02/95	Midnight Sun	Nanisivik		6:37:00	Canada	87
430	07/09/95	Calgary Stampede	Calgary		5:48:34	Canada	
431	07/23/95	Veterans Games	Buffalo/Niagara Falls	NY	5:41:03	Canada	
432	08/06/95	Millennium	Rochester	NY	7:51:00		
433	08/11/95	American Cancer	Rochester	NY	7:15:00		88
434	09/03/95	Newfoundland	St. John's	NF	7:58:43	Canada	
435	09/17/95	Tsawwassen	Tsawwassen	BC	7:51:09		
436	10/01/95	Wineglass	Bath/Corning	NY	8:09:20		
437	10/08/95	Valley Harvest	Kentville		8:50:35	Canada	
438	10/29/95	Cape Cod	Falmouth	MA	7:38:01		89
439	11/18/95	JFK 50 miler	Boonsboro/Wmspt	MD	7:10:45		90
440	12/30/95	Last Chance	Tampa	FL	6:58:42		
441	01/14/96	Fat Ass 50	Lake Worth	FL	8:11:00		91
442	01/28/96	Yours Truly	Lake Worth	FL	7:10:43		
443	02/18/96	Motorola	Austin	TX	6:47:36		
444	03/16/96	Shamrock Sportsfest	Virginia Beach	VA	6:20:36		
445	03/30/96	GNC 50 mile Challenge	NorthPark	PA	7:18:00		92
446	04/15/96	28th Boston	Hopkinton/Boston	MA	7:05:00		
447	05/05/96	Avenue of the Giants	Weott	CA	6:33:49		

No	Date	Marathon Name	Location	State	Time	Country	Ultra
448	05/12/96	Forest City	London		7:05:54	Canada	
449	05/17/96	American Cancer	Rochester	NY	7:03:00		93
450	05/25/96	Bay Shore	Traverse City	MI	7:04:01		
451	06/01/96	Team Up/Children's Health	Rochester	NY	7:52:00		94
452	06/23/96	Parade of Roses	Columbus	OH	7:05:00		
453	06/30/96	Nunavut Midnight Sun	Nanisivik		6:35:33	Canada	95
454	07/14/96	Ohio Michigan	Toledo	MI	5:56:08		
455	07/21/96	Sesqui-Millennium	Rochester	NY	7:48:00		
456	07/27/96	Kilauea Volcano	Volcano	HI	8:55:18		
457	08/18/96	Cambridge Bay	Cambridge Bay		8:01:10	Canada	
458	08/31/96	Brookville	Brookville	OH	7:30:00		
459	09/08/96	Saskatoon	Saskatoon		5:39:55	Canada	
460	09/15/96	Eriesistible	Erie	PA	6:05:00		
461	09/29/96	Island	Charlotte Town		5:48:02	Canada	
462	10/05/96	Graham's Farewell	Toronto		6:01:52	Canada	
463	10/13/96	Bay state	Lowell	MA	6:18:12		
464	10/27/96	Marine Corp	Arlington	VA	7:12:00		
465	11/10/96	Columbus	Columbus	OH	6:33:06		
466	11/23/96	JFK 50 miler	Boonsboro	MD	7:30:00		96
467	12/14/96	Tallahassee Ultra Distance	Wakulla Springs	FL	6:45:59		97
468	12/28/96	Last Chance	Tampa	FL	6:41:54		
469	01/05/97	Disney World	Lake Buena Vista	FL	6:14:00		
470	01/12/97	Lake Worth Fat Ass 50	Lake Worth	FL	7:04:14		98
471	01/26/97	Yours Truly	Jacksonville	FL	7:00:00		99
472	02/02/97	Tallahassee	Tallahassee	FL	6:11:16		

No	Date	Marathon Name	Location	State	Time	Country	Ultra
473	02/26/97	Austin Motorola	Austin	TX	5:55:51		
474	03/02/97	City of Los Angeles	Loa Angeles	CA	6:15:37		
475	03/29/97	March Madness	Vandalia	OH	7:01:00		
476	04/06/97	Hogeye	Fayetteville	AK	7:37:06		
477	05/11/97	National Capitol	Ottawa		7:11:14	Canada	
478	05/24/97	Bayshore	Traverse City	MI	6:44:44		
479	05/31/97	Team Up/Children's Health	Rochester	NY	8:00:00		100
480	06/06/97	American Cancer	East Rochester	NY	8:00:00		
481	06/22/97	Parade of Roses	Columbus	OH	7:25:00		
482	06/28/97	Niagara Ultra	Niagara Falls	NY	7:36:00		101
483	07/13/97	Ohio Michigan	Toledo	OH	6:39:16		
484	08/08/97	Khoury's 24 hr relay	Summersville	MA	8:02:24		102
485	08/17/97	Brookville Rails To Trails	Brookville	OH	6:34:00		
486	08/31/97	Scotty Hanton	Port Huron	MI	6:26:37		
487	09/06/97	Spitsbergen	Longyearbyen		6:53:33	Norway	
488	09/13/97	Oslo	Oslo		6:26:27	Norway	
489	10/05/97	Wineglass	Bath/Corning	NY	6:43:42		
490	10/11/97	First Global Autumn	Kokyo		6:23:36	Japan	
491	10/26/07	Niagara Falls Casino	Niagara Falls		6:23:26	Canada	
492	11/22/97	JFK 50 miler	Boonsboro	MD	7:30:00		
493	11/29/97	Kurt Steiner 50km	NYC	NY	7:53:56		103
494	12/13/97	Tallahassee Ultra	Wakulla Springs	FL	7:44:54		104
495	12/21/07	San Pedro Super 80k	Monterrey		7:09:00	Mexico	
496	01/04/98	Lake Worth Fat Ass 50	Lake Worth	FL	7:10:00		105
497	01/11/98	Walt Disney World	Orlando	FL	6:41:35		
498	01/18/98	Tallahassee	Tallahassee	FL	7:12:35		

No	Date	Marathon Name	Location	State	Time	Country	Ultra
499	01/25/98	Yours Truly	Pompano Beach	FL	7:02:23		
500	**02/01/98**	**Ocala**	**Ocala**	**FL**	**6:25:01**		
501	02/14/98	Austin Motorola	Austin	TX	6:15:22		
502	03/08/98	Ohio River RRC	Xenia	OH	6:50:45		
503	03/21/98	Shamrock Sportsfest	Virginia Beach	VA	7:03:10		
504	03/29/98	LA	Los Angeles	CA	6:57:20		
505	04/04/98	Hogeye	Fayetteville	AR	6:58:00		
506	04/26/98	Lake Waramaug	New Preston	CT	8:01:10		
507	05/10/98	National Capitol	Ottawa		7:08:00	Canada	
508	05/23/98	Bayshore	Traverse City	MI	6:54:58		
509	05/30/98	Team Up for Children's Health	Rochester	NY	8:00:00		
510	06/11/98	American Cancer	Rochester	NY	8:00:00		
511	06/21/98	Suzuki Rock and Roll	San Diego	CA	6:56:21		
512	06/27/98	Niagara Ultra	Niagara Falls		7:32:42	Canada	106
513	07/12/98	Ohio-Michigan Run	Toledo	OH	6:29:50		
514	07/25/98	Greenland	Nuuk		6:45:19	Greenland	
515	08/02/98	Rails To Trails	Brookville	OH	7:28:00		
516	08/08/98	Huntington's	Rochester	NY	7:35:00		
517	09/06/98	Scotty Hanson	Port Huron	MI	7:51:16		
518	09/13/98	Eriesistible	Erie	PA	6:56:31		
519	09/19/98	Air Force	Dayton	OH	7:30:42		
520	10/08/98	Wineglass	Bath	NY	6:57:23		
521	10/25/98	Marine Corps	Washington	DC	6:57:55		
522	11/01/98	Yodogawa Shimin	Osaka		7:27:27	Japan	
523	11/21/98	JFK 50 miler	Boonsboro	MD	7:53:50		
524	12/12/98	Tallahassee	Tallahassee	FL	7:11:18		107
525	01/03/99	Fat Ass 50k	Lake Worth	FL	7:51:00		

No	Date	Marathon Name	Location	State	Time	Country	Ultra
526	01/11/99	Walt Disney World	Orlando	FL	6:43:37		
527	01/18/99	Capitol City	Tallahassee	FL	7:15:41		
528	01/30/99	Blue Moon	New Port Ritchie	FL	7:52:00		
529	02/07/99	Ocala	Ocala	FL	7:20:00		
530	02/14/99	Motorola	Austin	TX	6:47:24		
531	02/28/99	Pafos	Cyprus		7:34:01	Cyprus	
532	03/20/99	Shamrock Sportsfest	Virginia Beach	VA	6:49:20		
533	03/27/99	GNC50k Nat. Championship	Cranberry	PA	7:13:12		108
534	04/11/99	Hogeye	Fayetteville	AR	6:53:07		
535	05/09/99	National Capitol	Ottawa		7:42:52	Canada	
536	05/23/99	Rock and Roll	San Diego	CA	6:45:15		
537	05/30/99	Millennium	Burlington		7:14:05	Ontario	
538	06/06/99	Strong Children	Rochester	NY	8:30:00		
539	06/11/99	American Cancer	Rochester	NY	8:30:00		
540	07/07/99	Niagara Ontario Ultra	Niagara Falls		8:17:45	Canada	109
541	07/11/99	Ohio-Michigan	Toledo	OH	7:03:06		
542	08/08/99	Rails to Trails	Brookville	OH	7:47:00		
543	08/22/99	Edmonton Festival	Edmonton		7:21:09	Canada	
544	09/12/99	Eriesistible	Erie	PA	6:51:57		
545	09/13/99	Air Force	Fairborn	OH	6:47:24		
546	09/26/99	Quad Cities	Moline	IL	6:52:00		
547	10/24/98	Marine Corps	Washington	DC	6:45:46		
548	11/14/99	Columbus	Ohio	OH	7:04:27		
549	12/01/99	!1st Aids Day	Waterloo		8 15 00	Canada	
550	12/11/99	Tallahassee	Tallahassee	FL	8:15:24		110
551	12/31/99	Last Chance Millennium	Tampa	FL	7:21:42		

No	Date	Marathon Name	Location	State	Time	Country	Ultra
552	01/09/00	Disney 2000	Orlando	FL	7:16:10		
553	01/15/00	New Port Ritchie	New Port Ritchie	FL	7 58 04		
554	01/23/00	Clearwater	Clearwater	FL	7:31:24		
555	02/06/00	Ocala	Ocala	FL	7:13:51		
556	02/20/00	Austin Motorola	Austin	TX	6:47:37		
557	03/05/00	ORRRC Xenia	Xenia	OH	7:34:29		
558	03/25/00	North Park, PA,50k	North Park	PA	7:25:21		
559	04/09/00	Buffalo 6 Hour	Buffalo 6 Hour	NY	7:23:00		
560	04/16/00	Glass City, Toledo	Glass City, Toledo	OH	7:45:04		
561	08/12/00	Brookville R/T	Brookville R/T	OH	8:20:00		
562	09/10/00	Eiresistable	Eiresistable	PA	7:42:35		
563	09/16/00	Toledo 24 hr	Toledo 24 hr	OH	7:57:58		
564	09/24/00	Quad Cities	Quad Cities	IL	7:53:27		
565	10/09/00	Asahikawa	Asahikawa		7:08:42	Japan	
566	10/21/00	Erie 12 Hour	Erie 12 Hour	PA	7:58:37		
567	10/29/00	Columbus	Columbus	OH	7:06:42		
568	11/12/00	JFK	JFK	MD	8:21:00		
569	12/30/00	New Port Ritchey	New Port Ritchey	FL	8:40:00		
570	01/07/01	Disney 2001	Disney 2001	FL	7:22:57		
571	01/14/01	Tallahassee	Tallahassee	FL	8:10:52		
572	02/04/01	Ocala	Ocala	FL	8:20:00		
573	02/16/01	Yours Truly	Galveston	TX	8:20:00		
574	02/18/01	Austin	Austin	TX	7:30:42		
575	02/24/01	Cowtown	Ft Worth	TX	8:09:00		
576	03/17/01	Virginia Beach	Virginia Beach	VA	7:30:22		
577	03/24/01	Cystic Fibrosis, Pittsburgh	Pittsburgh	PA	7:59:30		111
578	04/07/01	Xenia. ORRRC	Xenia.	OH	8:22:42		

No	Date	Marathon Name	Location	State	Time	Country	Ultra
579	04/22/01	Glass City	Glass City	OH	7:59:30		
580	04/26/01	Country Music Nashville	Nashville	TN	8:08:59		
581	05/06/01	Ottawa	Ottawa		7:53:38	Canada	
582	05/27/01	Burlington	Burlington,		7:55:05	Canada	
583	06/03/01	San Diego Rock & Roll	San Diego	CA	7:57:09		
584	06/30/01	Niagara-on-the-Lake	Niagara On The Lake		9:43:02	Canada	112
585	07/29/01	Carrollton Charity	Carrollton	MI	8:07:00		
586	08/11/01	Brookville	Brookville	OH	8:10:00		
587	09/09/01	Eriestistable	Erie	PA	8:06:06		
588	09/23/01	Quad Cities	Moline	IL	8:04:00		
589	10/07/01	Wineglass	Bath/Corning	NY	7:55:00		
590	10/14/01	Towpath	Peninsula	OH	8:19:00		
591	11/17/01	Tulsa	Tulsa	OK	7:59:34		
592	12/02/01	HOPS, Tampa	Tampa	FL	8:29:45		
593	12/08/01	Tallahassee Ultra Classic	Wakulla Springs	FL	8:16:00		113
594	12/30/01	Lunamatic	New Port Ritchey	FL	9:04:00		
595	03/16/02	Shamrock B	Virginia Beach	VA	9:01:27		
596	04/07/02	Xenia, ORRRC	Xenia	OH	8:38:50		
597	04/15/02	Boston	Boston	MA	8:19:27		
598	04/27/02	Nashville Country Music	Nashville	TN	8:21:41		
599	05/26/02	Burlington Rock& Roll	Burlington		8:36:08	Canada	
600	06/07/02	**Spencerport AmCan**	**Spencerport**	**NY**	**8:38:34**		

No	Date	Marathon Name	Location	State	Time	Country	Ultra
601	06/29/02	Niagara 50km	Niagara Falls		8:45:57	Canada	
602	07/28/02	Carrollton, Mi	Carrollton	MI	8:23:23		
603	08/09/02	Brookville, #1	Brookville	OH	8:25:00		
604	08/10/02	Brookville. #2	Brookville	OH	9:26:00		
605	08/25/02	Quebec City	Quebec City		9:50:28	Canada	
606	09/14/02	Olander 24 Hour	Sylvania	NY	8:47:00		
607	10/06/02	Wineglass	Bath/Corning	NY	8:24:16		
608	10/13/02	Towpath	Peninsula	OH	8:15:47		
609	10/20/02	Columbus	Columbus	OH	7:46:30		
610	11/22/02	JFK	Boonsboro	MD	8:37:53		
611	**12/14/02**	**Wakulla Springs**	**Wakulla Springs**	**FL**	**8:33:26**		
612	01/18/03	Charlotte Observer	Charlotte	NC	8:13:09		
613	02/02/03	Columbus Last Chance	Columbus	OH	7:59:38		
614	05/03/03	Ontario Shores	Greece	NY	7:58:51		
615	06/06/03	Spencerport AmCan	Spencerport	NY	8:45:00		
616	06/27/03	Niagara Ultra	Niagara Falls		9:08:16	Canada	114
617	07/11/03	Bath Relay For Life	Bath	NY	8:19:00		
618	07/18/03	Webster Relay For Life	Webster	NY	8:15:00		
619	07/24/03	Owego, Relay for Life	Owego	NY	8:38:34		
620	08/08/03	Brookville	Brookville	OH	8:15:00		
621	08/09/03	Brookville	Brookville	OH	8:30:00		
622	08/16/03	Reykjavik	Reykjavik		9:03:04	Iceland	
623	08/31/03	Potsdam, NY	Potsdam	NY	8:31:08		
624	09/13/03	Olander Park Toledo	Sylvania	OH	8:34:55		
625	09/28/03	Quad Cities	Moline	IL	8:19:55		

No	Date	Marathon Name	Location	State	Time	Country	Ultra
626	10/05/03	Wineglass	Bath/Corning	OH	8:18:24		
627	10/19/03	Columbus	Columbus	OH	8:22:42		
628	11/09/03	Harrisburg	Harrisburg	PA	8:10:01		
629	11/21/03	JFK	Boonsboro/Wmspt	MD	8:45:00		
630	12/13/03	Wakulla Springs	Wakulla Springs	FL	8:45:25		
631	01/31/04	Ocala	Ocala	FL	8:53:52		
632	02/15/04	Austin-Motorola	Austin	TX	8:24:06		
633	02/22/04	Your Truly	Galveston	TX	9:05:00		
634	02/28/04	Cowtown	Ft Worth	TX	8:21:29		
635	03/20/04	Shamrock	Virginia Beach	VA	7:59:43		
636	04/04/04	Xenia, ORRRC	Xenia	OH	8:59:44		
637	04/24/04	Nashville	Nashville	TN	8:58:46		
638	05/01/04	Ontario Shore	Greece	NY	8:46:22		
639	05/16/04	Mississauga	Mississauga		8:28:24	Canada	
640	05/30/04	National CAPS	Ottawa		9:24:00	Canada	
641	06/06/04	San Diego Rock/Roll	San Diego	CA	7:54:01		
642	06/11/04	Webster AmCan	Webster	NY	8:34:45		
643	06/18/04	Geneva AmCan	Geneva	NY	8:45:00		
644	06/26/04	Niagara 50km()	Niagara Falls		8:58:00	Canada	
645	07/09/04	Bath AmCan	Bath	NY	8:45:00		
646	07/26/04	Carrollton, MI	Carrollton	MI	8:31:00		
647	08/11/04	Brookville #11	Brookville	OH	9:10:00		
648	08/12/04	Brookville #12	Brookville	OH	8:40:00		
649	08/13/04	Brookville #13	Brookville	OH	8:59:56		
650	08/25/04	Sri Chinmoy Self-Transcendence	Nyack	NY	8:10:03		
651	09/11/04	Toledo 100 mile	Toledo 100 mile	OH	8:34:24		115
652	09/26/04	Quad Cities	Moline	IL	8:16:55		

No	Date	Marathon Name	Location	State	Time	Country	Ultra
653	10/03/04	Wineglass	Wineglass	NY	8:06:16		
654	10/10/04	Ottawa Fall Colors	Bath/Corning		8:29:52	Canada	
655	10/17/04	Columbus	Columbus	OH	8:36:48		
656	10/24/04	Casino Niagara	Niagara Falls		8:36:48	Canada	
657	11/14/04	Harrisburg	Harrisburg	PA	8:31:11		
658	11/20/04	JFK	Boonsboro	MD	9:01:34		
659	12/09/04	Wakulla	Wakulla Springs	FL	8:31:00		
660	01/31/05	Ocala	Ocala	FL	9:40:10		
661	02/11/05	Austin, Freescale	Austin	TX	8:43:23		
662	02/20/05	Yours Truly	Galveston	TX	8:52:45		
663	02/26/05	Cowtown Ft Worth	Ft Worth	TX	8:43:42		
664	03/03/05	Little Rock	Little Rock	AK	8:13:27		
665	03/19/05	Shamrock	Virginia Beach	VA	8:26:57		
666	04/10/05	Xenia, ORRRC	Xenia	OH	8:52:41		
667	04/18/05	Boston	Boston	MA	8:34:25		
668	04/30/05	Newcastle	Newcastle	DL	8:57:58		
669	05/14/05	Penn Yan AmCan	Rochester	NY	8:57:55		
670	05/29/05	Ottawa	Ottawa		8:50:51	Canada	
671	06/03/05	Spencerport AmCan	Spencerport	NY	9:20:00		
672	06/10/05	Honeoye Falls AmCan	Honeoye Falls	NY	8:54:00		
673	06/25/05	Niagara Ultra	Niagara Falls		9:38:38	Canada	116
674	07/01/05	Brookville 24 Hour	Brookville	OH	9:00:10		
675	07/31/05	Carrollton	Carrollton	MI	8:30:52		
676	08/12/05	Brookville Reunion #15	Brookville	OH	8:51:00		
677	08/21/05	Hornell AmCan	Rochester	NY	8:35:58		
678	08/28/05	Rochester	Rochester	NY	8:54:00		

No	Date	Marathon Name	Location	State	Time	Country	Ultra
679	09/10/05	Toledo 100 Mile, Olander	Sylvania	OH	8:36:59		117
680	09/25/05	Quad Cities	Moline	IL	8:46:12		
681	10/02/05	Hirosaki, Aomori	Hirosaki		8:31:00	Japan	
682	10/09/05	Portland	Portland	OR	8:01:xx		
683	10/16/05	Columbus	Columbus	OH	7:53:51		
684	10/23/05	Casino Niagara	Niagara Falls		8:46:34	Canada	
685	11/04/05	McNelly Birthday	Rochester	NY	8:47:41		
686	11/13/05	Harrisburg	Harrisburg	PA	8:55:13		
687	11/18/05	JFK	Boonsboro	MD	8:58:32		
688	12/10/05	Wakulla Ultra distance	Wakulla Springs	FL	9:12:01		
689	01/28/06	Yours Truly 50km	Galveston	TX	9:10:01		
690	02/11/06	Second Surfside Beach	Surfside	TX	8:39:42		
691	02/19/06	Austin-Freescale	Austin	TX	8:41:44		
692	02/27/06	Yours Truly, Mardi Gras	Galveston	TX	8:47:42		
693	03/05/06	Little Rock	Little Rock	AK	8:31:50		
694	03/19/06	Shamrock	Virginia Beach	VA	8:39:59		
695	03/31/06	Yours Truly	Newcastle	DL	8:33:10		
696	04/09/06	ORRRC, Xenia	Xenia	OH	8:57:14		
697	04/29/06	Nashville Country Music	Nashville	TN	9:03:21		
698	05/14/06	Mississauga	Mississauga		8:38:09	Canada	
699	05/28/06	National Capitol	Ottawa		9:30:39	Canada	
700	06/04/06	**San Diego Rock and Roll**	**San Diego**	**CA**	**8:46:15**		

No	Date	Marathon Name	Location	State	Time	Country	Ultra
701	06/17/06	Irondequoit for Phelps	Rochester	NY	8:46:27		
702	06/24/06	Niagara Ultra	Niagara Falls		8:52:58	Canada	
703	07/18/06	Irondequoit for Massey	Rochester	NY	8:50:00		
704	08/10/06	Brookville Reunion #16	Brookville	OH	9:11:31		
705	08/11/06	Brookville Reunion #17	Brookville	OH	8:36:18		
706	08/25/06	Sri Chinmoy	Nyack	NY	8:40:00		
707	08/27/06	Green Lakes Endurance Run	Syracuse	NY	9:15:00		
708	09/03/06	Rochester Course	Rochester	NY	8:43:23		
709	09/10/06	Erieistable	Erie	PA	9:28:34		
710	09/03/06	Rochester	Rochester	NY	8:29:23		
711	09/25/06	Toronto Scotia	Toronto		8:43:48	Canada	
712	10/01/07	Portland	Portland	OR	8:32:57		
713	10/15/06	Columbus	Columbus	OH	8:37:37		
714	11/22/06	Casino Niagara	Niagara Falls		8:44:24	Canada	
715	11/05/06	Huntington,	Huntington	WV	9:10:00		
716	11/12/06	Harrisburg	Harrisburg	PA	8:40:00		
717	11/19/06	Philadelphia	Philadelphia	PA	9:33:32		
718	01/10/07	Yours Truly	Rochester	NY	9:45:00		
719	01/19/07	Surfside Beach Run	Surfside	TX	9:10:42		
720	02/18/07	Austin	Austin	TX	9:03:11		
721	02/24/07	Yours Truly	Galveston	TX	9:45:00		
722	03/18/07	Virginia Beach	Virginia Beach	VA	8:52:49		
723	03/30/07	Yours Truly Wilmington	Newcastle	DL	8:50:00		

No	Date	Marathon Name	Location	State	Time	Country	Ultra
724	04/29/07	Yours Truly	Long Branch	NJ	9:00:00		
725	08/10/07	Brookville	Brookville	OH	9:50:00		
726	08/24/07	Sri Chinmoy	Nyack	NY	9:40:00		
727	10/07/07	Portland	Portland	OR	8:51:31		
728	10/21/07	Nationwide	Columbus	OH	9:23:17		
729	11/11/07	Harrisburg	Harrisburg	PA	10:07:07		
730	12/08/07	Tallahassee Ultra Distance Classic	Wakulla Springs	FL	9:42:18		
731	02/09/08	Surfside Beach Run	Surfside	TX	9:38:00		
732	02/17/08	Austin	Austin	TX	9:08:01		
733	03/30/08	Ocean Drive	Cape May	NJ	10:14:00		
734	06/13/08	Lake Placid Half Marathon & Relay	Lake Placid	NY			
735	08/12/09	Tromptown Run Hall Marathon	DeRuyter	NY			
736	09/05/09	Oak Tree Half Marathon	Rochester	NY			
737	09/05/09	Monster Marathon	Virgil	NY			
738	01/09/10	Arc of Onondaga Marathon	Syracuse	NY			
739	09/12/10	Westchester Marathon	White Plains	NY			
740	09/12/10	Rochester Marathon	Rochester	NY			
741	10/02/10	Hamptons Marathon	East Hampton	NY			
742	10/10/10	Marine Crps Marathon	Albany	NY			
743	11/01/10	Marine Corp Marathon	Albany	NY			
744	11/01/10	Red Baron	Corning	NY			

[i] Reserve Champion was second place

[ii] The Greater Rochester Track Club (GRTC) traces its origins back to July 1, 1958 when the old Rochester Track Club (RTC) was founded.

[iii] Information obtained from the Diabetes Foundation

[iv] The Earth Day Marathon in 1978, the start and finish were moved to Eisenhower Park in East Meadow, and the race was renamed the Long Island Marathon.

[v] Doing a quid pro quo, in 1984, the Olympics came to Los Angeles. The Soviet Union boycotted, citing concerns over the safety of their athletes in what they called an anti-communist environment. It was widely regarded as a retaliatory move for the 1980 boycott. The Los Angeles Games boasted 140 nations—more than at any previous Olympics, and up from eighty-one in Moscow. The US team won eighty-three gold medals and 174 medals overall.

[vi] International Association of Athletic Federations (IAAF)

[vii] The 50 States & D.C. Marathon Group is a unique group of individuals from around the world. The group all shares a goal of completing a marathon in all 50 States & D.C. To join this ONE of a kind group you must complete 10 marathons in 10 different states today but in 1989 it was set at 20.

[viii] The Distant Early Warning Line, also known as the DEW Line or Early Warning Line, was a system of radar stations in the far northern Arctic region of Canada, with additional stations along the North Coast and Aleutian Islands of Alaska, in addition to the Faroe Islands, Greenland, and Iceland. It was set up to detect incoming Soviet bombers during the Cold War, a task which quickly became outdated when intercontinental ballistic missiles became the main delivery system for nuclear weapons.

[ix] Personal computers came on the scene in 1981 and in 1987 there were only 10,000 websites. The internet as we know it today did not appear until 1990/1992 with the introduction of the world wide web.

[x] a term used for a group of culturally similar indigenous peoples inhabiting the Arctic regions of Alaska